FOR WHOM THE BELLS TOLL

The Unexplained Losses of S.S. Edmund Fitzgerald, M.V. Derbyshire, and Other Vessels of the Bulk-Cargo Silent Service

by

Raymond Ramsay M.Sc.

DORRANCE PUBLISHING CO., INC.
PITTSBURGH, PENNSYLVANIA 15222

All Rights Reserved
Copyright © 2006 by Raymond Ramsay M.Sc.
No part of this book may be reproduced or transmitted
in any form or by any means, electronic or mechanical,
including photocopying, recording, or by any information
storage and retrieval system without permission in
writing from the publisher.

ISBN-10: 0-8059-6914-4
ISBN-13: 978-0-8059-6914-6
Printed in the United States of America

First Printing

Also available through virtual retail website
www.DorranceEbooks.com

For information or to order additional books, please write:
Dorrance Publishing Co., Inc.
701 Smithfield Street
Third Floor
Pittsburgh, Pennsylvania 15222-3906
U.S.A.
1-800-788-7654
Or visit our web site and on-line catalog at
www.dorrancebookstore.com

*...with dedication to the
Great Lakes and deep sea mariners who
silently voyage in harm's way and the beloved
aggrieved families of those who may never return...*

Contents

Credo ix
Preface xi

Part One   A Personalized Prologue .1
                      Vessels of the Inland Marine Highway
                      Early History
                      The Marine Stairway
                      New Vessel Traffic
                      A Contribution

Part Two   Arrival in the U.S.A. 17
                      Great Lakes Engineering Works (G.L.E.W.) Company
                      G.L.E.W. Ecorse-River Rouge Shipyard (1903–1962)
                      Future Prospects and the St. Lawrence Seaway

Part Three   Bulk-Cargo Vessel Considerations 33
                      S.S. *Edmund Fitzgerald* Requirements
                      Great Lakes Environmental Conditions
                      20/20 Hindsight

Part Four   Design Office Revelations 40
                      Naval Architecture Consultancy
                      Enlightenment and Adjustment
                      Major Hull Structure
                      Vessel Loading Factors
                      And in Canada...
                      Fitzgerald Flexure

	Fitzgerald Side Launching
	Lake Erie Trials
	Delivery
Part Five	Design Office Practices .66
	The S.S. *Edmund Fitzgerald*
	The M.V. *Derbyshire* (OBO)
	Contrasting Practices
	The Bridge Class Shipbuilders
	End of a Notable Shipbuilding Era
	The Design Challenges
	Missing Modification Drawings
	Hull Stress Analysis
	Practical Factors
	Drafting Room Dilemmas
	Exposure of Global Bulk-Cargo Vessel Losses
Part Six	Cargo Terminal Interfaces 89
	Great Lakes
	Final Cargo Loading
	Oceangoing
	Parliamentary Debate
	M.V. *Derbyshire* Final Cargo Loading
	Samuel Plimsoll Revisited
	Merchant Shipbuilding Paradigm Shift
Part Seven	Plying the Great Lakes Trading Routes 110
	Load Lines
	The Operating Environment
	Clapotic Wave Formation
	Waves and Wedges
	Constructive Interference Waves
	Experience and Judgement
	In-service Operation
	Hull Separation
Part Eight	The Final Voyage of Fitzgerald 136
	Before Michipicoten Island

                Storm Warning
                U.F.O. Encounter
                Seek Safe Anchorage
                Final Moments
                M.V. *Derbyshire Ex Post Facto* Events
                Underwater Searches
                High Court of Justice (Admiralty Court) Hearing
                S.S. *Edmund Fitzgerald* Sinking Propositions

Part Nine   Summary 164

Part Ten   Epilogue and Epitaph .171

Reference and Sources 183
Glossary for Technical Bridging 186
Appendix 194

CREDO

As a retired third-generation shipbuilder, I firmly believe that a lifelong social contract should prevail between

    shipowners,

        designers,

            shipbuilders, and

                operating crews.

Few may aspire to a lifetime of extravagant wealth, but all can expect to find richness in those who proudly make their personal contributions to the maritime profession.

Raymond Ramsay, M.Sc.
2006

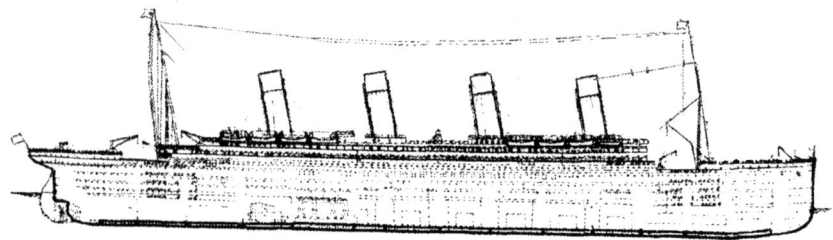

R.M.S. Titanic

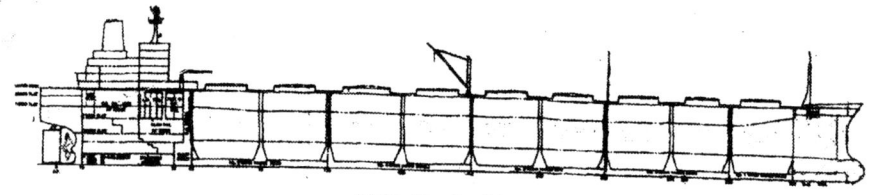

M.V. Derbyshire
(Ex - *Liverpool Bridge*)

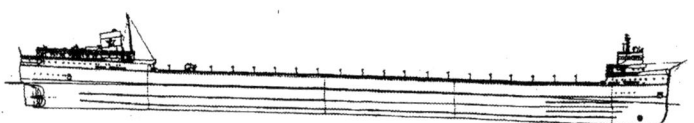

S.S. Edmund Fitzgerald

DIMENSIONAL PERSPECTIVE (Feet)			
VESSEL NAME	LENGTH OVERALL (Feet)	BEAM (Feet)	DEPTH (Feet)
* R.M.S. TITANIC	882	92	97 To Boat Deck
M.V. DERBYSHIRE	925	145	82 To Weather Deck
S.S. EDMUND FITZGERALD	729	75	39 To Spar Deck

* R.M.S.   Royal Mail Steamer
   M.V   Motor Vessel
   S.S.   Steamship

PREFACE

Throughout maritime history submarine forces have been respectfully referred to as the "Silent Service;" however, there are others who are equally deserving of the descriptor, such as the Great Lakes and oceangoing mariners who quietly operate mammoth bulk-cargo vessels without fanfare and frequently voyage in harm's way under hazardous environmental conditions, while conserving the economic vitality of national and international industries. Both military and commercial elements provide essential national services, albeit for different purposes.

This literary contribution gives specific recognition to the long history of the U.S.A.-Canada "marine highway" of the Great Lakes, which initially created commercial trading opportunities and continues to be essential for the industrial economies of both nations. In recent times the intra-continent opening of the St. Lawrence Seaway (1959), a marine equivalent of the Roman Appian Way, brought about significant design challenges and expanded access routes as increases in laker vessel length and bulk-cargo carrying capacity were made possible after new locks were installed with the deepening and widening of the Montreal to Lake Ontario navigational passage. These enhancements allowed lakers to transit from the head waters of Lake Superior to the Gulf of the St. Lawrence River, a distance of 2,342 miles with a vertical descent of 602 feet. Access was also facilitated for oceangoing ("saltie") vessels.

With recognition of the Seaway development, a newly constructed S.S. *Edmund Fitzgerald* bulk-cargo laker, of U.S.-flag and unique design (Fig. 1), was delivered to her owners, Northwestern Mutual Life Insurance Company, and she entered service in September 1958.

The "Big Fitz" rapidly established a leadership reputation as the longest, fastest, and largest-capacity vessel having compatibility with Seaway system capabilities. The vessel received classification by the American Bureau of Shipping (A.B.S.) and, over a period of about eleven years, she held Great Lakes ore-carrying transportation records. While some well-maintained Great Lakes vessels achieved an average service life of about forty-seven years in their limited-season freshwater operating environment, the seventeen-year young *Fitzgerald* catastrophically sank under abnormal storm conditions. Various U.S. government reports and unsolicited theories have been advanced for vessel sinking circumstances that have continued to defy full explanation.

The American-flagged S.S. *Edmund Fitzgerald*, fully loaded with 26,116 long tons of taconite pellets, sank on November 10, 1975, in the Canadian waters of eastern Lake Superior at position 46°59.9' N, 85°06.6' W. The vessel sank in a water depth of 530 feet, approximately seventeen miles from safe haven at Whitefish Bay, Michigan.

The vessel was listing after sustaining hull damage, at about 15.30 hrs., subsequent to passing Michipicoten Island while on trackline 141°T and downbound from Superior, Wisconsin. Disablement of both surface search radars occurred at about 16.10 hrs., when the vessel was operating at various speeds under severe storm conditions with degraded navigational capability caused by a snowstorm having duration from about 14.50 hrs. to 19.10 hrs. Under these extreme conditions the *Fitzgerald* successfully maintained radiotelephone communication with the downbound S.S. *Arthur M. Anderson*, which was following at about ten miles astern, and the oceangoing ("saltie") vessel M.V. *Avafors*, which was proceeding upbound with M.V. *Nanfri* and M.V. *Benfri* before deciding to seek safe haven at Whitefish Bay, Michigan.

In the area of wreckage, an underwater survey revealed that a 240-foot-long stern section was inverted and situated about 170 feet from a longitudinally-inclined and slightly heeled 276-foot-long bow section. The area between the bow and stern sections showed distorted structural material belonging to the separated 213-foot-long cargo-hold center section of the hull envelope.

All of the vessel's twenty-nine officers and crew members were reported as missing and presumed to be dead. There were neither witnesses nor distress signals, and the event appeared to be a catastrophic (vice incipient) casualty. The United States Coast Guard (USCG) Marine Board and the National Transportation Safety Board (NTSB) conducted thorough investigations and reached significant conclusions of merit, albeit the NTSB recommendations were made inclusive of dissenting opinion. The NTSB decisions were made independently of any recommendations proposed by the USCG Marine Board.

In a closely related timeframe, the British-flagged M.V. *Derbyshire* (ex-*Liverpool Bridge*) (Fig. 2), a unique oceangoing vessel designed for ore/bulk/oil (O.B.O.) carrier service, was delivered to Bibby Tankers Limited at Hamburg in June 1976. The O.B.O. type of vessel began to emerge as a distinct design type in the mid-1960s, and the Bridge Class was destined to become the largest and first of the O.B.O. vessels to be built in a British shipyard shortly thereafter. The *Derbyshire* was the last in a series of six almost-sister Bridge Class vessels constructed by the same shipbuilder, with the *Furness Bridge* being their first delivery in September 1971. All received classification by Lloyd's Register of Shipping (LRS) as ✠100A1 "strengthened for ore cargoes, holds 2 and 6 may be empty or oil cargoes." These vessels were also approved to load ore cargoes in alternate holds, with holds 2, 4, 6, and 8 empty. The four-year young *Derbyshire* catastrophically sank on or about September 9, 1980 with the loss of forty-four lives and without witnesses or distress signals.

Various British Government investigations and reports, academic treatise, professional fora, and unsolicited theories were advanced in attempts to explain the sinking, yet none satisfied all parties involved over a number of years. The investigations of both losses have not been fully conclusive, leaving considerable doubt in the minds of some free-thinking naval architects, seafarers, and the surviving kin of those mariners who perished.

VESSEL COMPARISON		
	S.S. EDMUND FITZGERALD (GREAT LAKES)	M.V. DERBYSHIRE (OCEANGOING)
L. Length B.P./LOA	711/729 ft.	925/926 ft.
B. Breadth	75	145
D. Depth	39	82
L/D Ratio	18.2	11.3
F. Freeboard	11.5 (Winter)	21.4 (Summer)
Displacement	35,000 tons	200,588 tons
Block Coefficient	0.88	0.84
Cargo Deadweight	26,116 tons	170,473 tons
Cargo Hold Capacity	860,950 cub.ft.	6,000,000 cub.ft.
V. Speed	14.15 knots (16.30 mph)	15.50 knots
V/L Speed-Length Ratio	0.53	0.51
Loss of Lives	29	44

Fig. 1 − SS. Edmund Fitzgerald. Photo - U.S. Coast Guard

Fig 2. – M.V. Liverpool Bridge (Renamed M.V. Derbyshire)
Photo - J.M. Evans

The British oceangoing ore/bulk/oil (O.B.O.) carrier vessel M.V. *Derbyshire* of the Bridge Class, loaded with 154,960 l.tons of iron ore concentrates, sank in a water depth of 13,812 feet (2.6 miles) after encountering Pacific Typhoon Orchid when about 350 miles southeast of Kawasaki, Japan, on or about September 9, 1980.

On June 8, 1994, Oceaneering Technologies, of Maryland, USA, under contract to the International Transport-workers' Federation (ITF), teamed their Ocean Explorer 6000 side-scan sonar and Magellan 725 Remote Operating Vehicle (ROV) systems aboard the Japanese survey vessel *Shin Kai Maru*. They searched for and sighted the letters "SHIRE" on the *Derbyshire* wreckage.

In the area of wreckage an underwater survey revealed that the bow section was approximately 1,670 feet from the stern section, with most of the hatch covers located within a 740-foot wide corridor between the two sections. The pattern suggested that no substantial section of the hull and none of the hatch covers completely separated from the main part of the vessel while on the surface. All of the forty-two officers and crew members, and two wives, were reported as missing and presumed to be dead. The sinking event received formal investigation by the British Department of Transport and was subsequently reopened by the British High Court of Justice (Admiralty Court) after other Bridge Class vessels experienced structural failures.

Almost concurrent with these losses, Lloyd's Register statistics (circa 1980–1990) of worldwide bulk-cargo vessel losses were brought to light and raised serious questions about structural adequacy and maintenance, classification society effectiveness, seamanship, shipbuilding quality, and seaworthiness concerns. Some experienced mariners also prognosticated that bulk-cargo vessels are oceangoing workhorses that could have singular problems not affecting other oceangoing vessels. Based on their service histories, this theory may be absolutely correct. In the foregoing timeframe, with worldwide scope, bulker losses surged for vessels over 15,000 tons deadweight, and many were sinkings having no survivors or witnesses. The statistics revealed losses averaging about twenty sinkings per year from identifiable causes, plus historical losses of about one bulker per year attributable to unexplainable events. Statistics developed by other marine analysts further suggested that navigational errors were accountable for about 35 percent of losses and that more than 75 percent of marine casualties may be possibly attributed to human errors. Thirty to 35 percent of losses were suggested to be attributable to inadequate hull structure.

The author's concern is not only for the lack of full explanation of the *Fitzgerald* and *Derbyshire* catastrophies and the high mortality rate of bulkers cited in the overview. Major projective concern is also expressed for the structural safety and quality standards for vessels now being constructed in the burgeoning construction programs currently underway in the expanding lower-wage industrial economies throughout China, Korea, Japan, India, and other Far Eastern countries. As their insatiable demand for bulk-cargo raw materials and oil continues to increase, these industrially-ascendant economic forces are also reformatting commodities markets throughout the world, with attendant straining of the systems that originate such commodities and those that expedite their shipment by land and sea.

In 2003, China eclipsed Japan to become the world's second-largest importer of oil after the United States, and this was partly reflective of the "China Syndrome" which is also characterized by a worldwide shortage of vessels to satisfy their ever-increasing raw material demands on any given day. Shortages have inevitably fostered increased costs of operation, and bulk-cargo transportation costs were reported to have at least doubled in the 2003–04 timeframe. The foreign industrial planning response to the rapidly rising raw material demand curve and the shortage of vessels is reflected by shipyards of Japan and Korea executing shipbuilding orders for bulk-cargo vessels through the year 2007. China is also building many shipyards, including the world's largest in Shanghai. Other shipyards in Vietnam and Indonesia are also participating in the shipbuilding boom and, in the year 2003, Lloyd's List showed that global orders had more than doubled to a record sixteen hundred vessels. The expansion and improvement of cargo loading and unloading facilities is also proceeding at a high tempo.

Such expansion of shipbuilding programs to satisfy national raw material needs is expected to continue and receive high national priority, similar to Japan's post-World War II industrial revolution, which could not have succeeded without massive importations of raw materials and oil. These commodities were mainly transported in government-subsidized, Japanese-built vessels having massive proportions that required advancement of the maritime state of the art and cargo-carrying economics. In retrospect Japan met the challenge through national commitment and by having centralized management vested in their Ministry of International Trade and Industry (MITI). This was coupled with the expertise of their legions of accomplished technocrats and industrialists, who designed and produced vessels having massive proportions that required technical scope expansion beyond that of prevailing classification society rule requirements—and the extant state of the art for jumbo-sized vessel design and construction. At the present time, scant evidence appears to be present in the Western world for the fostering of more sophisticated technical approaches to support safe and even-larger bulker designs in the interest of optimizing cargo-carrying cost effectiveness. The author considers that the present shipbuilding expansion could generate increased operational risk in the long term, should economic parameters predominate and dictate hastiness in producing even larger bulk-cargo vessels which could exceed the design criteria currently published by various construction and inspection classification societies.

Under such circumstances the attendant technical risk could become a by-product of excessive semi-empirical data extrapolations which, in the present environment, may *not* be supported by the needed research and development (R&D) to complement selected hull structural configurations, computerized simulations, iconic modeling, full-scale prototyping, stringent life-cycle surveillance, operator feedback, etc. Retrospectively, the rule-based semi-empirical modus operandi used by classification societies for many years has provided a blind-faith "comfort zone" for underwriters, vessel owners, and designers, when bounded by precedent technical criteria and with acceptance based on proven application experience with *conventional* vessel configurations. However, any deviance or misinterpretation of rule boundaries, by surveyors or designers, could expose vessels to undefinable performance deficiencies, whenever a full understanding of the physics and physical interactions has not been developed.

This status quo, conducive to rigid rule-book and government regulatory compliance with application of long-standing procedures, should *not* remain as the sole criteria for evaluating the effectiveness of classification societies, vessel designers, or investigators. Nor should such traditional design practices be allowed to inhibit technology transfer from other fields, or creative and justifiable reasoning associated with structural dynamics and the hydroelastic behavior of vessels, beyond classical still-water determinations of hull-girder strength and vessel behavior under fictitiously "normal" environmental conditions. Otherwise it is possible that the maritime community could experience more unexplained losses without survivors or witnesses in the future—and with further ex post-facto *cause majeur* conclusions of investigators as outcomes of "We don't know what we don't know" scientific and technical dilemmas.

In this vein, the S.S. *Edmund Fitzgerald*, M.V. *Derbyshire*, and other case histories and investigations appear to merit reconsideration from the point of view of assessing the (in)adequacy or (in)completeness of available baseline design criteria, and the identification of scientific data necessary to formulate and reinforce technical conclusions having judicial merit beyond a reasonable doubt. Keeping in mind that the subject short-lived vessels were conceived by entrepreneurs with multiple bulk-cargo transportation efficiencies in mind and that they were both designed beyond the limits of extant A.B.S. and L.R.S. classification society rules, it is possible that the necessary extrapolation and heuristic reasoning of surveyors and designers could have indeed contributed to their catastrophic losses.

Part One:
A Personalized Prologue

On March 15, 1958, I first set my immigrant feet on American soil, and it was with a measure of relief that the frigid but picturesque winter experiences of Quebec were left far behind. At that point in time I knew very little about American history and the social and industrial cultures of the shipbuilding profession within its framework. However, I was very conscious that the Windsor – Canada to Detroit – Michigan Ambassador Bridge was one of the busiest international commerce gateways in the world and that the Detroit River was a part of the inland marine highway that facilitated an uninterruptable flow of bulk-cargo raw materials to the dependent industrial heartland. In later years I was to learn that our U.S.-flagged bulk-cargo lakers are required to transport about seventy thousand tons of iron ore to keep a major steel mill running for about five days, and seventy thousand tons of coal would only satisfy the electricity-generating demand of Greater Detroit for about one day.

Apart from these national awareness shortfalls, my maritime heritage and good geography teachers had fortunately tutored me well, and I had awareness of the generous national shoreline, the inland waterway system, and the Great Lakes natural fresh water basins that are surrounded by about 75 percent of the North American continent's population. The designated Great Lakes region alone accounts for about 25 percent of that population. As a newcomer I quickly realized that considerable time and effort would be required for discovery and geographic spatial adjustments, commencing with an appreciation of the Great Lakes fresh water basin immensity and having an awesome surface area of about ninety-four thousand square miles and an intra-continent shoreline of about ten thousand miles. As an ex-Brit I was indeed fascinated by the combined land masses of England, Scotland, Wales, and Northern Ireland having about the same surface areas as the five Great Lakes, with these lakes representing about 20 percent of the world's fresh water supply. Especially notable is Lake Superior, which stores about 50 percent of the capacity within the Great Lakes basins and is given recognition as the largest fresh water mass in the world, covering an area of about 31,660 square miles. For added perspective, Lake Superior's volumetric capacity is equal to that of Lakes Huron, Michigan, Erie, and Ontario, plus three more Lake Eries for good measure.

Vessels of the Inland Marine Highway
Immediately before coming to the United States I was employed for two years (1956–1958) as a naval architect with the very reputable Davie Shipbuilding Company, located at Lauzon in the Province of Quebec, Canada. At that point in time, this established shipbuilder and repairer was a subsidiary of Canada Steamship Lines (C.S.L.) headed since August 1951 by the president and C.E.O. T. Rodgie McLagan. C.S.L. also owned and operated four other shipyards at Collingwood, Kingston, Midland, and Port Arthur, Ontario, under the presidency of Richard Lowery, who was a dynamic British-trained naval architect, innovator, and business executive.

It is historically coincidental that C.S.L. started to expand the size of vessels for their bulk-cargo carrying fleet in a similar timeframe as American shipowners, to take advantage of improvements within the planned St. Lawrence Seaway System. The C.S.L. designs were of similar length and draft as the American-built *S.S. Edmund Fitzgerald*, to expand cargo-carrying capacity as enabled by Seaway improvements, with the first vessel, *Murray Bay* delivered in 1959 (versus 1958 for *Fitzgerald*). The *Murray Bay* was built and side-launched at their Collingwood shipyard and, because of excess carrying capacity and vessel attrition, thirteen of the C.S.L. smaller "canaller" vessels were taken out of fleet service in 1959, thereby heralding a change in the composition of future Great Lakes marine traffic. The *Whitefish Bay* (a C.S.L. flagship) was built in 1961 at the Davie Shipbuilding Company and was followed by eleven more (1963–1968) for C.S.L. and other shipowners.

Built	Name	Builder	Original Owner
1959	Murray Bay	Collingwood	Canada Steamship Lines
1961	Whitefish Bay	Davie	C.S.L. (Flagship)
1963	Baie Saint Paul	Davie	C.S.L.
1964	Saguenay	Davie	C.S.L.
1966	Manitoulin	Davie	C.S.L.
1967	Richelieu	Davie	C.S.L.
1968	Frontenac	Davie	C.S.L.
1963	Frankcliffe Hall	Davie	Hall Corporation
1965	Lawrencecliffe Hall	Davie	Hall Corporation
1966	Beavercliffe Hall	Davie	Hall Corporation
1969	Ottercliffe Hall	Davie	Hall Corporation
1966	A.S. Glossbrenner	Davie	Labrador Steamships
1968	Lake Manitoba	Davie	Nipigon Transport

When all of these vessels were successfully stern-launched, they raised some traditionalist eyebrows because of longitudinal bending stress concerns during the launching process for vessels of such length, which, on the Great Lakes, would have normally followed side-launching procedures, as in the case of *Murray Bay*, *Fitzgerald*, and others.

While all had similar high-block coefficient (full) hull forms to maximize carrying capacity, many of the above Canadian vessels embodied a succession of technical improvements of merit including, but not limited to:

- labor and cost reductions through application of modular construction techniques with high-strength steel fabrication;
- multi-engine diesel (versus steam turbine) propulsion machinery installations, having contribution to reduced crew complements;
- centralized vessel control from the bridge, and
- self-unloading capabilities, which would become vogue in later years.

In typical unpretentious Canadian manner, their parallel ship-building and operational performance, from Thunder Bay, Ontario, to Halifax, Nova Scotia, for this new generation of St. Lawrence

Seaway-sized bulk-cargo carriers, appears to have quietly passed into marine history without the overt media coverage that was attendant to the post-delivery "mystique" of the *S.S. Edmund Fitzgerald* over her notable seventeen years (1958–1975) of Great Lakes service.

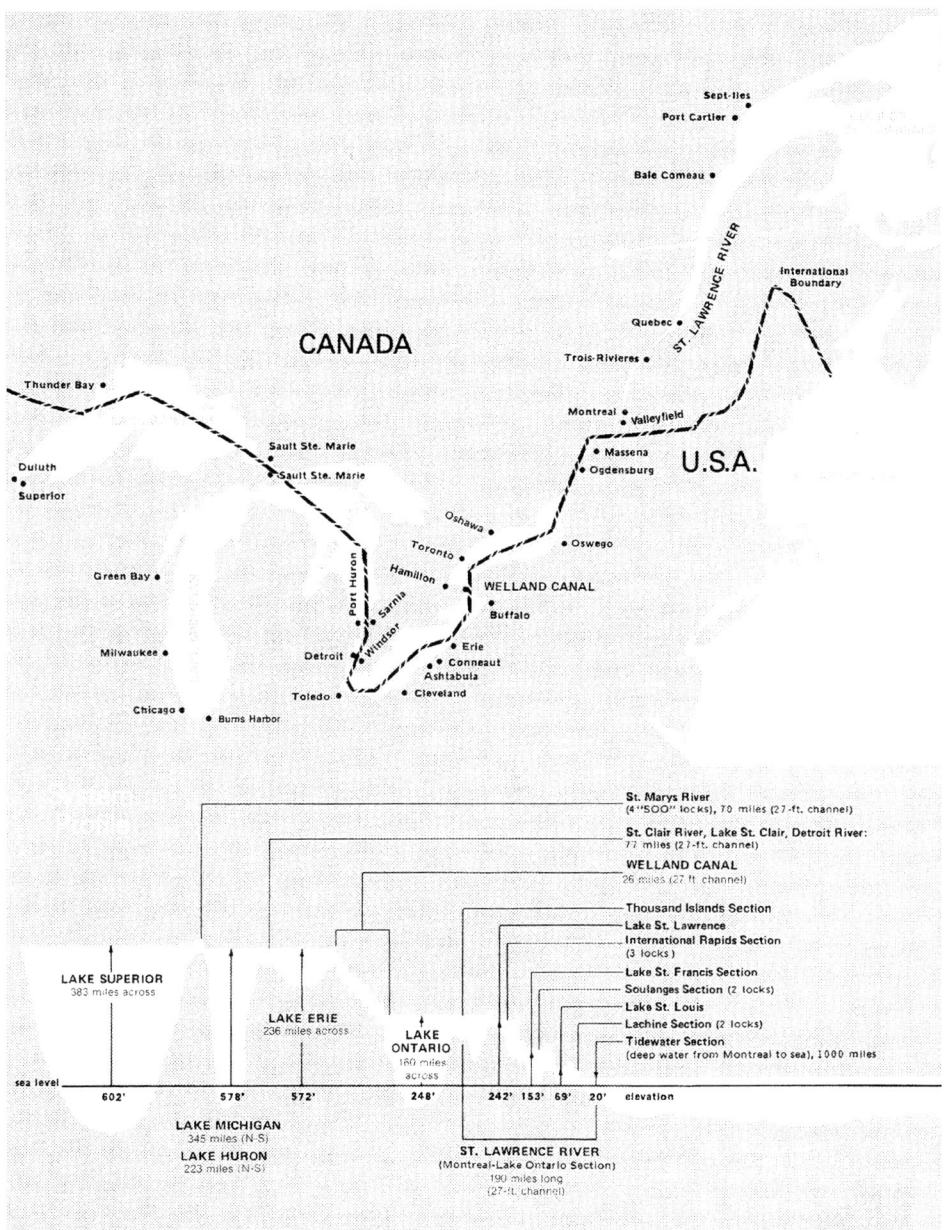

Fig. 3 – Great Lakes Trading Basins

Early History

During my Canadian residency, I availed myself of opportunities to research various historical Great Lakes maritime achievements of the 1600s, from the time when the French explorer LaSalle built the first land-locked *Griffon* sailing vessel for fur trading around three lakes, to enterprising French missionary engineers who pioneered construction of basic canals for shallow-draft barge traffic propelled by low-powered steam reciprocating machinery. Some of these barges carried "auxiliary" power in the form of horses to provide augmentation of the low-powered steam-driven plant when navigating areas having powerful rapids.

These visionary engineers, and others, constantly looked westward beyond Mount Royal (Montreal) with yearnings for ways to more easily access the Great Lakes trading basins (Fig. 3) without resorting to overland portage. Many years afterwards (1834–1904), significant waterway development was undertaken between Montreal and Lake Ontario to introduce a standardized lock size of 270'0" length x 45'0" width that eventually imposed limiting dimensional constraints for the subsequent design of "canaller" vessels to be used in connecting the St. Lawrence River to Great Lakes cargo-carrying services. This lockage system allowed vessels to bypass rapids and accommodate differences in water elevations between Montreal and Lake Ontario, and it was capable of raising vessels to 248 feet above sea level. Self-propelled and "boxy," steel-hulled "canallers" were specifically designed to utilize this early marine routing system, and they included a number of vessels delivered to Canada by British shipyards. These vessels were specially reinforced and cautiously certified for a risky (one-time) Atlantic crossing to Canada. As an immigrant who experienced rough weather conditions during a ten-day winter North Atlantic crossing (1956) from Liverpool, England, to Halifax, Nova Scotia, aboard Cunard Line's vintage R.M.S. *Scythia*, with drifting icebergs slightly North, I still have the utmost admiration and empathy for intrepid "canaller" crews who may have braved similar elements in their smaller, slower, and less-seakindly vessels.

One of these British-built vessels was the diesel-electric self-unloading *M.V. Cementkarrier* (Fig. 4) which was built by Furness Shipbuilding Company, my ship design apprenticeship alma mater (1947–1952). This vessel enjoyed a long and productive life (1930–1986) while operating in the brackish waters of the St. Lawrence River and the fresh water environment of the Great Lakes.

Subsequently many other "canallers" were designed and built by Canadian shipyards, including *M.V. Metis* (Fig. 5), *M.V. Coniscliffe Hall* (Fig. 6), and *M.V. Rockcliffe Hall*, which were delivered during my period of employment with the Davie Shipbuilding Company. These "canaller" vessels furthered the evolution of our intra-continent waterborne trade, even though their commissioned life was short, and their cargo capacity was limited by dimensional constraints (269' 0" length x 43' 10" beam x 22' 6" depth/14' 3" draft) due to the controlling lift lock dimensions at Cornwall, Ontario, Canada. This particular lock (No. 17) was completed in 1840, and it contributed to by-passing of the Long Sault rapids, albeit an inward shift of a lockwall imposed a perpetual limitation on the beam width of *all* "canallers."

The Marine Stairway
When inland trade expanded, larger bulk-cargo (and other) vessels and their shipbuilding industrial support base developed, it became evident that larger lockage systems would be necessary to facilitate expanded navigational access:

Fig. 4 - M.V. Cementkarrier – self-discharging cement carrier
Photo J.M. Evans

Fig. 5 - M.V. Metis
Photo Davie Shipbuilding

Fig. 6 M.V. Coniscliffe Hall
Photo Davie Shipbuilding

From Lake Ontario to Lake Erie:

Opening of the current twenty-six mile long eight-lock Welland Canal in 1932 bypassed the Niagara Falls and elevated vessels an additional 324 feet to 572 feet above sea level. This resulted in major shipping linkages from Lake Ontario to other lakes further inland.

From the Lower Lakes to Lake Superior Ports via Sault Ste. Marie:

A large capacity vessel-locking installation, generally known as the SOO Locks (Fig. 7) was constructed between 1914 and 1968 as follows:

- DAVIS LOCK (1,350 x 80 x 23.1 feet), constructed 1914.
- SABIN LOCK (1,350 x 80 x 23.1 feet), constructed 1919.
- Now closed, a proposed new lock would utilize the space occupied by the DAVIS and SABIN LOCKS.
- MacARTHUR LOCK (800 x 80 x 31.0 feet), constructed 1943.
- POE LOCK (1,200 x 110 x 32.0 feet), constructed 1968.

These locks elevated vessels a final twenty-four feet to 602 feet above sea level at the lakehead.

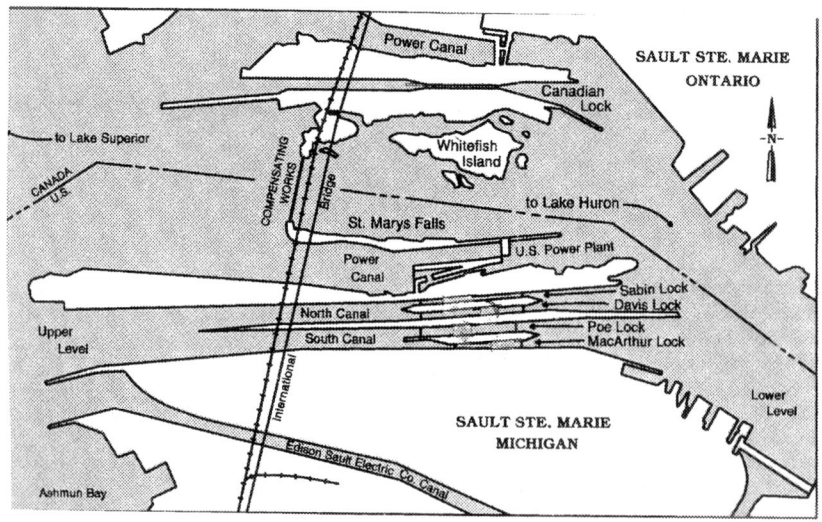

Fig. 7 - The "Soo" Locks

Bi-national Partners

Introduction of these inland marine trade routes would no doubt have partly satisfied the creative waterborne transportation visions of early French engineers and traders, although the final navigation routing for large, deep-channel, *oceangoing* vessels would not begin until ground was broken on August 10, 1954, for construction of the St. Lawrence Seaway System under joint United States-Canada sponsorship.

In the five years that followed:

- Twenty-two thousand American and Canadian workers excavated over two hundred million cubic feet of rock and soil (including destructive "blue mud" that significantly shortened the working life of excavating equipment and escalated program costs). Over six million cubic yards of concrete were poured.
- Almost forty thousand acres of mainly New York State and Ontario, Canada, farmland were permanently flooded. During my visits to the excavation sites, I recall seeing a (pre-submergence) Cornwall, Ontario, road sign optimistically proclaiming "We have to go, but watch us grow."
- The Moses-Saunders bi-national hydro-electric power plant was constructed.
- Ten new lift bridges were built.
- The Jacques Cartier and Mercier Bridges at Montreal were elevated.
- A canal was excavated along the South shore of the St. Lawrence River to bypass the Lachine Rapids.
- Forty-one miles of Canadian National Railroad mainline track and thirty-five miles of highway were relocated.
- Eight Ontario communities were relocated, with the displacement of 500 homes and 6,500 Canadians.
- A major new construction element was extended from Montreal to Lake Ontario, with excavation for seven new locks having a combined lifting capability of 248 feet over a distance of 190 miles. This was complemented by navigational channel

widening and deepening to a depth of 27 feet. In total, a deep-draft inland marine highway, extending 2,342 miles from the Atlantic Ocean to the most-westerly port of Duluth, at 602 feet above sea level, was made possible for larger vessels not exceeding the limiting maxima of the St. Lawrence Seaway System.

Lest it be forgotten, the approval, planning, and building of the St. Lawrence Seaway took over half a century to complete after U.S. Representative John Lind of Minnesota originally sponsored (in 1892) a Congressional Resolution for a joint U.S.-Canada investigation into the possibility of building a deep-draft waterway from the head of Lake Superior to the Atlantic Ocean. In 1895, it was determined that the St. Lawrence River could be a feasible route. When the Seaway was opened to traffic on April 25, 1959, with official dedication by President Eisenhower and Her Majesty Queen Elizabeth II, on June 26 and 27, 1959, the ceremonies were conducted with a great sense of accomplishment and optimism for future domestic and international trading benefits.

New Vessel Traffic
Over a period of time, the composition of Great Lakes and St. Lawrence River vessels gradually changed to take full economic advantage of the Seaway. Initially some "canallers" were lengthened for increased cargo-carrying capacity, before eventual phase out, to achieve balance in the supply-demand business profile.

Some oceangoing "salties" that cautiously utilized the Seaway System incurred damage and delays while in transit, and into this evolutionary arena American and Canadian vessel owners made large investments for new Seaway-sized bulk-cargo vessels, of which the *S.S. Edmund Fitzgerald* was the leader Some had certification to operate as far East as Sept Iles, located in the Province of Quebec and/or on limited Canadian coastal routes.

At that time some American and Canadian bulk-cargo carriers were designed with self-unloading capability and were able to capitalize on newly-emergent business opportunities offered in lower reaches of the St. Lawrence River by offloading coal cargo at deep-water docks or topping-off large oceangoing colliers stationed mid-stream (Fig. 8).

Fig. 8 – Self-unloading from Lakers to Oceangoing Bulk-cargo Vessel
Photo - St. Lawrence Seaway Development Corporation

Although *Fitzgerald* was designed as a "straight-decker" to transport a variety of bulk-cargoes such as iron ore, coal, wheat, etc., she mainly hauled taconite pellets from ports of western Lake Superior to steel mills in Detroit, Michigan, Cleveland, Ohio, and Gary, Indiana. Due to structural design constraints, oceangoing and coastal service were precluded.

Coincident with radically changed American heavy industry and business frameworks (since 1959), the supply/demand spectrum for bulk-cargo products has also undergone significant changes affecting industrial distribution, vessel dimensional increases with significant reductions in fleet population, and operating cost/ton-mile.

Today (2005), typical 1,000-foot supercarriers (thirteen in number for Upper Lakes service) each have a cargo carrying capacity of about four or more 600-footers and have considerably less fuel, crew, and other operating costs. A currently widespread use of "self-unloading" capability is generally the norm, with an unloading rate of about seventy thousand tons of iron ore or coal in less than ten hours.

In retrospect, the overall U.S. Great Lakes bulk-cargo fleet has become drastically diminished over the years, from about two hundred vessels in the 1970s to about one hundred (early 1980s), to about seventy-five (mid-1990s), and forty-two active vessels at the close of 2003. These reductions have had debilitating effects upon mariner employment and the supporting shoreside industries providing construction, repair, and maintenance services. Virtually every aspect of the American industrial base, including U.S.-flag operators on the Great Lakes have undergone restructuring since the 1980s and still operate without government subsidies.

Most of their difficulties are iron-ore related, since level playing fields of competition and free trade in the world steel market are as rare as Great Lakes ice in August. Reduced demand for domestically-produced steel products has had undesirable systemic effects throughout U.S. industry as dumping and predatory pricing on our shores have become vogue, whenever foreign exporters 'dump' surplus products during downturns in their own industries. There is an ongoing state of crisis as Great Lakes bulk-cargo fleets and the American steel-making industry have become seriously reduced in size and employment as the result of reduced demand. Correcting the iron ore supply-demand business deterioration, will require government intervention.

In light of the 1959 Seaway completion and certain shipyards having potential to build and repair large laker and oceangoing vessels, the late 1950s framework of reference *appeared* to bode well (from my career development viewpoint) for Great lakes shipyards to consider participation in the competitive international marketplace. The positioning and long-term achievements of the Great Lakes Engineering Works (GLEW) shipyard, River Rouge, Michigan, coupled with their selection to build the *S.S. Edmund Fitzgerald*, *appeared* to serve as a credible entry point for a naval architect to pursue his chosen career. Regrettably, and for macro-economic reasons, including the severe post-World War II decline of U.S. commercial shipbuilding industries (Fig. 9), the perceived professional opportunities could not be realized.

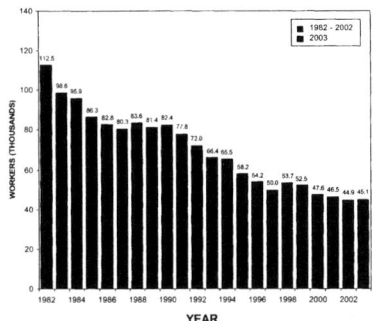

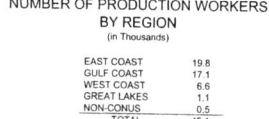

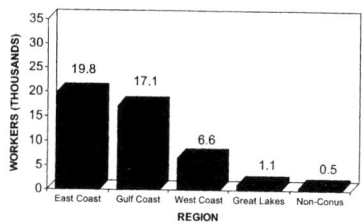

Fig. 9 - Private Shipyard Status
Source: U.S. Maritime Administration

A Contribution

With the foregoing as personalized prologue, and with career benefit from my association with higher-tech naval ship engineering in later years, I wish to contribute additional perspective to the catastrophic unexplained bulk-cargo vessel losses of the laker *S.S. Edmund Fitzgerald* (November 1975) while transiting in Canadian waters, with expansion to the British *M.V. Derbyshire* (September 1980) and others in worldwide operation. The *Fitzgerald* and *Derbyshire* losses occurred in a closely-related timeframe and, while each vessel subsequently received varying depths of inconclusive investigation, their losses still remain "riddles wrapped in mysteries inside enigmas," as would have been expounded by the late Sir Winston S. Churchill.

Restatement of prior findings, conclusions, theories, and recommendations will be minimized to avoid undue repetition, although appropriate references will be included (exclusive of other elements that feel a need for recognition of the "Devil's Triangle," flying saucers, and flights of extraterrestrial imagination).

Part Two:
Arrival in the U.S.A.

After clearance through Immigration and Customs Service control points prior to exiting the International Ambassador Bridge in Detroit, Michigan, I merged with Detroit's swiftly-flowing confluence of vehicular traffic, which appeared to be heading for the industrial downriver area via the westbound Edsel Ford Expressway. After hesitatingly taking a ramp marked SOUTH-SCHAEFER ROAD, CANADA (!?), I felt that I may have made a navigational error, because I knew that Canada was due *North* of the United States. Nevertheless I proceeded until grimy Schaefer Road, in mainly Ford Motor Company territory, intersected Jefferson Avenue at River Rouge. It was a relief to eventually arrive in the city of River Rouge, but unfortunately *no one* seemed to know where the shipyard was located.

At that time I had an initially alarming but serendipitous encounter, with an inebriated "Paul Bunyan-sized" individual who was staring at the Quebec license plate on my automobile. As I approached, he belligerently asked what I was doing in River Rouge. Rather than beard the lion in his den, I chose (what *I* thought) was the path of least resistance by answering that I was to start work at the Great Lakes Engineering Works shipyard—*if I could find it*. In short order I sensed that I had *not* chosen the path of least resistance when "Paul Bunyan" became very agitated and physically lifted me by the lapels of my jacket and, in no uncertain terms, told me to return to Quebec since he had lost his job at the shipyard. To him, it looked like I may have been his *replacement*!

I was certainly no physical match for my antagonist, so I was obliged to exercise discretion and diplomacy rather than valor. While still suspended, I asked what job he had lost at the shipyard and was informed that his trade was welding. After I told him that I was a ship designer, I was slowly lowered to the sidewalk and received an apology couched in terms of "I guess I can't do your job...and you wouldn't want to do mine. Welcome to the U.S.A." A serendipitous outcome ensued when he provided good directions to the shipyard on Great Lakes Avenue. I later considered this circumstance to be paradoxical, in that although no one was able to give me directions to the shipyard, the media reported over ten thousand people were later on-site to view the *S.S. Edmund Fitzgerald* launching event!

Great Lakes Engineering Works (G.L.E.W.) Company

When passing through a residential area along Great Lakes Avenue, I became very aware that I was entering the vintage G.L.E.W. marine property, which covered 33.64 acres in the city of River Rouge, Michigan, contiguous with an 11.66 acre tract in the city of Ecorse (Fig. 10). At a much earlier time, other shipbuilding and ship repair properties were operated at St. Clair, Michigan, and in Ashtabula, Ohio. These industrial facilities were augmented by a general office and an engine plant in the city of Detroit, the latter being engaged in the production of triple- and quadruple-expansion steam engines. After the company's founding in early 1903, the shipyard launched its first bulk-cargo vessel, the *S.S. R.W. England*, on May 5, 1905 (Fig. 11-1). By today's standards she was of moderate dimensions at 377' 0" length x 50' 0" beam x 28' 3" depth and had a cargo capacity of six thousand tons. Since that time the first self-unloading freighter, *S.S. Wyandotte* (Figs. 11-2 and 11-3) was built (1908) and some three hundred other vessels were either built or repaired, for Great Lakes and oceangoing commerce. These included bulk-cargo carriers, ferries, tugs, barges, yachts, and an underwater tunnel caisson. A listing of contracts (1903–1962) executed by the G.L.E.W. River Rouge Shipyard is shown in Fig. 11-4.

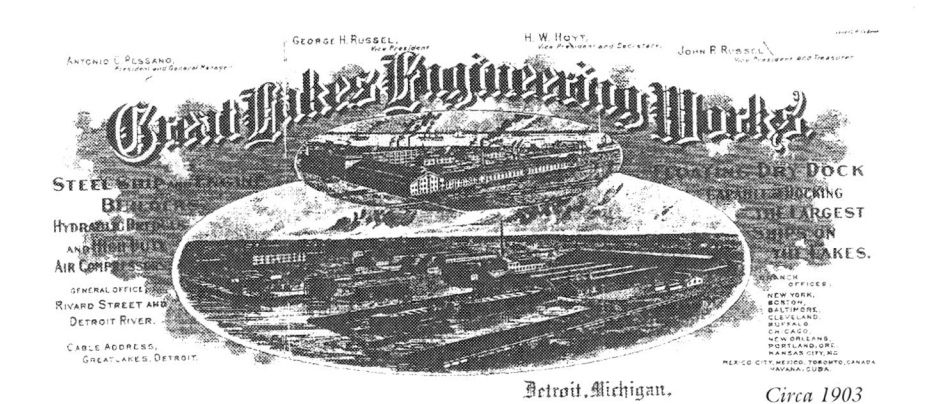

Fig. 10 – River Rouge, Michigan G.L.E.W. Shipyard Site. U.S. Army Corps of Engrs, U.S. Lake Survey -Detroit River Chart No. 41 (1958)

Fig. 11-1 – The R.W. England wsa the first vessel at GLEW and she measured 377' x 50' x 28' 3" (1905).

Fig.11-2 – Construction view of the Wyandotte, the first self-unloader built on the lakes.

Fig.11-3 – S.S. Wyandotte
Source: Dossin Museum Collection

#	Name	#	Name	#	Name	#	Name
1	R. W. England	58	F. J. Lisman	115	Lake Winona	172	Edward J. Berwind
2	Detroit	59	Grayson	116	Lake Crystal	173	Joseph H. Frantz
3	James E. Davidson	60	Borinquen	117	Lake Allen	174	William C. Atwater
4	Hoover and Mason	61	Yaguez	118	Lake Hemlock	175	William G. Mather
5	Superior	62	Bayamon	119	Lakehurst	176	John A. Topping
6	Peter White	63	Robert M. Thompson	120	Lake Mary	177	Halcyon
7	William G. Mather	64	A. A. Raven	121	Lake Conesus	178	Gt.Lks.Drge.&Dk.Co.54(scow)
8	Delaware	65	Ruby	122	Lake Silver	179	A. F. Harvey
9	Frank C. Ball	66	Boston	123	Lake Janet	180	S. T. Crapo
10	B. F. Jones	67	North American	124	Lake Pearl	181	police boat (for Detroit)
11	James Laughlin	68	A.& N.O.T.Co.Barge No. 1	125	Lake Gardner	182	140 (scow)
12	William P. Snyder	69	barge 2	126	Lakeville	183	141 (scow)
13	Michigan	70	barge 3	127	Craincreek	184	Cadillac
14	Ishpeming	71	barge 4	128	Cranenest	185	The Straits of Mackinac
15	J. H. Sheadle	72	barge 5	129	Crawl Keys	186	No. 142 (scow)
16	John W. McKerchey	73	barge 6	130	Craycroft	187	No. 57 (derrick scow)
17	E. L. Wallace	74	New Orleans (fuel lighter)	131	Corydon	188	No. 58 (derrick scow)
18	Thomas F. Cole	75	Multnomah (dredge)	132	Costilla	189	Handy Billy (derrick scow)
19	Wilpen	76	Wahkiakum (dredge)	133	Cote Blanche	190	No. 1 (scow)
20	D. O. Mills	77	Hibernia (scow)	134	Cotopaxi	191	derrick scow (unnamed)
21	Milinokett	78	Maitland No. 1	135	Cottonplant	192	Dunbar (derrick scow)
22	John J. Boland	79	Ann Arbor No. 6	136	Cottonwood	193	Myron S. Taylor
23	Jacob P. Kopp	80	Huron	137	Coulee	194	motor boat (U.S.GypsumCo.)
24	Josiah G. Munro	81	South American	138	Council Bluffs	195	Napper Tandy (scow)
25	Rochester	82	International	139	Couparle	196	Service (scow)
26	Burlington	83	Kerry Gow (scow)	140	Courtois	197	No. 2 (scow)
27	Bennington	84	cement barge	141	Coushatta	198	Eugene P. Thomas
28	W. A. Bradley	85	Harry J. (tug)	142	Coutolene	199	Dupuis No. 12 (scow)
29	Harry A. Berwind	86	barge	143	Covalt	200	Edgewater
30	William Livingstone	87	scow	144	Covedale	201	Chester
31	James Corrigan	88	scow	145	Covena	202	R. H. Goode (tug)
32	Daniel B. Meacham	89	International	146	Coverun	203	Empire (dredge)
33	Wyandotte	90	Yaque	147	Cowan	204	Dearborn (tug)
34	Ecorse (tug)	91	Yuna	148	Lake Elkwood	205	Margaret II (yacht)
35	Clifford F. Moll	92	Inca	149	Lake Elkwater	206	Dahlia (litehse tender)
36	Theodore H. Wickwire	93	No. 10 (scow)	150	Lake Ellendale	207	Green Island
37	Ulster (scow)	94	No. 11 (scow)	151	Lake Ellenorah	208	Norfolk
38	Munster (scow)	95	William A. McGonagle	152	Lake Ellerslie	209	Ralph H. Watson
39	North Sea	96	Conneaut	153	Lake Ellicott	210	John Hulst
40	Shenango	97	Norfolk	154	Lake Ellijay	211	Leon Fraser
41	G. A. Boeckling	98	Philadelphia	155	Lake Ellithorpe	212	Enders M. Voorhees
42	Leinster (scow)	99	Munisla	156	Lake Ellsworth	213	A. H. Ferbert
43	Conneaght (scow)	100	Aristobulo del Valle	157	Lake Ellsbury	214	Richard J. Reiss
44	Stadacona	101	P. L. M. 4	158	Lake Elmdale	215	Cadillac
45	Erie	102	P. L. M. 5	159	Lake Elmhurst	216	George A. Sloan
46	Ontario	103	Pontiac	160	Lake Elmont	217	Frank Purnell
47	Champlain	104	Frank H. Goodyear	161	Lake Slavi	218	Robert C. Stanley
48	St. Clair	105	Souk Ahras	162	Lake Elmsford	219	Lehigh
49	William J. Olcott	106	Lake Tahoe	163	Lake Elmwood	220	Vacationland
50	William B. Dickson	107	August Ziesing	164	Delphine (yacht)	221	Cason J. Callaway
51	William P. Palmer	108	River Rouge (flat scow)	165	Dupuis No. 6 (scow)	222	J. L. Mauthe
52	Willis L. King	109	Lakeland	166	139 (scow)	223	Reserve
53	Col. James M. Schoonmaker	110	Lake Dunmore	167	James McNaughton	224	William Clay Ford
54	William P. Snyder Jr.	111	Lake Elizabeth	168	Wayne	225	Edmund Fitzgerald ✱
55	Penobscot	112	Lake St. Clair	169	Frontenac	226	Herbert C. Jackson
56	Seaconnet	113	Lake Houghton	170	Benson Ford	227	Arthur B. Homer
57	W. E. Harper	114	Lake Owens	171	T. N. T. (drill scow)		

Fig. 11-4 – Great Lakes Engineering Works
Vessels Built at Ecorse/River Rouge 1903-1962
Source: River Rouge Historical Museum

Throughout the G.L.E.W. shipyard's lifetime, it had a reputation for flexibility in the cross-training of workers for the encouragement of craftsman diversity, improved employment stability, and the high-quality outfitting of crew and passenger accommodations.

Significant innovative achievements included the following:

1908 - The freighter *Wyandotte* became the world's first self-unloading vessel and started a trend that would change the way bulk cargoes were handled.

1912 - The freighter *Edison Light* became the first "sternwinder" with cabins directly over the stern and was developed for East Coast bulk-freight trade.

1918 - The steamer *Crawl Keys* was completed in a record-breaking twenty-nine days during World War I by increasing prefabrication and improving the coordination of construction.

1924 - The steamer *Benson Ford* became the first diesel-powered Great Lakes bulk-cargo carrier.

1925 - The freighter *William C. Atwater* became the first Great Lakes bulk-cargo carrier to use single-piece steel hatch covers and a travelling deck crane.

1958 - The *S.S. Edmund Fitzgerald* became the first bulk-cargo vessel specifically designed for Great Lakes and St. Lawrence Seaway service.

During World Wars I and II, significant contributions were made to support the war effort.

In the shipyard's twilight years, such attributes made the shipyard a well-qualified choice to build the *S.S. Edmund Fitzgerald* as the longest and fastest vessel having the greatest bulk-cargo carrying capacity. Any boarding visitor would quickly realize that the outfitting of passenger, officer, and crew accommodations was superb.

In retrospect, it is appropriate to acknowledge that the opening of the G.L.E.W. Company in 1903 was during a time of historical industrial and population growth in Michigan. The Company was one of many early enterprises that were able to capitalize on emergent business opportunities in an environment favoring innovation and labor-intensive undertakings by both skilled and unskilled workforces.

Historical records are most revealing and show that literacy and innovation were hallmarks of the early Michigan business environment, with the Detroit area as her principal industrial city, port, and staging post for the distribution of Michigan-produced goods and services. Practical innovation even extended to an unpaved Dearborn road in "Ford Country" being reinforced with cedar planks to carry commercial loads of heavy-duty wagon trains and occasional steam engines as industrial production abounded.

Shipyards were emerging as promising sites for young men to acquire training and gain experience in various trades having potential cross-fertilization with other industries. It should be noted that the first official mechanical apprentice training (1882) of automotive icon Henry Ford was at the Detroit Drydock Company, which pioneered Bessemer steel fabrication and the construction of iron vessels for Great Lakes service. It is also a matter of record that Mr. Ford was only paid a $2.00 weekly wage and his landlady charged $3.50 per week, so he "moonlighted" (like others) and was able to transfer his shipyard mechanical skills to the repair of timepieces and farm machinery. His shipyard apprenticeship was a prized appointment that was repeated by the author under an indentured five-year agreement that only had a weekly wage of $1.75 during the initial year of 1947. In reality, apprentices were paying their employer for their training and worked long hours.

The year 1903 was also a significant aviation milestone for the United States when one considers that the first airplane flight was made by Orville and Wilbur Wright at Kittyhawk in North Carolina. That same year, the first transcontinental road trip was made across the United States by the pioneering Dr. Horatio Nelson, driving a vintage Winton vehicle under daunting road conditions plagued with logistical difficulties while en route.

These are but a few of the achievements in the year 1903, with the Great Lakes Engineering Works Company also a participant as the United States progressed toward becoming a vibrant industrial giant.

G.L.E.W. Ecorse-River Rouge Shipyard (1903–1962)
When opened in 1903, the original shipbuilding and repair plant was the largest on the Great Lakes, occupying a land tract of about eighty-five acres and having a frontage of fourteen hundred feet on

the Detroit River. The Michigan Central and Detroit Southern railroads both had trackage into the shipyard. The shipyard plant had four shipbuilding berths of six hundred feet in length, to facilitate simultaneous construction of four of the largest vessels ever planned for Great Lakes services at that time in history. Between these berths there were two slips for the side-launching of new vessels.

The larger slip, at 600 feet length x 150 feet width x 30 feet water depth, was also used for operation of a floating drydock that was the first of its kind on the Lakes and was large enough to handle any vessel that operated in the inland waters. At such time as the slip was required for a new vessel side-launching event, the floating drydock was temporarily towed out into the Detroit River. The other side-launching slip was 600 feet length x 125 feet width x 14 feet water depth. Each shipbuilding berth had electrically-powered travelling cranes for the transfer of shipboard material and machinery from various shops, and two ten-ton steam locomotive cranes were run on tracks to service all parts of the yard when carrying out lifting or hauling functions.

So far as possible, electricity was used to operate shipyard machinery, and there were two large air compressors, each capable of furnishing 3,000 cubic feet of air per minute at a pressure of 160 pounds per square inch. This power ran all pneumatic drilling, chipping, riveting, and caulking tools. Plate fabrication tools, shears (including a 100-ton pair of shears), and punches were operated by electricity. Electric overhead gantry cranes served each production shop. Indeed, the original 1903 shipyard appeared to be well-equipped to present formidable business competition to others and was strategically positioned to service vessels plying the busy Detroit River.

Over many years, the plant operations also displayed diversification in that the company contracted for fabrication and erection of structural framing for steel buildings; construction of highway trailers for hauling automobiles; the assembly of railroad cars; and miscellaneous steel products. Locally the shipyard provided steel fabrications for many additions to the original Great Lakes Steel mills in Ecorse, the McClouth Steel Corporation plants in Trenton and Gibralter, and for Detroit Edison's River Rouge Power Plant. The company was better known, however, for its shipbuilding accomplishments especially during wartime conditions. As an aside, I recall that while researching the National Archives in Washington, D.C., I read some very personalized World War II correspondence between a River Rouge politician and President Franklin D. Roosevelt. It was reassuring to read that the shipyard, its workers, and the supporting steel industry had visibility at the highest Washington level in the local politician's letters requesting an increased shipyard workload. One request was aptly directed:

> "Dear Mr. President, we wish to make you aware that we want to contribute to the war effort and have a highly-skilled 2,000-man workforce, and steel mills next door who have to just pass their steel over the fence to build good ships. Other Great Lakes shipyards are receiving orders and we cannot understand why we are not receiving the same considerations...."

Regrettably, with the passage of time such memories of the many years of G.L.E.W. shipyard achievements appear to have passed into oblivion, albeit the *S.S. Edmund Fitzgerald* sinking catastrophe still has national remembrance through Gordon Lightfoot's commercialized ballad "The Wreck of the *Edmund Fitzgerald*" and the hearts of mariner families.

In later years, the shipbuilding plant became reduced in size, covering 45.30 (versus 85.00) acres but was still located about two miles South of the Rouge River. The two G.L.E.W. slips, indented at ninety degrees to the Detroit River, remained virtually unchanged, but only one of the four ship-construction berths was retained in an active status immediately adjacent to, and parallel with, a deactivated berth. The latter berth was innovatively used as a production platen for the prefabrication of hull modules and deckhouse sub-assemblies. In retrospect it may be fairly stated that the shipyard's production achievements were noteworthy and largely creditable to its employees, who carried out their duties without support from shipbuilding technologies available today. By this statement, I have in mind advancements such as Computer-Aided Design and Manufacturing (CAD/CAM); numerically-controlled (N.C.) machining; plate-cutting and forming processes; laser alignment; computer-assisted production, planning, and control; selective non-destructive testing (NDT); and formalized quality assurance measures, etc.

Those who have experienced a hands-on relationship with the industry may share my view that processes used by G.L.E.W. continued to demonstrate that Great Lakes shipbuilding was still very much an art form, as production tradesmen continued to traditionally practice "doing-the-best-with-the-tools-available." within the plant.

As with most Great Lakes shipyards operating in the *Fitzgerald* construction timeframe, the G.L.E.W. shipbuilding and repair practices could be characterized by a labor-intensive workplace environment requiring about 80 percent perspiration and 20 percent inspiration when contrasted with rapidly evolving "high-tech" industries. Production innovations, requiring minimum new capital investment, were made possible by the modular construction of major (side ballast tank) hull sections, which were fabricated on their sides to maximize down-hand welding, with attendant improvements in joint fitup and welding quality. These sections were rotated ninety degrees before crane transfer and positioning on the construction berth. (Fig. 12)

Prefabricated topside deckhouse structures were completed off-hull before being hoisted and positioned in their spar deck locations about fifty feet above ground level before ship launching. Some cellular double-bottom water ballast tank modules were actually fabricated by off-site contractors for avoidance of production-line flow congestion within the shipyard in way of the prefabrication berth platen.

These and other production practices made it possible for G.L.E.W. to meet their scheduled side-launching date of June 7, 1958 (Fig. 13), only K + forty-four weeks after keel laying. On launching day, Hull No. 301 (the *S.S. Edmund Fitzgerald*) was in a very high state of pre-launch completion, at about 7,500 tons weight and with the 140-ton main propulsion steam turbine and both of her 84-ton boilers already installed (Figs. 14, 15A, 15B). Lake Erie performance trials were successfully completed on September 13, 1958, followed by delivery to the Northwestern Mutual Life Insurance Company owners on September 22, 1958 (K + 58 weeks).

The subsequent timely deliveries of almost identical vessels, the *S.S. Herbert C. Jackson* and *S.S. Arthur B. Homer* to other owners also benefited from the innovative production practices prior to shipyard closure in 1962 as shipbuilding and repair business opportunities declined.

Future Prospects and the St. Lawrence Seaway

During that time there were pervasive rumors and speculations that the shipyard may be sold to parties having interest in transforming the site to an offloading terminal for oceangoing "saltie" vessels who were experiencing cargo unloading delays due to a paucity of dockside facilities.

Early Seaway System experiences (circa 1959) revealed that most Great Lakes ports, except for Toronto, were ill prepared to handle the increased flow of shipping. This situation also affected the port of Detroit when seagoing vessels, such as the *S.S. Santa Rosa*, decided to depart without discharging her cargo after many days of delay. The navigational constraints of the Seaway, coupled with offloading delays, were anathema to cost-effective commercial shipping operations. However, it was an expectation inter-alia that cargo offloading facilities would become improved, albeit seasonal icing limitations were expected to remain an obstacle to year-round operations.

Fig. 12 – Side Ballast Tank Module On Side (Rotated 90°)
K + 4 Weeks
Shipyard Photo – Dossin Museum Collection

Fig. 13 – Keel Laying August 7, 1957
Shipyard Photo – Dossin Museum Collection

Fig. 14 – K + 12 Weeks
Shipyard Photo – Dossin Museum Collection

Fig. 15 – K + 16 Weeks
Shipyard Photo – Dossin Museum Collection

Fig. 15A – K + 26 Weeks
Shipyard Photo – Dossin Museum Collection

Fig. 15B – Launching Day. June 7, 1958 K + 44 Weeks
Photo – Center For Archival Collections, Bowling Green State University

While it is evident that there has been considerably expanded "saltie" traffic flow and port facility enhancement over the years, there was no sign of an increased G.L.E.W. workload. It is also noted that the statistical data (circa 2004) still does not reflect exploitation of the containerized cargo-handling concept. To the observer, specialized intra-Seaway and intermodal *feeder* vessel designs appear to have potential for enabling cost-effective use of "saltie" vessels. Such satellite augmentation would release oceangoing containerships for their high-speed dedication to rapid transoceanic voyages only. Their container offloading could be handled at a "notional" quick turnaround St. Lawrence River port, with no locking required, and containers could be offloaded and transported by road, rail, or intra-lake feeder vessels as seasonal conditions permitted—as in productive *coastal ports*.

With the successful advent of Malcolm McLean's Sea-Land Corporation containerization concept in the early 1960s, a visionary businessman, Jeno Paulucci, foresaw the potential use of intermodal container transportation between Duluth-Superior, Cleveland, and Buffalo to move his company's canned good products. In 1959, the Browning Line, a Detroit carrier, provided a service using the steamers *W. Wayne Hancock* and *John C. Hay*, but for only part of the season, because sufficient back-haul cargoes could not be generated for the Duluth-Superior Twin Ports.

Much later, in October 1975, a new container facility was placed in commercial operation at the Clure Public Marine Terminal at Duluth, but despite heavy promotion, the venture was again unsuccessful. While containerization is embraced on a world-wide scale and at major U.S. coastal ports, it would appear that the Great Lakes region is missing an international commerce opportunity to benefit shipping and businesses of the hinterland.

In light of overall deteriorating national maritime industry circumstances, it was clearly evident that personal shipbuilding career prospects on the Great Lakes—and the G.L.E.W. shipyard's future—were at risk. Until I gained naturalized citizen status, it would be unlikely that a suitable naval architect position could be sought with military activities engaged in security-sensitive warship programs. I therefore temporarily changed my field and accepted a challenging automobile body stress analyst engineering position with the Central

Engineering Division of the venerable Chrysler Corporation and found many of my technical skills transferable, although the flotation principles of Archimedes were never called upon. As the saying goes, "When in Detroit, do what Detroiters do...build cars!"

The G.L.E.W. shipyard closed in 1962, and the *Fitzgerald*'s launch basin facility morphed into a part of the Great Lakes Yacht Club recreational site (Fig. 16). This event appeared to be the precursor of a very bleak national business environment for commercial shipbuilding and repair in general.

Fig. 16 – A Metamorphosis-
The Great Lakes Yacht Club. (Ex-Great Lakes Engineering Works Shipyard)
River Rouge, Michigan
Photo – River Rouge Historical Museum

PART THREE:
BULK-CARGO VESSEL CONSIDERATIONS

The practice of naval architecture has evolved over centuries and now has a wide range of technological complexity when applied to a broad spectrum of vessels, inclusive of highly sophisticated nuclear-powered combatant submarines operating globally in harm's way and simple commercial barges operating in low-risk marine environments. All vessels require unique consideration as effective and safe marine systems having compatibility with specific operating conditions within their realm and the achievement of economic goals for acquisition, operation, and life-cycle maintenance. Great Lakes and oceangoing bulk-cargo carriers lie within this broad spectrum, and the naval architect is usually expected to function as an overall system integrator for the design and construction of such vessels as the *S.S. Edmund Fitzgerald*.

S.S. Edmund Fitzgerald Requirements

With service restricted to the St. Lawrence Seaway System, her design was required to be in compliance with Great Lakes Load Line Regulations. Hull structural design and the selection of machinery installations also required approval by the American Bureau of Shipping (ABS) Ship Classification Society. A basic principle was followed that the vessel should meet structural strength, reserve buoyancy, and stability requirements to assure owners, shippers, and insurers of product soundness, seaworthiness, and crew safety.

The United States government did not enact legislation to extend the principles and requirements of compulsory Load Line Regulation to Great Lakes vessels until post-1935, at a time when newer vessels were evolving with requirements for increased size, speed, and cargo capacity. Published classification society rules for certain conventional oceangoing vessels would have been in use for many years, and under these conditions credible semi-empirical bases for the design of hull structures were developed. In the mid-1930s, a special committee was formed to draft regulations for Great Lakes vessels, following a pattern already established for oceangoing vessels in compliance with the International Load Line Convention. The committee gave careful consideration to hull structural strength as a primary factor in the assignment of vessel freeboard. In its review of pre-1935 designs, the committee considered that laker designers (in conjunction with classification societies) had demonstrated a satisfactory appreciation of the requisite structural strength requirements for Great Lakes service. Their conclusions were purportedly based on long-term designer and operator experience with earlier long-lived, smaller, and slower laker designs that were mainly developed through semi-empiricism, extrapolation, and limited surveillance for vessels less than about six hundred feet in length. Computational methodologies for the determination of hull longitudinal strength in oceangoing vessels and transferable criteria were used as guidance parameters in determining to what extent the strength standards applicable to oceangoing vessels could be transferred or modified for use in the design of Great Lakes vessels.

In retrospect this must have been a challenging task when determining viable limits for the judicious application of similitude principles and the appropriate use of extrapolations from existing (pre-1935) designs. The unimaginable future extension to much longer and more slender vessels, such as the 729-foot *Edmund Fitzgerald*, having a length/depth ratio of 18.2 followed by 1,000 foot (Fig. 17) Upper-Lake bulkers with L/D ratios up to 21.5, could not possibly have been on the committee's horizon, the latter vessel having an even larger carrying capacity of about seventy thousand tons whenever lake depth conditions permitted.

Fig. 17 – The Jones Act Fleet On The Lakes
Photo – Lake Carriers' Association

IN ONE TRIP, A 1,000-FOOT-LONG GREAT LAKES SELF-UNLOADER

CARRIES THE EQUIVALENT OF SIX 100-CAR UNIT TRAINS

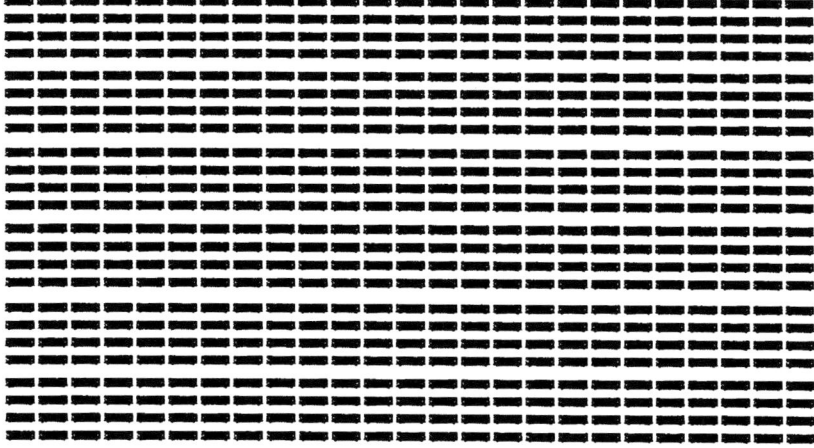

= 100 gross tons per railroad car

If the committee members were reconvened today, their assignment would be even more complex when endeavoring to develop regulatory approaches to the structural design of large lakers, using prevailing classification society rules for oceangoing vessels as a point of departure. Circa 1935, existing lakers had many similarities, and this may have provided an acceptable base for repeat designs and for some future extrapolations, even though their unregulated operating history was not without disasters.

Great Lakes Environmental Conditions
As apriori guidance, the original committee rightfully considered the Great Lakes seasonal environment as unique and made assumptions using a shallow scientific base, as follows:

> "Great Lakes vessels suffer less apparent damage (than oceangoing) because of shorter waves, while experiencing long life in a fresh water (less corrosive) operational environment."

While this may be acceptable as a general observation, it appears to have disregarded seasonal Great Lakes storm conditions that generate lethal "Constructive Interference Wave" heights and long fetches. Also, the longer vessel life had co-dependency with such factors as operational life-cycle maintenance, cargo load capacity, distribution effects on hull structure, and whether vessels were driven hard or at reduced speed under hazardous environmental conditions.

The "lesser-corrosive" operating environment observation may have been technically correct (in the 1930s) but should not have been interpreted as "corrosion-free" when one considers that advanced corrosion does occur in vessels and working harbors. For example: In 2004 the Duluth Seaway Authority identified a 95 million dollar funding requirement for replacement of sixty-five thousand lineal feet (twelve miles) of corroding sheet piling within the harbor to prevent expected failure in five to ten years.

The committee further noted:

> "Distances between terminals are comparatively short and vessels caught out in bad weather are seldom without a place to secure shelter."

Severe storm emergence can be very rapid on the Great Lakes, and large (post-1935) vessels have very limited safe haven choices.

> "Bulk-cargo carriers operate on eastern lakes where weather conditions are more favorable."

Pre-1935 and post-1935 losses of bulkers in all lakes are statistically high, with the majority attributable to severe cause majeure influences. The November storm season on Lake Superior is considered the most hazardous.

> "A lesser longitudinal stiffness factor (than oceangoing counterparts) could be adopted, based on successful operation of Great Lakes bulk-cargo vessels."

A paucity of (1935) environmental data prevented full appreciation of a vessel's multi-axial structural loadings induced by the unique and destructive Great Lakes wind, wave, seiche, and surge forces encapsulated within the static boundaries of land-locked water masses.

It is understood that open-ocean environmental data are quite different and more widely researched than for the Great Lakes, and their shoreside boundaries are infinitely distant. Great Lakes bulk-cargo vessels have practical depth constraints for lock transits and therefore have more slender length/depth (L/D) ratios and hull flexibility than oceangoing counterparts. Hydroelasticity is a key factor, albeit analyses have reliance on hypothetical (versus recorded) external forces. The St. Lawrence Seaway-sized *Fitzgerald*, (L/D ratio 18.2) was designed in accordance with regulatory requirements, to a longitudinal strength standard approximating slightly more than one-half of that required for oceangoing vessels. Such past premising still appears to be accepted by some but is considered highly questionable by others, including the *officers and crew members of every Great Lakes vessel, bereaved families of missing crew members, some of the knowledgeable politicians, citizens having maritime interests and this retired naval architect.*

20/20 Hindsight

The Great Lakes storms have claimed many lives, from the time when native Americans, traders, and explorers used canoes to those who subsequently established inland commerce with sailing ships and the leviathan bulk-cargo "long ships" thereafter. Within this historical envelope it is recognized that cause majeure (unexplainable Acts of God), human error, and vessel failure are but three of many factors that have contributed to sinkings and human losses in the November storm cycle alone, and most may forever remain unexplained when there are neither survivors nor witnesses. For improved understanding and technical advancement, it would appear that the manifest Great Lakes "calm pond" perceptions and other premising found in technical literature should be reviewed and modified to one of realism wherein our lakers and their crew members may safely voyage in harm's way when exposed to severe storm conditions unique to our inland "Eighth Sea." The casualty tolls of the past suggest that not all designers arrived at a satisfactory appreciation of laker strength requirements, for which post-1935 criteria were extrapolated.

The Great Lakes are not sheltered waters in the same league as waterways in the German Rhineland, where distances are short, the weather has good predictability, and there are places to seek refuge if necessary. The continuing perception of Great Lakes totally survivable mission envelopes can be factually disputed by the record of unexplained sinkings, and the general governmental passivity toward acceptance of significantly limber (flexible) and heavily-loaded hull structures, subjected to fatigue-inducing maximum speed operations, requires review. Such a review should be conducted using a multi-disciplined scientific approach inclusive of operator input.

During the *Fitzgerald* investigatory hearings, the author viewed with concern the general disregard for the input of operating crew members, who spoke of hearing failed rivets "popping" when underway, multi-strand, 5/8 inch diameter wire deck fences breaking because of hull hogging deflection, and, with additional concern, of the linear hull "bending and springing." Their disconcerting statements were not "sea story" hearsay, albeit Investigatory Boards showed little concern while taking such testimony in stride.

There should have been more concern, questioning, follow up, and reevaluation of design criteria, since it was readily apparent that certain governing standards and regulations for Great Lakes (and jumbo oceangoing bulk-carriers) were suspect and possibly inadequate… notably when design requirements exceeded published classification society parameters that were heavily dependent on extrapolations and semi-empiricism rather than thoroughly-researched scientific data. Without doubt, more violent storm conditions and even larger bulk-cargo vessels lie ahead for Great Lakes and oceangoing carriers in their search for minimization of the cost per ton-mile for bulk-cargo transportation and survival against predatory foreign steel exporting practices.

PART FOUR:
DESIGN OFFICE REVELATIONS

Naval Architecture Consultancy

Many American industrial practices, including those of the small Great Lakes Engineering Works (G.L.E.W.) design office were new to me. I was surprised when making a belated discovery that the *Fitzgerald* shipowner had provided tasking to an external consultant naval architectural firm to translate his requirements into detailed specifications, conceptual, and preliminary designs which were in compliance with Great Lakes Load Line Regulations. Past practice, during my British apprenticeship with the then-Furness Shipbuilding Company and later preliminary design office employment with the then-Davie Shipbuilding Company in Canada, had not followed this pattern, except in the case of vessels destined for government service and subject to competitive bidding by multiple shipbuilders. Customarily, a prospective shipowner would hold pre-contract discussions with a shipbuilder's Chief Naval Architect and *all* of the follow-on naval architectural work would be done by the construction shipyard's design staff.

Upon arrival at the G.L.E.W. shipyard (March 1958), I found that the (Hull No. 301) *S.S. Edmund Fitzgerald* conceptual and preliminary design gestation period with the consultant had expired, and most of the production drawings had been completed by drafting staffs of the shipyard's hull and machinery groups. Hydrodynamic model testing had also been completed at the Wageningen facility in the Netherlands, and propeller waterflow characteristics were already evaluated by the then-U.S. Navy David Taylor Model Basin at Carderock in Maryland. These were interesting, if not disconcerting, discoveries, because it certainly appeared that the preliminary design "train" had left the station considerably in advance of my coming aboard—and there were moments when I thought of Paul Bunyan's admonishment and the option of returning to Canada. My forte was preliminary design and estimating, and it did not appear that my expectations could be realized. In seeking other technical assignments, I was advised that there was neither a regulatory requirement nor common G.L.E.W. practice for the preparation of static or dynamic stability calculations, including cross-curves of stability. This may have been a blessing in disguise, because there was no evidence of an Amsler-type integrator instrument or an electronic desk calculator to perform the tasks. Computers for small businesses were still a developmental pipe-dream. The only "high-tech" desktop equipment appeared to be one antiquated (hand-cranked) calculating machine, one coveted slide-rule-on-a-helix (Fuller's Barrel), my personal slide rule, and a prized office planimeter. In addition, a vessel inclining experiment would not be performed to determine the metacentric height (GM) for lakers because of their inherently high level of stability, especially with the concentration of high density iron ore cargo occupying only the lower half of the three cargo holds—and because it was also *not* a requirement of the Great Lakes Load Line Regulations.

Enlightenment and Adjustment

As part of the cultural and technical adjustment, I proceeded to perform an ad-hoc review of the structural design and scantlings developed by the consultant and had considerable difficulty for the lack of familiarity with their heuristic reasoning and their premising for extrapolations made *beyond* the limits of existing regulatory criteria for smaller bulk-cargo vessels. This included midship section modulus assumptions and any strength additions that a vessel with propulsion machinery located aft could require. Through past experience I accepted that classification societies usually provided a sound basis for the design of vessels within a *conventional* range of dimensions and performance requirements and tacitly acknowledged that the *Fitzgerald* was *beyond* the norm. My ad-hoc review proceeded with a measure of trepidation, since I felt that neither the American Bureau of Shipping (nor *any* other classification society) could be expected to assess this massive vessel's structural requirements by extrapolation alone.

Such a laker vessel, having the greatest size, cargo deadweight, and speed, required technical analysis from first principles, iconic modeling, and learned evaluation of structural extrapolations proposed by experienced naval architects (or multi-disciplined consortia), plus an operational input from laker and shore-base terminal communities.

It was noted that the following laker and oceangoing vessel hull structures tables of "Factors For (Midship Section) Modulus Calculations" were far from identical, and the author had no technical basis on which to assume linearity above tabulated maximum values, which were mainly based on precedent empiricism. Albeit such license appeared to have been taken in the actual vessel design process, at a time when theoreticians were a long way from determining the magnitude of multi-axial hull girder loadings and responses under hydroelastic conditions.

LAKER VESSELS			
Factors for Modulus Calculations			
L (ft.)	f	L (ft.)	f
100	1.70	360	8.10
120	1.95	380	8.70
140	2.20	400	9.30
160	2.50	420	9.90
180	2.90	440	10.50
200	3.40	460	11.10
220	3.90	480	11.70
240	4.50	500	12.30
260	5.10	520	12.90
280	5.70	540	13.50
300	6.30	560	14.10
320	6.90	580	14.70
340	7.50	600	15.30
		620	15.90

Notes: This applied where the ratio L/D does not exceed 13.5 in vessels of 325 ft length and under and 19 in vessels of 600 ft length and above. Intermediate values between lengths of 325 and 600 ft. length were to be obtained by interpolation.

OCEANGOING VESSELS

Factors for Modulus Calculations

L (ft.)	f	L (ft.)	f
100	1.80	360	9.40
120	2.00	380	10.30
140	2.35	400	11.20
160	2.70	420	12.15
180	3.15	440	13.10
200	3.60	460	14.15
220	4.20	480	15.15
240	4.80	500	16.25
260	5.45	520	17.35
280	6.20	540	18.45
300	6.95	560	19.60
320	7.70	580	20.80
340	8.55	600	22.00

For example: For the laker *Fitzgerald*, tabular extrapolation from the foregoing laker table yielded an 'f' value of 18.63 which was codified by Code of Federal Regulations C.F.R. 45.15–17(c)(5)(ii). The Load Line Regulations provided a guidance standard for longitudinal strength, and requiring a *minimum* midship section modulus (I/y) for effective material, as expressed by the formula:

$$I/y = f.d.B$$

in units of inches^2-feet.

Where,

- I = Midship section moment of inertia (inches^2-feet^2)
- y = Distance to extreme deck fiber (feet)
- f = A factor from the foregoing (laker) table
- d = Molded draft (feet)
- B = Molded beam (feet)

and,

Minimum required midship section modulus (I/y value) was based on the following dimensions (see Footnotes)

Length Between Perpendiculars	(LBP)	=	711.00 ft.
Length to Depth Ratio	(L/D)	=	18.23
Breadth molded	(B)	=	75.0 ft.
Depth molded	(D)	=	39.0 ft.
Draft molded	(d)	=	26.56 ft. (summer)
			27.22 ft. (midsummer)
Midship section modulus factor	(f)	=	18.63 per Laker Table.
Section modulus (min) I/y	(f.d.B)	=	37,110 inches^2-ft.
+15% ABS requirement		=	+5,570 inches^2-ft.
Minimum design I/y required			42,680 inches^2-ft.
Actual I/y provided			42,592 inches^2-ft.

It was also important to realize that the emergence of larger Seaway-sized lakers made it difficult to realistically apply simple beam theories to hull structural design in the absence of directly-applicable American Bureau of Shipping (ABS) Classification Society Rules (circa mid-1950s). This necessitated a need to extrapolate from a semi-empirical data base, with infusions of past experience and heuristic "guesstimating."

Footnotes:
(i) Derived from Great Lakes Engineering Works Midship Section Drawing No. 113-1183 dated October 1956. (Fig. 18)

(ii) If *Fitzgerald* had been designed for *oceangoing* service, an extrapolated 'f' factor would have yielded 28.38 (versus 18.63), thereby showing that the laker vessel would have had lesser longitudinal strength, only slightly more than one-half of that for an oceangoing counterpart and a pattern believed to be extant on other lakers of that era. A lesser longitudinal bending strength would have contributed to increased hull flexibility, vibration, and the impaired fatigue life of structures.)

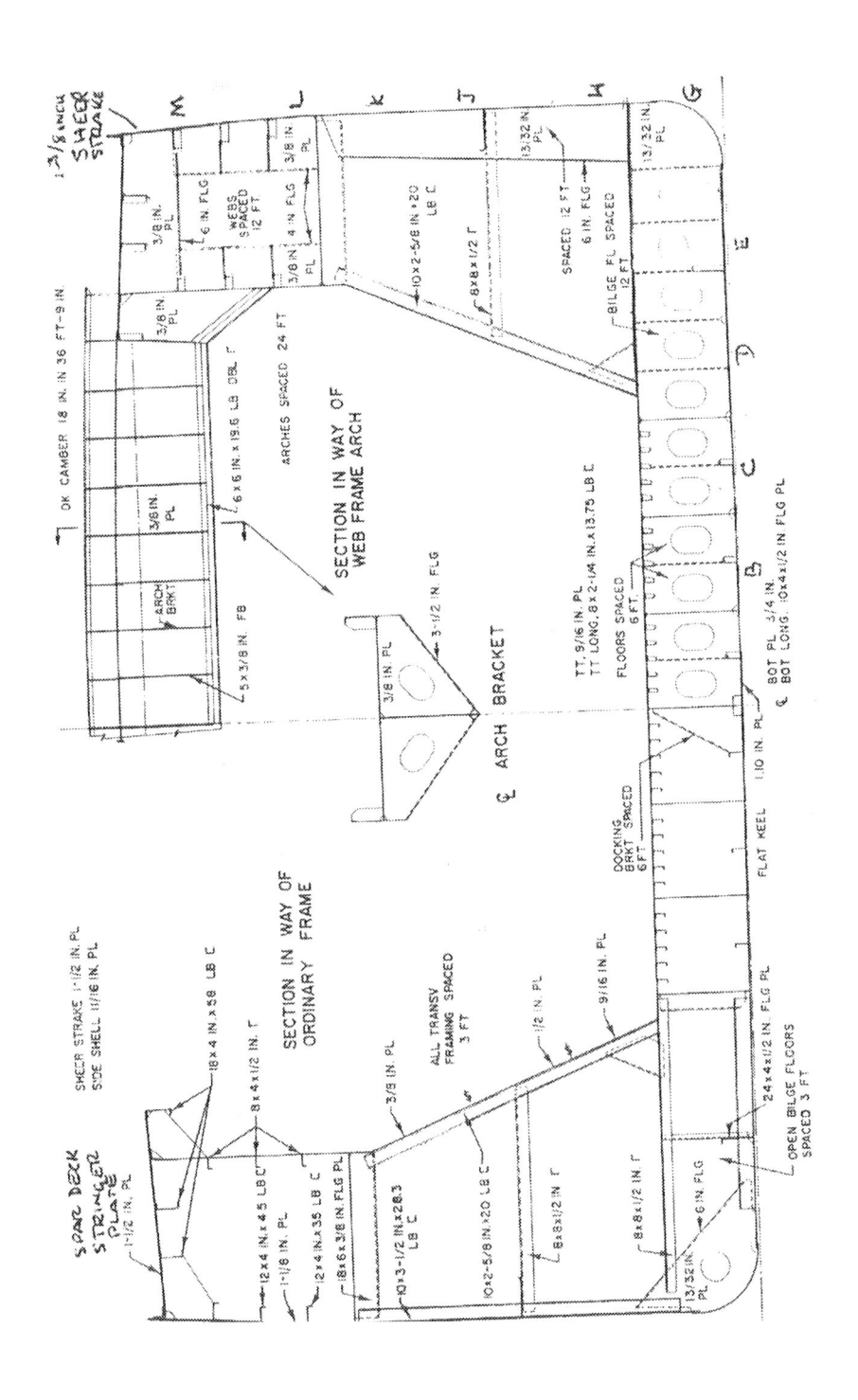

Fig. 18 – Typical Great Lakes bulk carrier.

The foregoing considerations were apparently given recognition during the initial estimation of bending stress capabilities of *Fitzgerald*'s longitudinal hull girder, under still-water (versus dynamic) conditions, and having a midship section structural configuration similar to Fig. 18.

Major Hull Structure
This midship section structure was replicated throughout the three cargo holds, extending over about 70 percent of the vessel's length. They reflected practicality for cargo handling and the accommodation of the shipyard's innovative modular construction processes. From a production engineering perspective, the mix of welding, riveting, and the multiplicity of non-complex structural details appeared reflective of traditional laker shipyard practices. The accumulative tolerances, however, associated with the multiplicity of structural details, had potential for affecting intermediate and final on-berth alignments. Welding joint fitup, quality control, and structural joint efficiency could have also been affected, especially with a paucity of non-destructive testing (NDT) in evidence. Indeed, it was apparent that laker ship design and construction were reflective of a traditional, practical, and labor-intensive art form rather than revolutionary technological advancement requiring major investments of capital.

Considerable attention was paid to improving productivity and the quality of installations made on the building berth by having prefabricated hull modules and deckhouse structures constructed on the adjacent off-hull assembly platen. Many of the shell-side and bottom-shell plating-welded butt joints were contiguously aligned (not staggered) in the interest of uninterrupted field welding. During the vessel construction process, shipyard planning and production managers consulted with design staff regarding module hoisting weights and centers of gravity, while developing rigging strategies as necessary for the execution of safe heavy-lift shipyard operations. Good structural design and practical shipfitting considerations were also apparent by installation of a double-riveted shell seam connection between the upper shell-side sheer strake (Strake 'M') and the adjacent side-shell plating (Strake 'L'). The radiused bilge plate (Strake 'G') also had double-riveted connections to the bottom-shell plating. These riveting features demonstrated good shipbuilding practice by enabling latitude in plating seam alignment fitup during final hull assembly, while simultaneously providing "crack arrestor" mitigation benefit should welded shell plating butt joints fail and seek paths of crack propagation.

The unobstructed main cargo holds were subdivided by two *non-watertight* "screen" bulkheads. The open spaces at the lower corners of each bulkhead enabled hose washdown should different bulk cargoes, such as ore, grain, or coal, be carried. Residual deposits from each cargo would be manually flushed to the after end of No. 3 Cargo Hold, where they were removable.

The hull structural configuration was longitudinally stiffened within the cellular double bottom and was complemented by transverse floor structure. Longitudinal stiffening was additionally used internal to each access tunnel and below the spar deck stringer plates. The side-plating, in way of the eight side ballast tanks, had transverse (twelve-inch channel-section) framing, complemented by deep web-plate shell stiffening at twelve-foot intervals with internal strut bracing internal to each tank.

From a hull stressing point of view, it is generally known that the shearing force in a vessel's hull girder generates a maximum stress level at a vessel's neutral axis and about one-quarter length (1/4L) from bow and stern. In a bygone era, as fully-riveted vessels aged, stress sometimes revealed itself through the loosening of rivets in these locations on large vessels, and dynamic force vectors could occur in opposite directions whenever a vessel was in a wave trough (sagging) or on a wave crest (hogging).

At that earlier time, Lloyd's Rules (LR) required vessels exceeding six hundred feet in length to have treble riveting in three shell plating seams, at about one-half the vessel depth (neutral axis region) for one-fourth of a vessel's length (1/4L) in the fore and aft bodies. While riveting was superseded by welding in these locations on the *Fitzgerald*, there was *no* evidence of special reinforcement consideration at the 1/4L locations from the vessel's bow or stern, unless one considers the minimal contribution of shell fenders and their backup shell stringers. The *Fitzgerald* midship section modulus was increased to reflect an historical design philosophy that, on vessels with after propulsion machinery, the upper side and deck plating should be augmented to obtain longitudinal hull girder strength 15 percent above the standard for vessels with machinery amidships. This design philosophy was an outgrowth of an existing precept that vessels with after propulsion machinery would be "sagging" when in a fully loaded condition, with exposure to higher longitudinal bending moments and having potential for elastic instability ("buckling").

It was noted that spar deck plating continuity was interrupted by twenty-one closely spaced cargo hatch openings with each having a 48-foot (64 percent of vessel's beam width) x 11-foot length and a 24-inch high coaming. With such deck openings, outboard stringer plating and the longitudinal hatch-side girders were continuous, but the interspaced spar deck plating was not.

Under these conditions, the port and starboard deck stringer plates (each of 151 inches width) became the effective extreme spar deck fibers for stress analysis purposes (Fig. 19). This justified the heavy spar deck stringer plate (1-1/2 inches thick) and the riveted sheer Strake 'M' (1-3/8 inches thick) extending throughout the parallel hull body to the after boiler room before transitioning to lesser thickness in the stern and bow sections. The stringer and sheer strakes of plating were connected to an 8" x 8" double-riveted gunwale angle.

Fig. 19 – Spar Deck
-Continuous Outboard Stringer Plate.
-Hatchway Openings (21) With 24-inches
High Peripheral Coamings
K + 52 Weeks
Photo – Shipyard Photo – Dossin Museum Collection

While primary longitudinal bending stresses in laker hulls will always require experienced consideration, the overall hydroelasticity, elastic instability (buckling) resistance, and design details for a large bulk-cargo vessel having semi-monocoque, thin-shell structure require comprehensive scientific support as the state of the art advances. A practical point of interest was the oversizing of certain structural material, based on long-standing Great Lakes ore-carrier design practices, to accommodate rough treatment by cargo loading/unloading equipment, and the use of mobile apparatus for final cleanup of three cavernous and obstruction-free cargo holds having a combine extent of 519 feet and comprised of No. 1 Hold (177 feet), No. 2 Hold (144 feet), and No. 3 Hold (198 feet). The cargo holds had an overall combined capacity of 860,950 cubic feet. Since the cargo holds were separated by two non-watertight "screen" bulkheads, the vessel safety was reliant upon the reserve buoyancy contributed by eight side ballast tanks, having integral double bottom tankage that formed a double-hull watertight boundary.

Vessel Loading Factors
As follow-on to the structural review, I performed preliminary trim and loading calculations for *Fitzgerald*'s full-load and ballasted conditions while making many assumptions, although:

(1) I was unaware that the (pre-1975) Load Line Regulations had *no* requirement for a loading manual; and

(2) I was advised that the masters of Great Lakes vessels would not use a design office-prepared cargo loading manual even if it was provided.

This was a case of *déjà vu* for me, because many years ago (1950), I recall an oceangoing supertanker master advising me that he would load his vessel as he wished "with the objective of delaying immersion of the Plimsoll Line as long as possible to maximize [his] on-board cargo load upon departure from the oil terminal." He claimed that *his* tanker's bunker fuel consumption would cancel the departure "hogging" condition while in transit.

On another occasion (May 1958), I recall having an opportunity to review a profile and deck drawing for the thirty-one year-old self-unloading laker *S.S. Carl D. Bradley* (Fig. 20), which was engaged in the limestone and coal trade on Lakes Michigan and Erie. The drawing was provided to allow the G.L.E.W. shipyard to plan their floating drydock ballasting and docking configuration and to submit a contract bid for execution of a scheduled five-year survey during the 1958–59 winter layup availability. At that time I was very surprised to see that the guidance drawing showed a recent cargo distribution. The bulk cargo appeared to be concentrated at the ends of the vessel and therefore would have been contributory to a hogging condition that may, or may not, have represented the master's normal dispersion of cargo or water ballast weight.

Fig. 20 – S.S. Carl D. Bradley under the Ambassador Bridge
Photo – Kenneth E. Smith

Owner - Bradley Transportation Company.
Built - 1927 American Shipbuilding Company, Lorain, Ohio.
Lost - November 18, 1958 in violent Lake Michigan storm.

Due to foundering under severe storm conditions; with loss of life in Lake Michigan on November 18, 1958, the scheduled drydocking survey did not take place. The USCG Marine Board of Inspections marine Casualty Report dated July 7, 1959, determined that the vessel was in a ballasted condition at the time of sinking, and included two germane statements:

> "...the vessel heaved ("hogged") upward near Hatch No. 10 when in a ballasted condition, and broke in two sections approximately three hundred (300) feet in length...[and]...present management knew of *no* company instructions issued concerning the sequence of loading, unloading or *ballasting* of their vessels. They (the owners) considered that the responsibility in these matters was *vested in the ship Masters*...."

With machinery aft and full capacity ballasting of after tankage with lesser ballasting forward, could this have also contributed to an over-stressed "hogging" condition and the abnormal forces of unique "Constructive Interference Waves"?

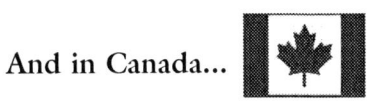

And in Canada...

The Great Lakes vessels of our good Canadian neighbor have also experienced bulk-carrier hull failure through non-adherence to supplied "Trim an Stability Books with Loading Calculations." An example is cited by the Transportation Safety Board Report No. M00C0026 (T.S.B.) of Canada in the case of self-unloader *M.V. Algowood* (Fig. 21), which sustained hull buckling and cargo-hold flooding while loading aggregates and manufactured sand when on-berth at Bruce Mines, Ontario, on June 1, 2000. The 729-foot vessel, owned by Algoma Central (Marine) Corporation, was built (1981) by Canadian Shipbuilding & Engineering Limited of Collingwood, Ontario. There was no loss of life.

Fig. 21 – Algowood being towed by the tug Progress at Bridge #5 on Welland Canal – July 14, 2001
Photo – Jim Morris

The T.S.B. investigation determined that:

> The Lloyd's-supplied "Trim and Stability Book with Loading Calculations" was on board for guidance of the vessel's Master.
>
> The loading/deballasting operation did *not* follow an on-board, computer-generated procedural plan...which could have eventually produced a hogging/bending moment of 1.9 times the maximum permissible bending moment approved by Lloyd's.
>
> Immediately before hull failure the *Algowood* was subjected to a calculated hogging bending moment about 2.3 times the maximum permissible...[and] adoption of similar loading cargo distribution in previous voyages could have *eventually* led to fatigue in the hull structure.
>
> The magnitude of induced hull stresses were neither known nor appreciated by shipboard personnel.
>
> Although loading instrumentation is not a regulatory (Canadian) requirement for Great Lakes

bulk-cargo carriers, the T.S.B. does encourage the use of such installations.

For the *M.V. Algowood* hull failure to occur at the loading berth in still water, and with so many other quantifiable technical conditions present, the circumstances removed many of the traditionally unknown factors attendant to open-water "mysteries" which are sometimes listed as "unknown cause with loss of life." From these episodes it was evident that the earlier-cited seagoing supertanker master's (1950) loading manual philosophy was still alive and well—and what goes around, comes around.

Fitzgerald Flexure

The process of developing loaded and ballasted condition calculations required the use of lightship hull weight and displacement distribution data. With such data available, it also provided an opportunity to make preliminary estimates of shear forces, bending stress levels, and the amplitude of longitudinal hull deflection. The calculated (still water) stress levels were low and gave no cause for concern, although the vertical hull deflections were sufficiently large to merit further consideration and later physical measurement with transit (theodolite) surveying equipment after the vessel was waterborne.

On personal initiative, I made post-launching sightings with the vessel in still water and having an abnormal stern-trimmed lightship condition. The sighting range (519 feet) extended between the poop and forecastle front, immediately above the outboard deck stringer plates and side ballast tankage.

After graphically plotting deviations from a datum, with extrapolation over the full length (729 feet) of the vessel, the hogging (deflection upward) was estimated to be almost eight inches...an amount of significance to myself, but apparently not so for experienced masters of Great Lakes bulk-cargo vessels who have claimed hogging observations of about eighteen inches during winter layup. Their observations may not be uncommon for the structures of older vessels that were subjected to cyclic flexure over a period of time under in-service conditions; however, in the case of the new *Fitzgerald*, she was still a "tight" vessel, having a hull structure with zero service life at the time of hogging measurement, and she could therefore be expected to be initially more resilient to flexure.

Fitzgerald Side Launching
With over fifty years of side-launching experience to their credit, the G.L.E.W. shipyard was required to meet the challenge of safely launching the eight million dollar vessel of 75-foot beam and weighing about 7,500 tons into a slip (Fig. 22) having only 150-feet width—and open to the Detroit River at one end. As was customary practice, the floating drydock was temporarily removed from the launching slip area.

The launch preparation and execution for such a long, heavy vessel was a sequence calling upon the combined skill and experience of shipyard managers and tradesmen, in cooperation with design staffs when appropriate. As is often the case, these parties inevitably had to arrive at compromises when pursuing a middle course between opposing viewpoints, with mutual understanding that undue deference by any side could have negative consequences for the launching process, which is irreversible.

Many land-situated and afloat spectators, who were strategically positioned on elevated positions to view side-launching of the "longship" laker, may have accepted the scene as a routine event, since almost all Great Lakes shipbuilders traditionally follow this practice. In this particular instance, however, considerable pre-outfitting work had been done, especially with regard to achieving a high level of completion for the pre-launch condition. This condition was inclusive of the man propulsion installation comprised of a 140-ton x 7,500 horsepower steam turbine, both 84-ton coal-fired boilers, and her massive (19-1/2 foot) propeller and rudder. During launching preparations, the design staff collaborated with shipyard management by providing:

- Hoisting weight and center of gravity information for crane-rigging purposes.
- Technical support for the sizing and arrangement of sliding ways, which would be coated with a synthetic grease to ensure low-friction sliding and a uniform bearing pressure of about two tons per square foot. One had to carefully consider that a launchweight of about 7,500 tons would not be

uniformly distributed over the vessel's length because of the concentrated propulsion plant machinery weight located aft. These stern sliding ways required an increase in area to prevent over-pressurization of the grease lubricant, which could cause temperature elevation under launch motion conditions with unacceptable effect on the coefficient of sliding friction.
- Proper placement and sizing of launch-arresting draglines were necessary for horizontal vessel braking during the final phase of side launching.

No technical literature could be located having direct applicability to the side-launching of large vessels within the configuration and dimensional constraint of the G.L.E.W. shipyard, and the design staff innovatively installed a simple, tracking apparatus for the recording of vessel travel, motion, and acceleration. The apparatus was basically a taut horizontal line from which evenly-spaced pennants were strung across the closed end of the launching slip, with a large sweep-hand clock face in the foreground for time-motion observation.

Immediately upon the commencement of vessel sliding movement across the line of sight, a videographer tracked the *Fitzgerald*'s lateral movement, transverse oscillation, vertical displacement, and restraining dragline effects.

The data were reduced to a graphic form that was used to develop a baseline to technically assist subsequent G.L.E.W. launchings of the *S.S. Herbert C. Jackson* and the *S.S. Arthur B. Homer*. On June 7, 1958, at 12.34 P.M., the hull commenced sliding toward the tranquil water-filled slip shortly after the sponsor, Mrs. Edmund Fitzgerald, wife of the chairman of the board of Northwestern Mutual Life Insurance Company, christened the vessel. (Fig. 22-1, 22-2, 22-3, 22-4, 22-5) Launching release was expedited by the activation of electrically-operated guillotine blades that operated hold-back mechanisms.

The launching dynamic of the *S.S. Edmund Fitzgerald* was smooth, with minor roll and heave oscillations. In the final stages, when completing a starboard roll after most of her lateral energy was expended, there was a slight buffering of port side bilge plating when encountering the far wall of the slip.

FIG 22 – GREAT LAKES ENGINEERING WORKS
1000 EAST GREAT LAKES AVENUE
RIVER ROUGE, MICHIGAN

ADMIT _____

TO WITNESS THE LAUNCHING OF THE
S.S. EDMUND FITZGERALD
ON SATURDAY, JUNE 7, 1958 AT 12 O'CLOCK NOON, E.S.T.
UNDER CONSTRUCTION FOR
THE NORTHWEST MUTUAL LIFE INSURANCE COMPANY — OWNER
AND
OGLEBAY NORTON COMPANY
COLUMBIA TRANSPORTATION DIVISION — CHARTERER

SPONSOR: MRS. EDMUND FITZGERALD   ADMITTANCE TIME: 11:15 A.M. E.S.T.

Fig 22-1 – Launching Day. June 7, 1958
K + 44 Weeks
Photo – Dossin Museum Collection

Fig. 22-2
Sliding Toward Launching Slip

Fig 22-3
Almost Clear Of The Launching Ways

Photos – Center for Archival Collections, Bowling Green State University

*Fig 22-4
Launching Day. June 7, 1958
K + 44 Weeks*

*Fig. 22-5
Fully Afloat And Almost Stopped*

Photos – Center for Archival Collections, Bowling Green State University

While the G.L.E.W. shipyard met its goal of achieving a successful launching after careful preparation, this is not always the case for other shipbuilders, as exemplified by the 1907 capsizing of the *S.S. Principessa Jolanda* at La Spezia, Italy (Fig. 23).

Instability at launching would be catastrophic. The *S.S. Principessa Jolanda* poised for the launching at La Spezia, Italy in 1907. This vessel was practically complete and ready for trials. Thousands of people were in attendance both on the ground and in yachts clustered about the ends of the ways. (*Courtesy of the Mariners Museum, Newport News, Va.*)

A few moments after the vessel was waterborne, she took a sharp list to port and tugs and yachts rushed to the rescue.

A few moments later the huge 500-ft vessel lay on her side and began to settle in the waters of the harbor. The vessel was almost a complete loss; only the boilers were salvaged.

Fig. 23 – An Unsuccessful Launching (1907)

Lake Erie Trials

Almost every person involved with the *Fitzgerald* hoped to be aboard during acceptance trials in Lake Erie, when all systems would undergo service testing and the overall performance would be measured. The interest became heightened as she was observed to be starting propulsion machinery trials at dockside shortly before proceeding to open water, where there would be operating vessel traffic. During the dockside trials, final checklists were also being prepared to ensure that outfitting inventories were complete. This dockside trial was held at the G.L.E.W. shipyard for initial reduced power operation of the main propulsion plant and the checking of auxiliary machinery installations.

It was during this phase that I met Captain Bert Lambert, who was destined to become the first master of the vessel, when we were both assessing the amount of fuel stowed in the coal bunker. (During the 1971–72 winter layup, while at Duluth, the vessel underwent a coal to oil conversion.) While I was at the coaling hatch rim taking actual measurements of the heaped coal for use with calculations related to coal capacity calibration and consumption, Captain Lambert was casually studying the coal height and its angle of repose with his experienced eye. We later compared our coal estimates, and they proved to be essentially the same; with other events related to his unassuming confidence and judgement, this gave me great admiration for the gentlemanly mariner.

Most of those on board, including V.I.P.s, operating crews, and technical staff members who were participants in the Lake Erie trials, welcomed the opportunity as a combination of work, pleasure, and a memorable learning experience. In the case of technical staffs (including myself) it was a moment of truth to compare engineering predictions with actual vessel performance through underway correlations of speed and power; evaluations of turning circle and maneuvering space requirements; anchoring system operation and emergency stopping capabilities; navigation aids adjustment; etc.

The Lake Erie trial course and schedule of events are shown in Fig. 24.

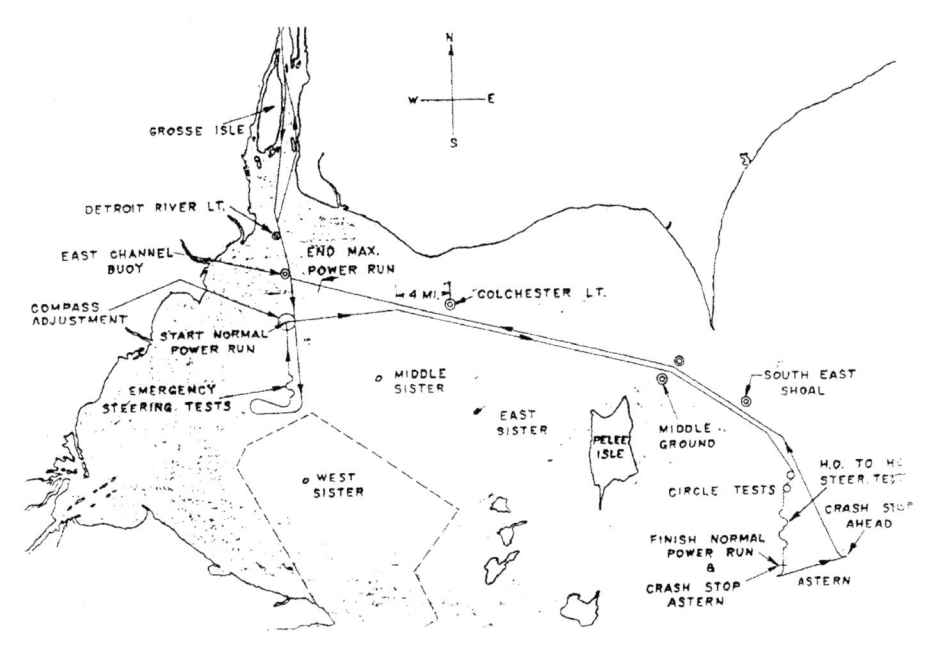

THE PRIDE of the AMERICAN FLAG

On September 22, 1958 she was officially delivered into the hands of Northwest Mutual Life Insurance as owners and to an Oglebay-Norton crew as operators and charterers for the Columbia Transportation Division.

The Fitz passed through the Soo locks for the first of many times on September 24, 1958.

G.L.E.W. HULL 301 - Str. "EDMUND FITZGERALD"

SCHEDULE

		Start	Finish	Elapsed
A-1	Check Drafts	7:00:00 AM	7:15:00 AM	15:00
A-2	Leave Dock & turn around	7:15:00 AM	7:45:00 AM	30:00
	Pass Shipyard & Proceed to E. Ch. Buoy	7:45:00 AM	9:30:00 AM	1:45:00
	Run South about 2-1/2 to 3 Mi.	9:30:00 AM	9:40:00 AM	12:10:00
	Compass Adjustment, etc.*	9:40:00 AM	11:15:00 AM	1:35:00
B-1 B-2	Anchor Tests - Ford. & Aft.	11:15:00 AM	12:15:00 PM	1:00:00
	Course various, increasing speeds: 12 Nozzles - 15 Min. 13 Nozzles - 15 Min. 14 Nozzles - 15 Min. 15 Nozzles - 15 Min.	12:15:00 PM	1:15:00 PM	1:00:00
C-1	Check House Top & Trick Wheel			
C-2	Steering during this period Finish period about 3 Mi. South of East Channel Buoy.			
D-1	Courses toward Colchester Light & S.E. Shoal at about 7500 SHP with 18 Nozzles. Check speed at Colchester, Middle-ground and S.E. Shoal.*	1:15:00 PM	4:15:00 PM	3:00:00
D-2	Figure Eight Circle Tests (After passing S.E. Shoal Light)			
D-3	Normal Power Steering Tests			
E-1	Crash Stop Astern		4:20:00 PM	12:05:00
E-2	Astern Endurance & Steering Test	4:20:00 PM	4:50:00 PM	12:30:00
E-3	Crash Stop Ahead, then increase power to abt. 8250 HP - 20 Nozzles.*	4:50:00 PM	5:10:00 PM	12:20:00
F	Start maximum Power Test Run. Return to E. Channel Buoy at 20 Nozzle speed. Check speed at S.E. Shoal, Middle Ground and Colchester*	5:10:00 PM	7:30:00 PM	2:20:00
	Return to Shipyard at normal or reduced power as required by Navigation	7:30:00 PM	10:00:00 PM	2:30:00
	Tie up at Shipyard	10:00:00 PM		

Fig. 24 – Sea Trials of the Fitz
September 13, 1958

On September 13, 1958, at 0700 hrs., the *Fitzgerald*'s drafts were checked before departure from the shipyard in a ballasted condition and subsequent to turning into the Detroit River before following a downbound track to Lake Erie. The initial departure momentarily churned-up bottom mud and caused some propeller-induced vibration, which gradually dissipated as the vessel became aligned with the deep-water channel. As we proceeded toward the trial course, other upbound lakers greeted the *Fitzgerald* with whistle salutes normally reserved for their own fleets.

Each trial event was successfully executed under ideal weather conditions, and one rapidly grew to respect the challenging command responsibility of a laker master when navigating, stopping, and maneuvering such a ponderous vessel requiring multiple ship lengths of lake-space when executing a crash-stop evolution. Later, on every trip, the fine control for entering and transiting various minimal-clearance locks would be very exacting to avoid sustaining hull damage.

As a matter of personal interest, I availed myself of an opportunity to visually observe anticipated cyclic hull flexure when walking through the lighted bow-to-stern underdeck tunnels (2) that provide protection from rough weather. Qualitative observations were made when undergoing a full-power (16.3 mph) steady-state endurance run having minimal wave influence. The rhythmic vertical deflections of overhead illuminating electric light fixtures were noticeable and disconcerting and were creditable to vertical longitudinal "bending and hull springing" action.

In the case of "long ships," such as *Fitzgerald*, hull "bending and springing" actions are probably related to longitudinal girder flexibility due to the reduced midship section modulus permitted for lakers having a characteristically slender length/depth (L/D) aspect ratio (Fig. 25); water ballast weight distribution; propeller-induced excitation; the period of wave encounter; and other disturbing forces.

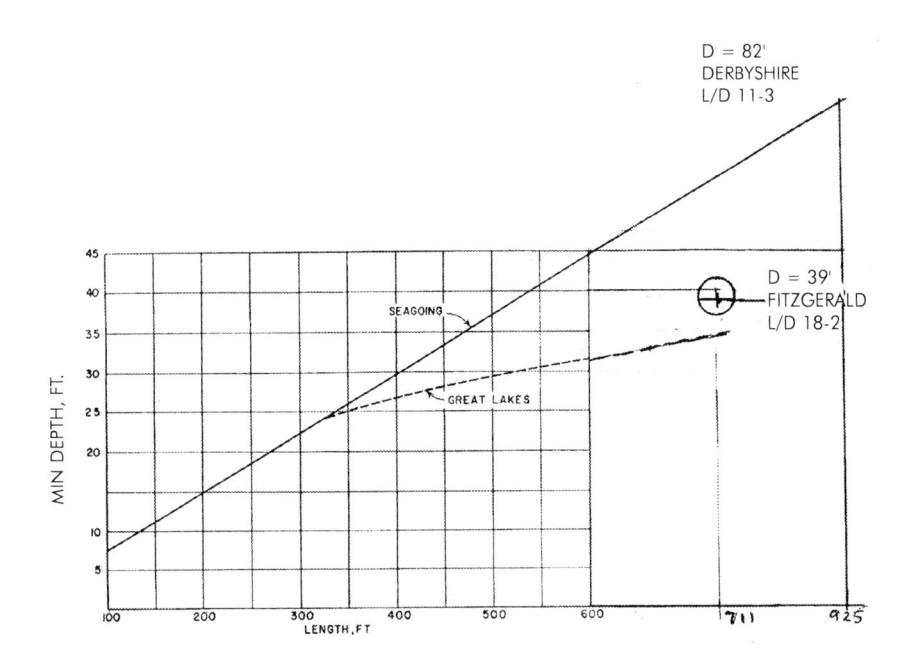

Fig. 25 – Ratio L/D for seagoing and Great Lakes ships
The L/D Ratio Is a Rough Measure of Hull Stiffness

For *Fitzgerald*'s future in-service operations, when severe storm conditions would be experienced, it was anticipated that variations in the amplitude of hull flexure and cyclic frequency would be evident and, after a critical number of (unknown) flexing cycles, fatigue cracks and/or elastic instability (buckling) could occur—leading to repairs or catastrophic failure. Since in-service operations would rarely be conducted under still-water conditions, for which the vessel was designed, multi-axial stressing effects on the vessel's structure would be expected to emerge.

Similar "bending and springing" observations were made by former crewmen Richard Orgel and Delmar Webster and became part of testimony before the USCG Marine Board investigative hearings when they testified that "*Fitzgerald*'s springing was like a diving board," and "Springing and bending during a storm was not unusual." Even though cyclic hull motions have visibility as recognized naval architectural concerns, the crewmen's testimony did *not* appear to receive the technical consideration it so deserved.

When trial events were completed, the *Fitzgerald* proceeded on an upbound course, at reduced power, to the G.L.E.W. shipyard. This was a good time to take a leisurely tour through the splendid accommodations and to partake of the social activities in the lounge and recreation rooms. The time was well spent in allowing an overall appreciation of such a majestic vessel, the production of which had given participants a sense of pride and facilitated a unique learning experience. As the twilight began to take effect, it produced a changed surrounding scene of silhouettes and range marker lights not previously noticed. With Captain Lambert's permission, I was able to spend the remainder of the trip enjoying a panoramic view from the pilot house, where he was confidently seated in his starboard side high-stool command position. This was also an excellent vantage point to make first-time observation of the unique laker docking maneuver required for turning such a large vessel through ninety degrees and using a "winding" procedure when entering the G.L.E.W. shipyard property. During this docking maneuver, it was possible to rationalize why lakers have a stem bar that is close to being plumb for a number of practical reasons, inclusive of the "winding" procedure for turnaround in a narrow channel. During conduct of this procedure the engine speed was briefly ordered full-ahead with the rudder hard over, and a bow line was secured to the dock by a seaman previously swing over the side through use of the man-overboard "monkey" boom. As the vessel was swung around, the steel stem bar experienced local loading as it pivoted against the dock wall, and the dockside groaned. Because of this bow contact, the stem bar and attaching shell-plating welds of lakers require regular inspection for damage during their operational lifetimes.

Delivery

On September 22, 1958, the *S.S. Edmund Fitzgerald* was officially delivered to her owner, Northwestern Mutual Life Insurance Company, before being conveyed to Oglebay Bay Norton Company under a Bare Boat charter and bearing the flag of their Columbia Transportation Division.

Columbia Transportation Division-Charterer

With Captain Lambert in command, she departed the G.L.E.W. shipyard on the following day, upbound for the Soo Locks and underway at a speed that was faster than about 90 percent of Great Lakes bulk-cargo carriers. She transitted the Soo Locks on September 24, 1958, at about 1400 hrs., en route to Silver Bay in Minnesota to receive her first loading.

At that time, most ore cargo was in the form of taconite pellets, which were high-density "tailings" having low-iron content. From the beginning, "Big Fitz," as she became known, broke Great Lakes cargo-transportation records on an annual basis for about eleven years, and this became a challenging expectation for a succession of masters, including Captains Bert Lambert (1958–59), N.C. Larsen (1959–65), Peter Pulcer (1966–1971), and Ernest McSorley (1971–75) when million-ton seasons became the norm.

PART FIVE:
DESIGN OFFICE PRACTICES

The *Fitzgerald* was the largest bulk-cargo vessel to be built at a Great Lakes shipyard when delivered in the year 1958. Throughout a beyond-the-norm design process, an experienced American consultant and construction shipyard design staffs became obligated to resort to the traditional application of heuristic judgement when extrapolating beyond the limits of existing American Bureau of Shipping (ABS) Classification Society Rules for hull structural scantlings applicable to earlier, slower, and smaller bulk-cargo lakers.

An absence of directly-applicable structural criteria for this size of vessel made such a technical approach necessary in the development of preliminary design calculations and drawings submitted for review and approval by the consultant naval architect. Such approvals were required prior to the construction shipyard's follow-on drafting of production shop drawings to be used in the planning and fabrication of steel hull structures.

A similar situation confronted British designers of six oceangoing Bridge Class Ore/Bulk/Oil (O.B.O.) vessels, including the *M.V. Derbyshire*. This type of vessel emerged as a distinct type in the mid-1960s and had alternate hull loading arrangements for ore cargo stowage (Fig. 26). With such cargo hold arrangements it was anticipated that high shear forces would be generated in the hull girder. For this reason special Rules and Class notations such as "Strengthened for Heavy Cargoes-Specified Holds May be Empty" were introduced by Lloyd's Register in 1964. The first true O.B.O. vessel designs that appeared in 1965–66 were destined to carry ore, oil, or less-dense cargoes while still obtaining their full deadweight capacity.

The Bridge Class Design

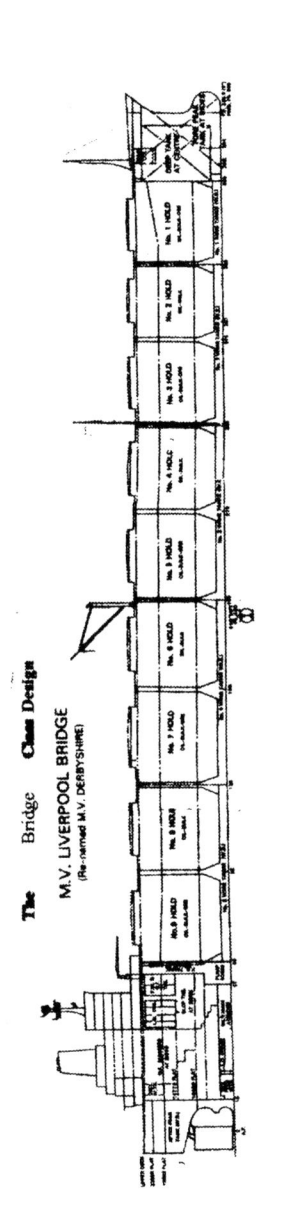

M.V. LIVERPOOL BRIDGE
(Re-named M.V. DERBYSHIRE)

The design was for an ore/bulk/oil carrier of approximately 170,000 tonnes deadweight. The ships were to be capable of carrying:

Ore cargoes in alternate holds with appropriate heavier scantlings.

Oil cargoes in all holds with surfaces pressed up to hatch coaming levels.

Bulk cargoes in all holds.

Certificates

At the time of her loss the following certificates had been issued in respect of the M.V. DERBYSHIRE.

(a) Cargo Ship Safety Equipment Certificate.
(Issued at Oslo, Norway, by the Norwegian Directorate of Shipping on the 6th April 1979. Valid until the 9th April 1981).

(b) Cargo Ship Safety Radio Certificate.
(Issued at Sasebo, Japan, by the Japanese Ministry of Transport on the 16th April 1980. Valid until the 15th April 1981).

(c) Cargo Ship Safety Construction Certificate.
(Issued by Lloyd's Register of Shipping on the 25th October 1977. Valid until the 30th June 1981).

(d) International LoadLine Certificate.
(Issued by Lloyd's Register of Shipping on the 4th June 1976. Valid until 3rd June 1981. Last annual survey carried out at Sasebo, Japan, on the 17th April 1980).

On completion of her construction the *DERBYSHIRE* was classed " $\cancel{1}$ 100 A1 strengthened for ore cargoes holds 2 and 6 may be empty or oil cargoes" by Lloyd's Register of Shipping. She thereafter continued to maintain this classification with Lloyd's Register of Shipping until the date of her loss.

Between the 3rd and 17th April 1980 the DERBYSHIRE was at Sasebo, Japan. During this period surveyors from LRS carried out annual and dry-docking surveys for classification purposes. In addition, a special classification survey was commenced and a general examination was made for the purposes of permitting a postponement of the completion of the special survey until sometime prior to April, 1981. The vessel had been in service only for about three years by the time of her last voyage.

Fig. 26 – The M.V. DERBYSHIRE was the last of a series of six sister ships.

Unfortunately by the end of the 1960s, structural problems were identified as being due to:

(a) high shear force generation in the side shell structure;
(b) large hull girder bending moments;
(c) extremely high bending and shear loads in transverse watertight bulkheads, especially in way of lower stools, because of the absence of horizontal stringers;
(d) torsion of the upper wing tank structure, resulting in elastic instability (buckling) of web frames and distortion of hatch openings; and
(e) considerable hydrodynamic loading on the upper parts of hold structure due to the free-surface swashing of oil cargo.

The occurrence of these problems was linked to the rapidly increasing size of O.B.O. vessels, severe collisions, and the effect of abusive cargo handling practices. on the structural configuration. Solutions included the selective use of high-strength steel in structures.

It was evident that designers of the six Bridge Class (O.B.O.) vessels were thrust into a complex evolutionary matrix and were required to work within a structural envelope *exceeding* the scantling criteria limits of existing Lloyd's Ship Classification Society Rules. In this situation, the shipbuilder endeavored to adapt 1971 Rules for tankers and dry cargo vessels, in the absence of O.B.O. criteria specific to the technical requirements. It is noted in retrospect, that the reputable Swan Hunter Shipbuilders, located at Wallsend on the River Tyne, was attuned to the increased world-wide demand for oil and the evolving demand for much larger tanker vessels during the continued closure of the Suez Canal. In May 1969, the VLCC (Very Large Crude Carrier) *Esso Northumbria*, having a deadweight of 253,000 tons, was launched, and she was one of a number of VLCCs that required venturing into vessel design areas close to the limits envisioned by evolving Lloyd's Rules. It would appear that this tanker precedent became an experience pattern to be closely followed during the preliminary design of Bridge Class (O.B.O.) vessels—but with even greater technical risk.

Throughout these processes it was not readily apparent that the preliminary design and production shop drawing preparation phases, for either vessel, were augmented by original research and development (R&D) procedures for the advanced hull structures. Nor was it evident that test and evaluation (T&E) protocols were initiated for proof of concept "build and bust" verification of hull scantling selections and decision making outcomes. Essentially there appeared to be related advanced-development technical voids that apparently placed all involved parties in a dilemma of "not knowing what they didn't know" about the dynamic loading and related structural requirements for each vessel—whose gargantuan proportions and unique cargo loading (unknowingly) placed them closer to durational risk boundaries for fatigue, cracking, buckling, etc.

Contrasting Practices

As an aside observation, such adventurous commercial design practices for advanced state-of-the-art vessels provide stark contrast with more-costly, but necessary system development and effective, methodologies used for most (U.S.) military vessels and many offshore structures having dynamically-loaded prototypical structural configurations. Under these circumstances, multi-disciplined cadres of graduate engineers would work in collaboration with researchers, academia, laboratories, designers, and drafting personnel. Lest my intent be misconstrued as seeking an impossible Utopian technical environment, it should be made clear that—as one who practiced in commercial and military shipbuilding during his career—I remain a technical and economic realist who fully recognizes that bulk-cargo vessels designed to Military Specifications (MilSpec) requirements could never be compatible with economic constraints attendant to commercial shipbuilding affordability. The selective involvement of multi-disciplined engineering teams and their practices for prototypical design development does, however, appear feasible and merited.

Traditional commercial vessel design processes have evolved over many years, with the primary goal of satisfying the requirements of insurers and shipowners while fully complying with *directly applicable* regulatory requirements. In brief, during a pre-construction gestation period, naval architects and others in the ship design field should normally conduct parametric studies, develop alternative conceptual designs, and formulate final vessel design characteristics by making at least one iteration of a basic design spiral (Fig. 27).

Fig. 2-7 Basic design spiral

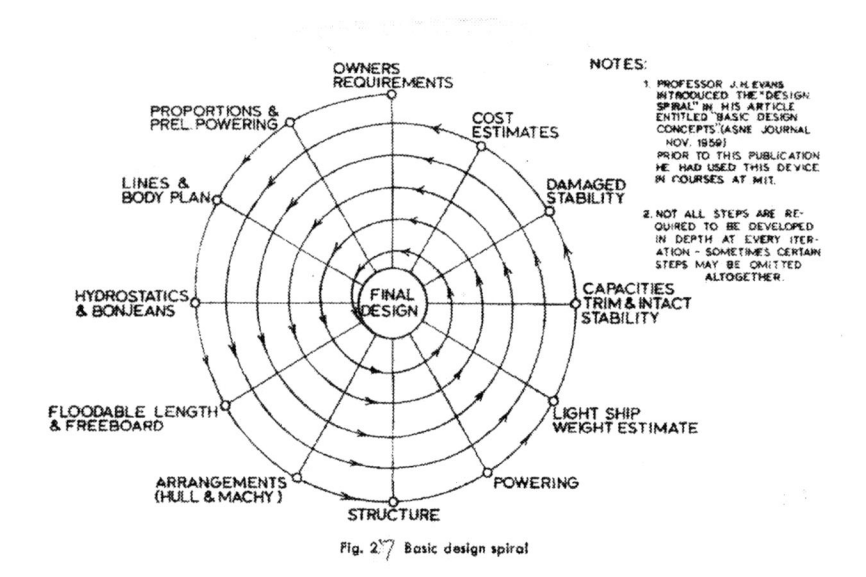

There are times when some steps in the cycle may be omitted altogether and, especially for lakers; their process may be considerably abbreviated when cargo handling, navigational, and other system constraints are already definable in detail from many years of operational experience. For example: In the past, lakers normally were given long-lived (about forty-seven years) ranges of service during operations in a closed intra-continent fresh water environment. Also, a measure of laker design standardization can be consistently forecast to suit shoreside facilities that are not usually subject to frequent changes (e.g. dimensional limits are known for locking evolutions along lake transit routes). Based on experience, hull reinforcement requirements for locking and ice navigation are reasonably predictable.)

On the other hand, the designs of oceangoing bulk-cargo vessels, operating in unrestricted corrosive saltwater environments are expected to be structurally capable of surviving storms having great intensity during long-haul global transits without opportunity for safe haven. Vessel design compatibility is also required for a considerable variety of higher-capacity shoreside cargo-handling facilities, including those on the St. Lawrence River when water depths and environmental conditions permit.

From a safety perspective, most of us have familiarity with the adage that "If one does not learn from the past, one is likely to repeat the same mistake(s) in the future." With this in mind, it was most gratifying to observe that *Derbyshire*'s protracted investigations and Court Hearings into her loss *did* introduce historical structural repair evidence for others of her Bridge Class in their search for possible multi-ship pattern(s) of design deficiency. Regrettably a similar approach did not appear to have been taken in developing similar corroborative evidence from almost-sister vessels to *Fitzgerald*, which could have been made available from the *S.S. Herbert C. Jackson* (prior to self-unloader conversion in 1975) and from the *S.S. Arthur B. Homer* (prior to layup in 1980 and dismantling 1986). With benefit of 20/20 hindsight, such a discovery process could have had the potential of isolating any negative *Fitzgerald*-unique perspective(s), since these vessels did not become catastrophic losses and were immediate follow-on constructions at the Great Lakes Engineering Works shipyard, sharing *Fitzgerald*'s design, fabrication, and operational features.

The *M.V. Derbyshire* (Fig. 26), a British oceangoing Ore/Bulk/Oil (O.B.O.) bulk-cargo vessel, of new design and owned by Bibby Tankers Limited, was lost under unexplained circumstances on or about September 9, 1980, a timeframe not far removed from that of the *Fitzgerald* loss on November 10, 1975. The *Derbyshire* had almost completed an eleven thousand mile voyage, and her unexplained loss occurred when encountering Typhoon Orchid in the Western Pacific, about 350 miles southeast of Kawasaki, Japan. All forty-four persons aboard perished.

She was the last of a series of six Bridge Class vessels and the largest British merchant ship ever lost, and like others of the Class she had structural deficiencies. Results of an initial formal investigation, shown in the following statement by British Department of Transport, were met with strong public protest.

Not only were the conclusions disputed, the legal and ethical propriety of having a Lloyd's representative serving as an official assessor in the Wreck Commissioner's cadre, as stated in the Report of Court No. 8075, was subject to challenge. At the time, one of the assessors was also representing the Royal Institution of Naval Architects (RINA) on the Executive Committee of Lloyd's, when Lloyd's, as the classification society which assigned the *Derbyshire*'s Certificate of Seaworthiness, had vested interest in the outcome of the case.

The Official Report

The following statement was issued by the Department of Transport on January 23 1989

The *Derbyshire* was a large, relatively modern (built 1976) fully equipped and well manned oil-bulk-ore (OBO) combination carrier which disappeared virtually without trace in the North West Pacific while on voyage from Canada to Japan in September, 1980. At the time, it was the most serious UK marine casualty for many years because of the heavy loss of life (42 crew members and two wives).

While at the time evidence as to the cause of the loss of the vessel was inconclusive, during the following five years the Department commissioned extensive research into the structural design of the *Derbyshire* and also investigated reports of defects in some of her sister-ships. Despite this work, no firm evidence arose as to the cause of the loss. On December 12, 1986, the Department announced that it was the government's intention to hold a formal investigation into the loss of the vessel. The investigation, under Wreck Commissioner Mr Gerald Darling, QC, started on October 5, 1987, and sat for 46 days, eventually closing on March 10, 1988. It reached the following conclusions:

The *Derbyshire* was properly designed, properly built and constructed from material of approved standard.

No inference can safely be drawn from the absence of any distress signal.

The condition of the cargo when loaded and its loading were within the existing recommended parameters.

The *Derbyshire* was caught in the worst part of Typhoon Orchid and may have encountered local freak weather beyond what can be "hindcast".

The actions of her master were not unreasonable.

The possibility that the *Derbyshire* was lost as a result of torsional weakness in her hull is extremely low.

The combination of circumstances necessary to postulate separation of the hull at frame No 65 is very unlikely, though some doubt must remain.

It is improbable that immediate or even sudden structural failure of the forward hatch covers caused rapid sinking.

Sequential flooding of holds is a possible cause of loss but not thought probable.

If cargo liquefaction did occur, which is doubtful, it still cannot be concluded that that was a prime cause of the loss.

If the *Derbyshire* got beam-on to the weather, structural failure and/or cargo shift would have become much more likely. It is quite possible that that happened but it cannot be proved.

This assessor's participation appeared to demonstrate potential conflict of interest and the absence of a prerequisite clean slate, which could influence the outcome of the case. As a Lloyd's representative, with possible prejudgments favorable to this party, the assessor could have been tainted with partiality toward favoring the technical and financial interests of Lloyd's. Participation by this assessor appeared to have compromised the Rule of Bias, which prescribes that any party having a vested interest in the outcome of a case is precluded from any part of the judgement process itself.

If the *Derbyshire* Formal Enquiry had reported that Lloyd's and/or the shipbuilder were to be held culpable for technical deficiency and/or workmanship deficiencies causing the loss, then Lloyd's with other parties would have been vulnerable to large claim actions in suits for compensation. Inaction by the Court and Lloyd's to remove the assessor cast a dark shadow over every subsequent *Derbyshire* endeavor and had effect on the mantle of respect and unquestioned fairness authority of historic maritime institutions involved.

A subsequent motion to reopen the case was supported by seventy-seven members of Parliament and, regrettably, the cognizant High Court of Justice (Admiralty Court) remained inconclusive and controversial even though they pursued their mission with the assistance of seafarer representatives and the *Derbyshire* Family Association (DFA), with various learned institutions and marine experts who performed analyses and seakeeping model testing. It was noted that the High Court was extremely selective in their acceptance and rejection of certain technical studies, some of which were justifiably critical and raised various complex concerns about the vulnerability of bulk-cargo vessels in general. In the course of these hearings, Lloyd's Register (L.R.) statistics on world-wide bulk-cargo vessel losses were also embarrassingly brought to light for the 1980–1990 timeframe, portraying deficiencies in structural adequacy, life-cycle maintenance, inspection, general seaworthiness, and operating crew safety concerns.

It again should be acknowledged that the *Fitzgerald* and *Derbyshire* were unique, prototypical design and construction ventures in their own right, placing challenges on each shipbuilder to:

- adapt to enlarged structural envelope dimensions with both vessels *beyond* existing structural scantling limits established by the American Bureau of Shipping (*Fitzgerald*) and Lloyd's Rules (*Derbyshire*) for O.B.O. vessels;
- fabricate Grade A steels (*Derbyshire*) having inconsistency in toughness and higher tensile steels with lesser thickness commensurate with superior structural properties, albeit potentially prone to elastic instability (buckling) and cracking; and
- introduce modified production practices and quality control procedures for the fabrication, welding, and shop-to-berth handling of prefabricated hull modules having fifty to seventy tons weight.

The *Derbyshire* oceangoing vessel and her five almost-sister vessels were claimed to be the largest and first true Ore/Bulk/Oil (O.B.O.) carriers to be built in a British shipyard at that time (1971–1976). It was indeed coincidental that Swan Hunter Shipbuilders on the River Tyne decided to select the ex-Furness Shipbuilding Company as the construction shipyard on the River Tees. Furness was my apprenticeship alma mater (1947–1952), enabling me to claim familiarity with their design office practices and a measure of practical awareness regarding the production facilities, which had undergone modernization.

The Bridge Class Shipbuilders
During fifty years of business operation (1919–1969), the Furness Shipbuilding Company built a considerable variety of merchant vessels and also established a sound reputation for the innovative design and construction of oil tankers for domestic and foreign owners. The company was also ever-vigilant for emergent business opportunities, such as the construction of vessels for the carriage of bulk-cargo grain, ore, or coal, when shipping entrepreneurs were developing renewed interest in the acquisition of larger and specialized types of oceangoing bulk-cargo vessels. About that time, Furness decided to undertake a shipyard modernization program (1963–1965) in preparation for these potential business opportunities. Upon completion, Furness secured an order to build the bulk-cargo carrier *M.V. Essi Gina*, having a cargo capacity of 55,400 tons deadweight. At that

time this vessel was the largest ever to be built in the shipyard—and a quantum leap from the staple 18,000 and 24,000 tons deadweight tankers of early-1950s vintage. Subsequently Furness satisfied market demand for follow-on 32,000 tankers, but the company's cautious conservatism in undertaking 40,000 tonners, was deferred until 1961 because of necessary construction facility modification and potential stern-launching constraints.

End of a Notable Shipbuilding Era
In 1963, the *M.V. Essi Gina* was the final vessel to be delivered under the Furness Shipbuilding masthead prior to the shipyard's announced closure in mid-1968. Later, in January 1969, Furness became an industrial element within the Swan Hunter Shipbuilders Group before their nationalization under British Shipbuilders in 1975 and their separation and final closure in 1979, shortly before the loss of *M.V. Derbyshire* in September 1980.

When the Department of Transportation convened the initial Formal Investigation on June 11, 1987, the Wreck Commissioner experienced considerable difficulty in gathering together dispersed witnesses, evidentiary documents, and information germane to the *Derbyshire* and other O.B.O. vessels of the Bridge Class. The situation further deteriorated when the Formal Investigation was later reopened in the High Court of Justice (Admiralty Court) and reported out on November 8, 2000, over *twenty* years after the loss.

When Swan Hunter Shipbuilders entered liquidation in 1993, the new owners of the shipyard received indemnification against any future claim action (re: *Derbyshire*) in a privatization agreement with British Shipbuilders. (i.e., Any claim action would become British tax payer responsibility since British Shipbuilders was a government owned entity).

In reviewing the fifty-year shipbuilding history of the ex-Furness Shipbuilding Company for tanker and other vessel deliveries, it is evident that their design and construction commitments were met with conservatism and competence.

The following table illustrates their typical tanker and bulker vessel delivery history, which reflects progressive increases in principal dimensions, nominally conservative length/depth ratios of about 14.0, and compliance with published classification society structural scantling requirements. *At all times the designers were provided with directly-applicable ship classification society Rules.* (Excluding Derbyshire)

Year	Type	Principal Dimensions (Feet) L B D	L/D	Cargo Deadweight (Long Tons)	Life (Yrs)
1942	Tanker	483.8 x 68.3 x 36.1	13.4	14,710	18
1952	Tanker	533.0 x 71.4 x 39.1	13.6	18,100	22
1954	Tanker	572.3 x 80.3 x 42.4	13.5	24,600	26
1955	Tanker	639.8 x 87.4 x 45.9	13.9	31,100	23
1961	Tanker	691.5 x 95.6 x 48.9	14.1	40,200	16
1963	Bulker	775.2 x 101.7 x 52.7	14.7	55,400	15
1969	Bulker	792.0 x 104.5 x 58.9	13.4	77,250	17
1971	O.B.O.	925.0 x 145.0 x 82.0	11.3	170,473	4*

* *M.V. Derbyshire*

Oceangoing bulker service life was generally less than that for tankers, and this may be partly attributable to design configuration, rougher cargo handling and distribution, and a varying degree of maintenance and upkeep contingent upon the stringency or laxity of the selected classification society, the national flag and the operators.

The L/D (11.3) ratio for *Derbyshire* reflected conservatism, possibly to maximize capacity and/or provide added longitudinal stiffness for end-launching; otherwise all extrapolative scantling judgements and experience would appear to merit a "leap-of-faith" designator, since the management and technical responsibilities would have been significantly compromised by an absence of *directly applicable* classification society rules for O.B.O. vessels in the configuration and dimensional range under consideration.

Adaptation of 1971 Lloyd's Rules for *dry-cargo* and *tanker* vessels without advance research and extraordinary engineering support, is deemed to have *overwhelmed* drafting staffs when called upon to function *outside* the "comfort zone" of conventional drafting practices for merchant vessels when using directly-applicable rules.

The Design Challenges
The Bridge Class was composed of:

Original Name	Completed	Original Owner	Status	Age
Furness Bridge	Sept. 1971	Furness Withy	Shipbreaker 1992	21
Tyne Bridge	Sept. 1972	Huntings	Shipbreaker 1987	15
English Bridge (renamed 1985) *Kowloon Bridge*	Mar. 1973	Bibby Line	Total Loss 1986	13
Sir John Hunter	Jan. 1974	HilmarResksten	Shipbreaker 1997	23
Sir Alexander Glen	April 1975	HilmarResksten	Shipbreaker 1994	19
Liverpool Bridge (renamed 1978) *Derbyshire*	June 1976	Bibby Line	Total Loss 1980	4

* All names were subsequently subject to change.
** Age includes considerable off-line time for repairs and other inactive periods.
Author does not hold final data regarding maintenance history, material conditions, national flagging, or cognizant classification societies.

While the design and construction of jumbo-sized Bridge Class vessels would prove to be a much greater shipbuilding challenge than conventional oil tankers, bulk-cargo vessels, or even lesser-sized combination ore/oil vessels, the economic gain in shipowner revenues had the potential for offsetting increased acquisition costs. This challenging shipbuilding venture could have considerably strained the limits of any shipbuilders heuristically-acquired experience and technical extrapolation skills; therefore, a need for innovative design and construction approaches was of the essence, since published Lloyd's Ship Classification Society Rules had *no* direct applicability to these vessels.

In the absence of directly-applicable Rules for the Bridge Class, submitted drawings were checked by Lloyd's for conformity with (hybrid) Rule standards applicable to *tanker* and *dry-cargo* vessels built in 1971! *Such a circumstance begs the question of how Lloyds and the cognizant shipbuilder could have ever obtained a Certificate of Classification when NO directly-applicable baseline standards were published for shipbuilder use.*

With such premising, a risk analysis associated with developing such a unique O.B.O. vessel (*without* dimensional precedent); *without* the use of directly-applicable published Rules; and *without* scientific research or in-depth first-principle engineering should have been cautionary signs for all concerned. Based on life-cycle repair events and catastrophic losses within the Bridge Class vessels, the chosen design strategies and apparently dissonant classification rules for structural strength and integrity, the appendages, and the reliability of main propulsion, auxiliaries, and power generation could have been in jeopardy at the outset, with contribution to the loss of ocean-going seafarer lives.

It is recognized that Lloyd's Register of Shipping (L.R.) did not physically design the vessels but, by making appropriate amendments and approvals to documentation submitted to them by the Swan Hunter Shipyard Group, they were able to maintain an oversight position to assure a vessel's seaworthiness. In this role, groundwork was laid for the eventual issuance of a Certificate of Classification to demonstrate that Lloyd's standards had been met. Such a certificate does not imply, nor should it be construed as an express warranty of safety, fitness for purpose, or seaworthiness of a vessel.

Ship classification is but one element within a network of maritime safety partners. Other elements are parties such as the shipowner, the shipbuilder, the flag State, port States, underwriters, shipping financiers, and charterers, among others. Under these circumstances, the Swan Hunter (Tyneside) Group Technical Department appears to have followed conventional design office practices while (perhaps unknowingly) assuming high-risk responsibility for preliminary calculations, and drawings.

(For reader clarification: All Ship Classification Society Rules are expected to reflect proven requirements for *usual* types of vessels having *conventional* proportions and structural characteristics and under normal operating conditions. The Rules essentially provide *minimum* standards for the design development of preliminary and working shop drawings for structure and equipment. Designing from first principles, requiring long-term complementary scientific research and engineering investment, is not usually evident in staffing plans or financial commitments in the extant modes of operation throughout domestic or foreign *commercial* shipbuilding sectors. Albeit "spin-off" benefits from simultaneous military design and construction programs may accrue. Traditionally the classification society rules are *not* expected to serve as handbooks to serve this purpose.)

Concomitantly with this process, the preliminary design drawings were further developed by Swan Hunter Shipbuilders (Teeside) Haverton Hill (ex-Furness) construction shipyard design offices, where production shop drawings were prepared as the basis for planning, steel ordering, and hull unit production in the fabrication sheds and on-berth for each Bridge Class vessel.

Missing Modification Drawings
It has been my experience that it was not unusual for deviations from production drawings to be found necessary in any shipyard to improve productivity and accessibility or to circumvent physical interferences. Requested deviations are normally transmitted from production managers via technical liaison with a cognizant design office, where supplemental "as-built" auxiliary drawings would be prepared for review and approval by Lloyd's surveyors and serial use by various shipyard tradesmen. Under established practice this should have been the case for questionable changes to continuous longitudinal structure in way of the highly controversial Bulkhead 65 during construction of the first Bridge Class vessel and inclusive of *Derbyshire*. The degree of "as-built" modification would have determined whether the condition should be either retained on a separate drawing or incorporated into the original master drawing applicable to the Bridge Class. In reviewing the investigatory history of *Derbyshire*, it became evident that Lloyd's Register denied ever having sighted any "as-built" drawings for structural modification in way of Bulkhead 65, on vessels following completion of the first vessel *Furness Bridge*, which was delivered in 1971. None was ever located by Lloyd's or Swan Hunter Shipbuilders for use as key evidence when requested by the *Derbyshire* Family Association (DFA). Letters of intent were known to exist, however, between the vessel owners and Swan Hunter, which refer to the submission of Bulkhead 65 modification drawings for the purpose of seeking Lloyd's review and approval.

It would be unconscionable if Lloyd's surveyors would not have had involvement with the modification of such a vital structural element for hull structural integrity. Such irregularity was not only contrary to good administrative practice, it also carried a dangerous implication that structural changes may have been made by shipyard tradesmen levels *without* design office or Lloyd's involvement. As a sidebar comment, I recall that the storage of drawing records was meticulously maintained in a secured (Furness) vault within the Main Administration Office. Immediately prior to demolition of that building; certain ex-employees noted that the vault contents had been *ransacked*, and this poses a belated question whether legerdemain forces may have been active to seek, remove, and dispose of the Bulkhead 65 "as-built" drawing evidence because of their legal sensitivity throughout the hearings.

Hull Stress Analysis
To estimate the stresses in these extraordinarily large specialized hull structures for global oceangoing service, Swan Hunter *et al* embraced the emergent "Finite Element Analysis" (FEA) technique, which was being successfully introduced in other design fields as computer usage continued to surge within industry. FEA analyses were also made by Lloyd's and design consultants.

In principle the FEA is a very rational analytic approach, although application selectivity and caution are necessary. For example, my professional exposure to automobile, combatant submarine, and deep submersible design processes enabled personal insight regarding grossly contrasting developmental environments with those of the commercial shipbuilding industry.

In all of these cases, viable FEA estimates were coupled to large multiple-year Research, Development, Test and Evaluation (RDT&E) financial commitments. These commitments supported computerized and iconic (scale and full-size) modeling, followed by rigorous laboratory, proving ground, and in service testing, manufacturing, methodologies, quality standards, research, etc. This was often referred to as the "Build and Bust" approach to pre-acceptance proof of concept. Without such a systemic technical approach, FEA implementation become vulnerable if viewed as a "stand-alone" panacea or "silver bullet" stress analysis solution. Responsible designers should have kept in mind that new technology in inadequately-prepared hands can become more of a liability than old technology in the same hands.

Practical Factors

On the practical side of the FEA equation, surety for material and welding control, employee training, rigorous non-destructive testing (NDT) standards, and consistency in the chemical, mechanical, and quality properties of received materials, etc., are required by shipbuilders and suppliers. These critical factors could have had serious impact on FEA estimates for performance of Bridge Class structural design if absent from the systemic network. While the practical factors were vigorously defended by Lloyd's and shipbuilder officials, some tradesmen witnesses, and a retired Lloyd's Surveyor (Mr. D.H. Swift), furnished dissenting statements that called attention to installations of *delaminated* steel plating, poor welding quality, hull structure misalignment, etc., all of which had potential occurrence during shipyard production processes and with contingency on overall process control:

Metallurgists and other technically-qualified individuals had concern for the general use of Grade A steel in primary hull structures because no toughness testing was required. Toughness quality was variable, and there was brittle fracture susceptibility in the low ambient temperature regime that would be experienced under stressful dynamic conditions while in service. The serial prefabrication of hull structural assemblies in shipyard production sheds was followed by their subsequent handling and integration with other (fifty to seventy-ton) units on the outside building berth.

This proved to be a great challenge when massive units were prone to temporary distortion and misalignment. Forced fitup actions, on a scale not previously experienced, were frequently necessary to forcibly push/pull flexible units back into shape and to achieve the correct alignment of welded joints—all of which had the potential of inducing residual prestressing conditions. These critical final assembly processes were further exacerbated by a nomadic welder workforce composed of good welders and others of lesser experience. Many were prone to migrate to nearby companies, having much higher-paid offshore and other construction contracts. The author has witnessed this phenomena in other shipyards where employees did not hesitate to avail themselves of better working conditions, welder training, or higher piece-work rate opportunities with other companies. Ultimately a price is paid by the shipbuilder and

© 1990 The Royal Institution of Naval Architects

A THEORY ON THE LOSS OF THE DERBYSHIRE

by R.E.D. Bishop, C.B.E., F.Eng., F.R.S.*(Fellow),
W.G. Price, F.Eng., F.R.S.**(Fellow) and
P. Temarel*** (Fellow)

*   Vice-Chancellor and Principal, Brunel University, Uxbridge, UK, died 12.9.89
**   Professor of Applied Mechanics, Brunel University (to 30.9.90); Professor of Ship Science, University of Southampton (from 1.10.90)
*** Lecturer in Mechanical Engineering, Brunel University

Mr. D.H. Swift, C.Eng (Member): I was prevented from giving evidence at the Court of Inquiry. I was the Surveyor concerned with the earlier ships in this Class, not with the DERBYSHIRE, and the outcome of the inquiry so shattered me that I have been ill for two years. I have been waiting since 1970 to try and bring attention to the disastrous things that were liable to happen as a result of the poor quality in construction. I am no longer employed by Lloyd's Register, so therefore I am no longer bound by my Contract of Employment which prevented me from applying to join the inquiry. I made matters known to my senior staff; in fact one of them whom I approached is present here tonight.

I wish to ask whoever is representing the relatives if there is any way that I can help at all and give evidence; it is important that the information I have is made available to them.

I am not highly qualified on the theoretical side, but there are three things that arose during the construction.

Basically misalignment was almost chapter and verse throughout the whole of the construction. The so-called checks and building maintenance of form checks were virtually non-existent. Radiography: at no time when my recommendations were made to see radiographs where they presented for me; they were looked at by the Senior Surveyor. I have no idea upon the quality of workmanship that went in as a result of my request for non-destructive testing techniques.

The amount of work that the Surveyor had to cope with was absolutely ridiculous. I had four ships; I was the only Surveyor in the yard, and it was impossible to dispute all the photographs that the gentlemen presented here. It is almost without question that those sorts of defects occurred throughout the ships of which I had experience and the thing that horrifies me is that there has been very little attention until the previous speaker who highlighted the problems of the deckhouse.

One of the things about which I had terrific arguments with the Senior Surveyor and I could achieve no improvement on it, was the supporting arrangements beneath the deckhouse at the forward end. The drawing might have shown that there was alignment, but the number of hard points that occurred at the whole of the front area of the deckhouse had to be seen to be believed. Whether this contributes any evidence to the sort of cracks that could be propagated, I do not know.

I am rather emotional about this; I have been ill as I say. I wanted to give evidence and I was prevented from doing so. I only hope now that I can correct that. I have been under terrific emotional stress for years.

vessel owner, in the form of reduced quality, structural failures, delays, and expensive rework.

From the testimony of hearing witnesses, welding porosity, slag inclusions, and *random* non-destructive testing (NDT) on welded joints were also significant harmful observations. It boggles my mind that a Lloyd's representative charged with inspecting the alignment of intercostal structural alignment would state that his evaluation was (aurally) based on the sonic response from *hammer* testing. This was beyond the pale. However, it did serve as a low-tech/high-tech FEA paradox capable of generating risk factors not considered in theoretical stress analysis methodologies or during the operational life cycle of a vessel—until failure occurrence.

It is hoped that, with the passage of time and the anticipated continuance of bulk-cargo vessel dimensional growth, this relatively untrodden commercial shipbuilding ground will be given international recognition.

Drafting Room Dilemmas
For reader clarification and general awareness, commercial ship design draftsmen at consultancies and shipyards were not usually graduates of naval architecture or any other engineering discipline. This is not intended as derogatory comment, because they have fulfilled a vital mission in the history of shipbuilding. Whereas a Chief Naval Architect and a Master Shipwright once made unilateral decisions in their respective fields of training and responsibility, the advent of complex steel self-propelled vessels brought with it a need for teams of specialist ship draftsmen charged with the development of numerous drawings and technology adaptation.

During my ship design apprenticeship, I observed that, while some liaison did take place between "the yard" and "the office" operatives, very few group leaders, journeymen draftsmen, or ship design apprentices had ever physically experienced the *outside* production trade environment and practices of the mold loft, the steel fabrication sheds, the building berths, or the fitting-out basins. There was a definite white collar/blue collar schism of elitism based on a "them" and "us" class structure… which I subsequently found to be seriously flawed leaving an indelible mark on my character. This discovery was made (at Furness) over the final six months of training in the shipyard before entering compulsory military service when my deferment period expired. The experience allowed me to become aware of the lines of demarcation between a tradesman using his personal skill to produce a specific product designed by others and a craftsman who exercised control over the design of his own product, as in the case of a ship design draftsman. The 1980s emergence of Computer-Aided Design/Manufacturing Management (CAD/CAM) did bring about changes requiring ship draftsmen to divest themselves of their *individual* craftsmanship identities and to become skilled technicians within an interdependent computerized electronic network—and seeing even less of the ship construction site.

Some contemporaries and journeymen considered me irrational for requesting shipyard exposure during a (1952) Winter/Spring inclement weather season, but I felt the endurance challenge would become valuable training for the future. Many things were learned in the process, including a lifelong respect for shipyard tradesmen and an awareness that *most ship production difficulties originated in the design process*. I found a similar philosophy to be espoused by Japanese shipbuilders of Mitsubishi Heavy Industries, whom I visited at a later time (1975). Their design *managers* were regularly sent into the shipyard production environment to resolve problems originated by their design divisions. Having served a five-year apprenticeship, including six months of shipyard trade experience, I may claim a "been-there-done-that" level of "hands-on" credibility in comments made.

Without doubt, ship draftsmen may rightfully claim to be highly competent in their application of *directly*-applicable classification society rules (when available), as demonstrated by their successful performance on delivered vessels over many years. Regrettably, when published rules were unavailable for the Bridge Class (O.B.O.) vessels, the same draftsmen would probably have been euphemistically "adrift" and left mainly to their own devices while adhering to an historic rubric that vessel cost, performance, and ease of fabrication should start on their drafting tables. Partial dependency on past concepts that (perhaps) provided design similitude and were considered suitable for application of heuristic reasoning may have proved to be dubious and unsuitable in the absence of a sound scientific base. Moreso in the case of *Derbyshire* than *Fitzgerald*, because of the degree of extension beyond the state of the art. Even if all ship draftsmen had been graduate engineers, the absences of proven and directly applicable O.B.O.-specific classification society rule criteria and advanced research for understanding the physics and physical interaction mechanisms would have still prevented pragmatic resolution of the beyond-the-norm design dilemmas.

In retrospect the quantum change from previously non-O.B.O. vessel design experiences and especially the (mis)directed adaptation of Lloyd's Rule criteria for tanker/dry-cargo vessels to the *Derbyshire* and other O.B.O. vessels of the Bridge Class appeared to be deserving of definition as a "*camel masquerading as a horse designed by committee.*" In both of the *Fitzgerald* and *Derbyshire* design situations, the absence of primary underpinnings for their structural design could have unknowingly introduced risk.

When designing beyond Rule limits, thorough advanced research should have been merited and executed but was not readily recognizable, probably due to conflicts with traditional practice or potential impact on cost and schedule constraints. Under such circumstances certain well-worn sayings appear to be appropriate, such as: "Work in haste and relent at leisure," and "Whenever time, funding, and expertise are not available to perform necessary tasks in the first instance, the corrective requirements for these elements could become magnified in the aftermath should design deficiencies occur." With or without supportive research, shipowners and designers should have followed a "hasten-slowly" policy and sought compromise with cognizant classification societies and their on-site surveyors, with anticipation that there may be a divergence of opinion born of weak scientific justifications on both sides.

While it is generally accepted that classification societies are not normally in the business of designing vessels, their surveyors do have specific interest and responsibility in providing guidance and the monitoring of Rule compliance for fabrication details associated with sound hull structures and other vessel elements subject to their certification. Under normal commercial shipbuilding circumstances, whenever ship classification society rules customarily have *direct* applicability to the type of vessel being designed, experienced ship draftsmen are quite capable of developing drawings in accordance with stipulated rule requirements (a proven traditional and moderately-technical "cookbook" practice). For vessels not having precedent and *not* supported by directly-applicable

Rules, this circumstance would severely challenge talented designers, as in the case of *Derbyshire*. Their capabilities could have been overwhelmed when called upon to also function in a quasi-graduate engineer role while following their routinized drafting practices.

Investigatory bodies failed to give due recognition or scrutiny to this keystone element in structural design decision-making processes for the advancement of ship concepts to safe physical reality.

Until more pragmatic approaches are taken to designing beyond-the-norm structural configurations, backed by basic and applied research, a first-principle engineering approach will undoubtedly remain in the orbit of limbo.

Exposure of Global Bulk-Cargo Vessel Losses
Investigations of the unexplained *Fitzgerald* and *Derbyshire* losses drew attention to the need for domestic and global recognition of many other bulk-cargo vessel losses on the Great Lakes and the high seas. The former vessel being accorded a period of national attention with subsequent commemoration by historical societies. The latter receiving scant publicity throughout the media, even though in the 1990s, these essential vessels represented about 7 percent of the oceangoing fleet but were sustaining about 57 percent of the casualties, as officially recorded by Lloyd's Register (L.R.).

Within the framework of various studies, investigations, and hearings covering structural and other facets of the controversial *Derbyshire* design, it became public knowledge, from Lloyd's Register and other credible sources, that bulk-cargo fleets were experiencing losses at an abnormally high rate throughout the 1980s and early 1990s. The statistics indicated that twenty bulkers per year were written off by insurance underwriters from all causes, including war losses, collisions, groundings, contact damage, fire, explosion, capsizing due to cargo shifting, inundation by flooding through hatches, known structural failures, etc. At that time the average bulker loss from *unexplained* circumstances was cited by Lloyd's at about one per year.

The age of vessels varied, from eight to thirty-nine years, with an average age of eighteen with 78 percent of them fifteen years or older. By selective data analysis, the following are presented as excerpts of losses for various time envelopes:

- During the years 1990–1991, the pace of losses increased dramatically as twenty-five vessels of over 15,000 tons cargo deadweight were lost, with some circumstances having possible structural failure as recorded by Lloyd's Register.
- At least 273 crew members perished, and these were inclusive of 99 crewmen who were lost on board three of these vessels. It was estimated that 750 seafarers lost their lives in the 1988–1994 timeframe.
- During the period 1980–1996, forty-three "standard" ocean-going bulkers of over 20,000 tons deadweight were lost in circumstances where structural failure could have been a contributory factor. (A "standard" bulker configuration is defined as having a single skin, transversely-framed sides, a double bottom, and with topside and hopper tanks running throughout the cargo holds.) Other bulkers sustained structural casualties but were not lost.
- For the period 1990–1998, the Lloyd's Register 98, Table A4 showed a number of *unexplained* losses for oceangoing bulkers, including eight missing vessels, all carrying iron ore with holds 70 percent empty, and all with weak hatches.

This situation appeared to be a "very large skeleton in a very dark closet" and one of the best-kept secrets within the spectrum of maritime activity. It had all the trappings of technological failure for vessel design, operation, and incompatibility with damage inducing cargo-handling at terminals. Causal factors for the loss pandemic were probably systemic, ranging from design rooms to the cargo-handling facilities.

Within this matrix, the most disturbing aspect is represented by erroneous attempts to apply (*ex post-facto*) theoretical analysis with minimal regard to a shipbuilder's practical design and construction processes, the documented feedback data from which is usually almost minimal or non-existent.

The following summary shows a percentile distribution of probable loss causes for bulkers, based on interpretation of data accumulated over a broadened time spectrum and made available from various credible sources:

Attributable Causes	1960–1994	1990–1994
Possible hull damage	29.9%	28.6%
Wrecked or stranded	28.3	24.1
Fire and/or explosion	18.6	20.5
Collision	9.6	8.9
Missing unexplained	5.2	9.8
Machinery damage	3.9	3.6
Engine room flooding	3.4	4.5
Cargo shifting	1.1	–

It was not until 1990 before Lloyd's Register publically conceded that the then spate of losses signaled a need for investigation of this vessel type. One Lloyd's spokesman claimed that the losses were "atypical" and another stated that "Lloyd's Register did not believe the vessels had a fundamental design fault; they believed that the ship's sides *simply wear out* because of corrosion and punishment as cargo is loaded and unloaded." These statements carry a measure of truth but are far from complete when considered in priority context within a systemic failure matrix. Also, the statements were surprising since ship designers do rely on classification societies to provide criteria and standards compatible with corrosion, wastage, and operational attrition. If not the classification society, then *who?*

All of in-service bulk-cargo vessels, and those in the future, are indeed the type of workhorses that will continue to experience damaging environmental and operational forces during their lifetime. It would appear that time is of the essence for cerebral, technological, and design renaissance beyond the extant unwavering dependency and trust in inadequate "cookbook" methodologies and approaches that have provided a "comfort zone" for commercial vessel designers over many years. The efficient and safe movement of bulk cargo remains vitally important for global trading and is continually expanding to support the demands of ascendant industrial powers of Far Eastern nations. Unless bold scientific and financial commitments are forthcoming in the very near future, it is postulated that bulkers and their operating crews will continue to be at heightened risk on the tumultuous high seas.

PART SIX:
CARGO TERMINAL INTERFACES

Great Lakes

On the Great Lakes, where bulk cargoes such as ore, coal, limestone, and grain (Table 1) are extensively handled, several time-proven methods of vessel loading and unloading are employed, with each cargo and handling facility exerting its own influence upon the design features of various transporting vessels.

Table 1. Typical Bulk Cargoes.

Bulk Cargo	Stowage Rate Cub. Ft./L. Ton	S.S. Edmund Fitzgerald		
		Max Cargo Volume in Cub. Ft.	Max Cargo Weight in L. Tons	Water Ballast Required
Grains*				
Oats	65 - 75	860,950	12,300	Yes
Barley	53 - 85		14,800	Yes
Rye	48 - 52		17,200	Yes
Maize	45 - 49		18,300	Yes
Wheat	44 - 48		18, 700	Yes
Non-Grains				
Coal	40 - 45		20,500	Yes
Taconite	16 - 17		26,118 - 27, 402 (Load Line Varies)	No

* Grain Cargoes

These cargoes are susceptible to shifting and can also become compacted during a voyage due to vibration and ship motions.

Lake Carriers' Association

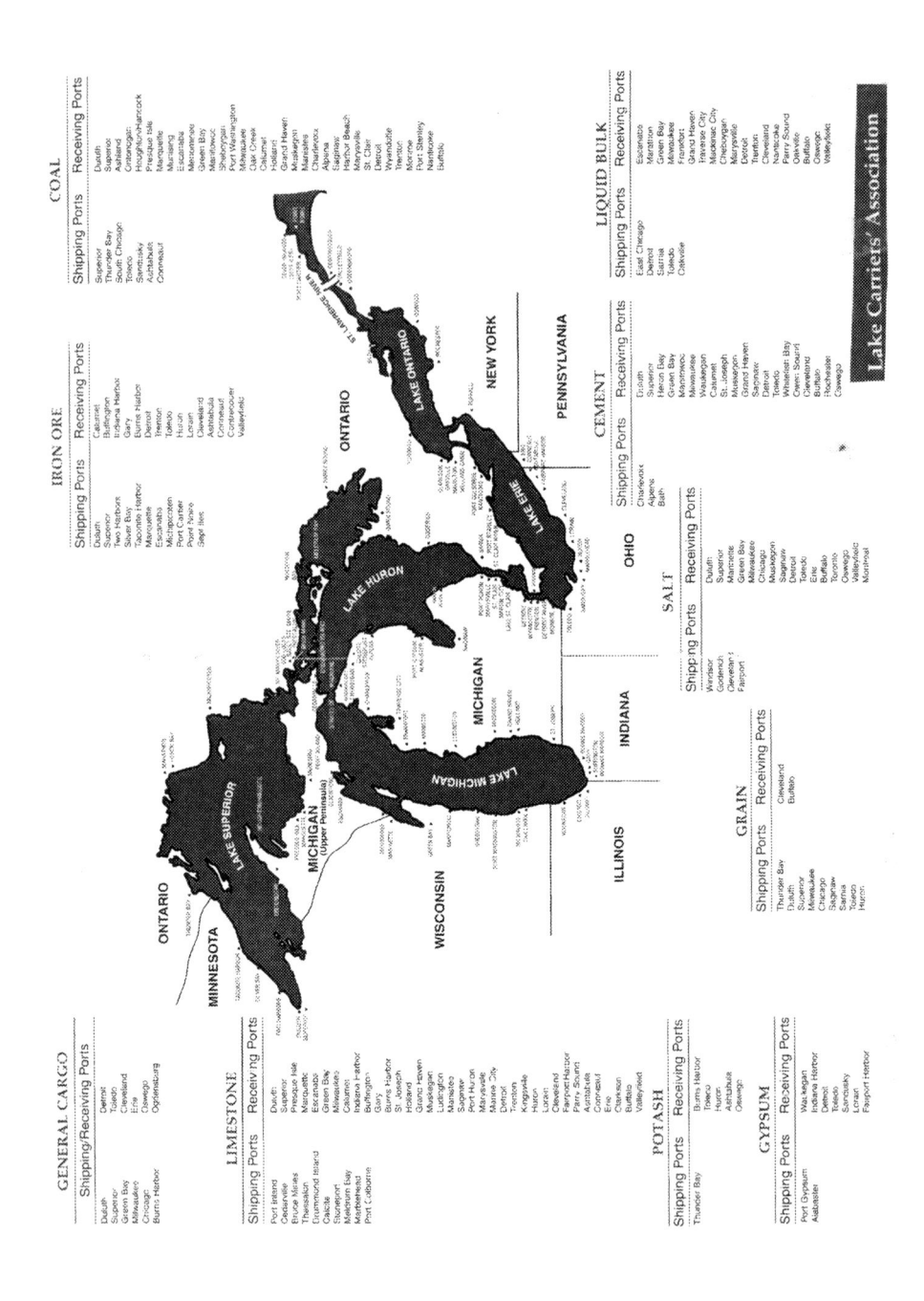

GENERAL CARGO

Shipping/Receiving Ports
- Duluth
- Superior
- Green Bay
- Milwaukee
- Chicago
- Burns Harbor
- Detroit
- Toledo
- Cleveland
- Erie
- Oswego
- Ogdensburg

LIMESTONE

Shipping Ports
- Port Inland
- Cedarville
- Presque Isle
- Bruce Mines
- Thessalon
- Drummond Island
- Calcite
- Stoneport
- Marblehead
- Port Dolomite
- Port Colborne

Receiving Ports
- Duluth
- Superior
- Presque Isle
- Marquette
- Escanaba
- Green Bay
- Milwaukee
- Calumet
- Indiana Harbor
- Buffington
- Gary
- Burns Harbor
- St. Joseph
- Holland
- Grand Haven
- Muskegon
- Ludington
- Manistee
- Saginaw
- Port Huron
- Marysville
- Marine City
- Detroit
- Trenton
- Kingsville
- Huron
- Lorain
- Cleveland
- Fairport Harbor
- Parry Sound
- Ashtabula
- Conneaut
- Erie
- Clarkson
- Buffalo
- Valleyfield

POTASH

Shipping Ports
- Thunder Bay

Receiving Ports
- Burns Harbor
- Toledo
- Huron
- Ashtabula
- Oswego

GYPSUM

Shipping Ports
- Port Gypsum
- Alabaster

Receiving Ports
- Waukegan
- Indiana Harbor
- Detroit
- Toledo
- Sandusky
- Lorain
- Fairport Harbor

IRON ORE

Shipping Ports
- Duluth
- Superior
- Two Harbors
- Silver Bay
- Taconite Harbor
- Marquette
- Escanaba
- Michipicoten
- Port Cartier
- Point Noire
- Sept Iles

Receiving Ports
- Calumet
- Buffington
- Indiana Harbor
- Gary
- Burns Harbor
- Detroit
- Trenton
- Toledo
- Huron
- Lorain
- Cleveland
- Ashtabula
- Conneaut
- Contrecoeur
- Valleyfield

CEMENT

Shipping Ports
- Charlevoix
- Alpena
- Bath

Receiving Ports
- Duluth
- Superior
- Huron Bay
- Green Bay
- Manitowoc
- Milwaukee
- Waukegan
- Calumet
- St. Joseph
- Muskegon
- Grand Haven
- Saginaw
- Detroit
- Toledo
- Whitefish Bay
- Owen Sound
- Cleveland
- Buffalo
- Rochester
- Oswego

SALT

Shipping Ports
- Windsor
- Goderich
- Cleveland
- Fairport

Receiving Ports
- Duluth
- Superior
- Marinette
- Green Bay
- Milwaukee
- Muskegon
- Chicago
- Saginaw
- Detroit
- Toledo
- Erie
- Buffalo
- Toronto
- Oswego
- Valleyfield
- Montreal

GRAIN

Shipping Ports
- Thunder Bay
- Duluth
- Superior
- Milwaukee
- Chicago
- Sarnia
- Saginaw
- Toledo
- Huron

Receiving Ports
- Cleveland
- Buffalo

COAL

Shipping Ports
- Superior
- Thunder Bay
- South Chicago
- Toledo
- Sandusky
- Ashtabula
- Conneaut

Receiving Ports
- Duluth
- Superior
- Ashland
- Ontonagon
- Houghton-Hancock
- Presque Isle
- Marquette
- Munising
- Escanaba
- Menominee
- Green Bay
- Manitowoc
- Sheboygan
- Port Washington
- Milwaukee
- Clair Creek
- Calumet
- Holland
- Grand Haven
- Muskegon
- Manistee
- Charlevoix
- Alpena
- Saginaw
- Harbor Beach
- Marysville
- St. Clair
- Detroit
- Wyandotte
- Trenton
- Monroe
- Port Stanley
- Nanticoke
- Buffalo

LIQUID BULK

Shipping Ports
- East Chicago
- Detroit
- Sarnia
- Toledo
- Oakville

Receiving Ports
- Escanaba
- Manistee
- Green Bay
- Milwaukee
- Frankfort
- Grand Haven
- Traverse City
- Muskegon
- Cheboygan
- Marysville
- Detroit
- Trenton
- Cleveland
- Nanticoke
- Parry Sound
- Oakville
- Buffalo
- Oswego
- Valleyfield

For most of her short life the "straight-decker" *Fitzgerald* hauled pelletized taconite cargoes from Lake Superior loading terminals to satisfy the insatiable appetite of a steel-making industrial heartland, having major steel mills with a capability to consume about seventy thousand tons of ore every five days. Each round trip was of about five days duration. A coal cargo of similar amount would also be necessary to generate Great Detroit's electricity needs on a daily basis. Without doubt, U.S-flagged lakers do make a major contribution to the employment and economies of many States, with cargo movement reserved between U.S. ports for U.S.-owned, built, and crewed vessels. These reservations are in accordance with The Jones Act (Section 27 Merchant Marine Act 1920) provisions, a long-standing U.S. Maritime Policy.

From this it is apparent that user-producer relationship must prevail between all activities, wherever variable business cycle demands can have immediate effect upon bulk-cargo production, shipment, consumption, product manufacturing and employment levels.

Loading of cargo is accomplished in about five hours by using either:

(a) conveyor systems as used at Escanaba, Michigan, and the Reserve Mining Company dock at Silver Bay, Minnesota; or
(b) typical "ore docks" (Fig. 28) using pierside storage "bin" pockets that are incorporated into the docks at Superior, Wisconsin, and at Marquette, Michigan. Special chutes are used for directing the ore or other mined bulk-cargo from the "bins" into the hatches of a loading vessel. Each "bin" contains from 250 to 400 tons of taconite pellets that are replenished by hopper-bottom rail cars from above. The gravity-flow loading rate was controlled by a chute-operated gate as ore is fed into a vessel's cargo hold.

Ore was also loaded at the facilities by belt conveyors, spouts and buckets.

A laker's loading hatch arrangement is required to match the spacing of pierside loading chutes and spouts, as in the *Fitzgerald* design, which had twenty-one cargo hatches, with each opening

Fig. 28 – Typical Ore Loading Dock
Photo – Larry Van Dusen

Fig. 29-1 – Unloading Terminal
Photo – Paul C. LaMarre

measuring eleven feet length and forty-eight feet breadth, with a center-to-center spacing of twenty-four feet. Such a layout facilitated uniform spreading of ore while permitting the lowering of chutes for free-flow loading.

Unloading could be accomplished in about twelve to fourteen hours at terminal facilities by:

(a) Hulett unloaders (originally introduced circa 1900), having a capability to unload ten thousand tons of ore in about four hours, operated in batteries for the simultaneous unloading of several hatches. Each unit (Fig. 29-2) consisted of a large gantry crane mounted on rails running parallel with the dock edge. Located on top of each gantry is a travelling tower surmounted by a large counterbalanced boom, whose lower end has an operator's cab and a large clamshell-type bucket (Fig. 29-3) for the unloading operation. A receiving hopper, mounted on the gantry base, transfers offloaded ore by chute to railway cars or to on-site stockpiles by conveyor belts; or

Fig. 29-2 – Hulett unloaders (now obselete)
Photo - Cleveland State University Library

*Fig. 29-3 – Hulett Unloader Clamshell-typle Bucket.
Photo – Cleveland State University Library.*

(b) Bucket unloaders consisting of a bucket and boom gear with an approximate capacity of seventeen tons and performance averaging three thousand to four thousand tons per hour.

This type of dockside equipment is flexible in operation and does not have an appreciable effect upon the design of the served ship, except for a requirement that wide hatches be used in order to access as much of a cargo hold as possible. The length and width of hatches must permit the unloaders to reach cargo-hold corners.

Final Cargo Loading
The *Fitzgerald* loaded her final cargo at Burlington Northern Railroad Dock No. 1 East, in Superior, Wisconsin, on November 9, 1975. The docks at Superior were equipped with storage pockets ("bins") built into the dock, and chutes were used to direct cargo from the pockets into the twenty-one hatch openings (Fig. 28).

The pockets on the dock were preloaded, before the vessel arrival, with approximately three hundred tons of pellets, although there were a few two hundred-ton and one hundred-ton pockets that were used in the final phase of loading to trim the vessel. Each ore pocket had its own chute which was lowered to service each hatch opening when readied for loading. Communication between the experienced Chief Mate John H. McCarthy, having responsibility for vessel loading, and the loading dock supervisor was accomplished by voice. The Chief Mate had been in the employ of the vessel's operator since 1947 in various capacities, including relief master in 1966 and 1971, and had served aboard the *Fitzgerald* as Chief Mate since April 1975. The vessel was moored starboard side to, on the inner end of the eastern side of the loading dock with the forward hatch opening of No. 1 Cargo Hold lined up with the furthest inshore pocket on the dock. Actual loading commenced with the aftermost hatch (No. 21) then was worked forward for the first run. Upon completion of each loading run, the vessel was shifted sternward to align hatch openings for the next run, again starting aft and working forward. Upon completion of the second run, the vessel was shifted again and took five or six pockets in the after hatches. This was expected to maintain the required trim by the stern until the final loading was completed.

As further background, the Load Line Regulations did *not* require the *Fitzgerald* to be furnished with a Loading Manual upon delivery in 1958, thereby allowing the vessel's Chief Mate (as cargo loading officer) to have considerable latitude with respect to the distribution of all cargoes. A documented record of the taconite cargo tonnage and distribution would have been entered in the Chief Mate's notebook (if used) and would have been lost at the time of vessel sinking. In the absence of a loading manual, the Chief Mate reportedly monitored *Fitzgerald*'s cargo loading operation by innovatively using a row of shirt-collar stiffener tabs to keep track of the amount and location of cargo hatch ore distribution. It is not known if this tracking approach was in addition to or in place of a notebook. Factual data on the final loading condition therefore remains unknown. In the absence of a documented record, a theoretical cargo capacity profile reveals that, with apportionment based on the relative capacities of No. 1, No. 2, and No. 3 Holds (over a total volume of 860,950 cubic feet), a cargo distribution could have been 36 percent in No. 1 and No. 3 Holds, and 28 percent in the No. 2 center Hold.

The vessel did have a slight trim by the stern based on her loading terminal departure drafts of 27' 2" forward and 27' 6" aft. An amidship draft reading was *not* available, nor was it known to have ever been taken, therefore, the hull sagging or hogging vertical flexure condition at departure could not be reconstructed. To fairly rationalize the vessel's loading condition, and with recognition that an experienced Chief Mate was in charge of loading operations, it appears reasonable to assume that if either zero hog or one inch of sag "belly" were attained after final ore cargo adjustments, then pre-stressing of the hull could have been insignificant.

The final Bill of Lading showed that 26,116 long tons of taconite pellets were received, but this figure was only considered an *approximation* since:

- About one-half of the received cargo was dumped into the dock pockets directly from ore cars, and the *actual* amount of taconite in each car was *not* known. An assumption was made that each ore car would be loaded with the average load for that type of car.
- The remaining half of the cargo was loaded into pockets via conveyor belt, and for these pockets, the load was more accurately weighed before reaching the pockets.

Although the author (and others) do not believe that in-transit shoaling or dockside grounding contributed to the *Fitzgerald* loss, there was awareness that deeper seasonal drafts permitted by the 1973 Great Lakes Load Line Regulations and/or reductions in lake water levels could have increased the frequency of dockside "groundings." Some bottom damage could have also been sustained at loading or unloading berths. (As an aside, it is recognized that self-unloading, boom-equipped lakers are more susceptible to "grounding" damage when executing fine-maneuvering evolutions to discharge bulk cargoes at a greater variety of shoreside installations).

Taconite iron-ore tailings, in pelletized form, are very dense and have a stowage factor of about sixteen to seventeen cubic feet per ton, thereby requiring only part-utilization of cargo hold space in a laker vessel. For example, the cargo-hold capacity of *Fitzgerald* was 860,950 cubic feet, of which only slightly over 50 percent of the volume was utilized when in a full-load condition, and care was needed to effect cargo dispersion that would avoid deleterious hull stressing and vibration.

The almost-spherical pellets, containing low-grade iron ore, have a water absorption rate of about 6 percent to 7 percent and may contain up to 27.5 pounds of water in the interstitial spaces within each cubic foot of pellets (without any free-surface water being observed in a cargo hold). The angle of repose for taconite pellets is approximately 26 degrees, whether wet or dry. The pellets are produced by an "oxide-pelletizing" process, which begins with the initial mining of low-grade iron ore (magnetite) concentrate. With the addition of bentonite, they are processed into spherically-shaped pellets of 3/8-inch to 5/8-inch diameter and fired at temperatures of 2,200–2,400 degrees F., which changes their composition to relatively non-magnetic hematite.

Over the *Fitzgerald*'s short seventeen-year workhorse career, she appeared to have fully met her operator's expectations and was reported to have completed 748 round-trip voyages covering over one million miles when mainly transporting nineteen million tons of ore pellets on the Great Lakes. Praiseworthy though this may have been, the notable achievement could have had *non-detectable* debilitating structural effects whenever the vessel was driven too hard in bad weather conditions, and fatiguing multi-axial forces would be juxtaposed on steady-state normal stress levels. While full-power settings do enable vessel masters to meet schedules and (perhaps) keep ahead of storms, the practice should not be favored for full-lined (block coefficient 0.88) vessels, which also become less seakindly and more difficult to control.

While the Great Lakes fresh water operating environment was favorable for the minimizing of corrosion, the vessel's hull was not immune from brittle fracture; damage sustained during cargo handling at terminals; bow slamming during transit; underway collisions; and hull damage during lock utilization. As a U.S.-flagged vessel, however, regulatory requirements and inspections should have provided a measure of assurance that maintenance and repair standards would be complied with for safe operations.

Oceangoing

The international bulk-cargo handling facilities servicing oceangoing vessels are on a mega-scale compared with those used by Great Lakes vessels, with some vessels of advanced age becoming operationally vulnerable when more (rather than less) inspections and maintenance are technically merited. From the 1990s onward, the inspection standards and practices of some ship classification societies for oceangoing vessels were also the subject of serious debate by masters having knowledge of registry-switching, with the express purpose of evading stringent inspection and maintenance for vessel classification purposes. (An isolated case was even reported of a classification society that made an offer to classify a vessel by fax, sight unseen *without* a prerequisite inspection! Some vessels chose to operate under other national Flags of Convenience (FOC), having less-costly registration, liberal laws, and safety compliance laxity.

Alarming vessel vulnerability and sinking loss issues were brought to the highest national attention in a number of countries, and early in 1992, Australia's two main ore exporters, Hammersley Iron and Broken Hill Pty, banned bulk-cargo vessels in excess of fifteen years of age from loading at their terminals to defray inferences that it was *their* loading that had contributed to sinkings. The Norwegian authorities, meanwhile, had started compulsory inspection of Panamanian and Maltese-flag bulk-cargo carriers and, subsequently, older vessels under other flags, in an attempt to reduce casualties. About that time, their Norway-Narvik terminal was reportedly visited by about 225 bulk carriers each year.

As the cargo loading rates and traffic at some terminals dramatically increased, there was heightened concern over the deteriorating structural capability of ore-carrier hulls to withstand more rapid and concentrated cargo-hold loadings. There was also the issue of severe attritional damage by the cargo and/or the heavy (thirty-five ton) grabs on hold structures during unloading evolutions.

The loading rate capabilities and hull damage potential may be typified by terminals at Dampier, Australia, where the Hammersley Iron shiploaders were able to load ore at a rate of 9,000 and 7,500 tons per hour, and at Tubarao, Brazil, having similar-type machines but of 16,000 tons per hour capacity. Hull damaging experiences were exacerbated by some vessel operators who were known to limit their loading dock time, at the expense of safe cargo distribution for some vessels reputed to be overworked and under-maintained. Examples include:

- The *Trade Daring*, a twenty-two-year old bulker that broke in two pieces whilst alongside a showpiece Brazilian port, fortunately without loss of life. Half of her crew were flown home and the remainder were imprisoned. Brazil did introduce a law requiring bulk-carrier vessels over eighteen years of age to undergo compulsory checks before loading iron ore—very correct in principle but weak in real-world service practicality.
- Over the lifetimes of all Bridge Class vessels (inclusive of total-loss *Derbyshire* and *Kowloon*) extensive repairs were required to maintain an operational status with various new owners, Flags of Convenience (FOC), and classification societies having a considerable range of structural inspection standards. One of the renamed operating vessels was reported to have "161 frames wasted like paper, all main structure in the forepeak wasted, bulkheads either cracked or wasted...."
- In many parts of the world, some vessels are delivered to a shipbreaker who may trade his low-cost acquisition to an unscrupulous shipowner who then seeks an insurer, backed by seaworthiness certification from a lax classification society.

With such modus operandi, the new shipowner is usually able to undercut freight rates of reputable seagoing competitors while trading in an expendable currency of dead seafarers as vessel losses proliferated. There is shipowner awareness that if the vessel reaches port they will be paid; if lost while in transit, a shipowner may often be paid more than a vessel is worth.

The maritime intent seems to have changed little since the days of Samuel Plimsoll (1890) when he wrote on the crux of this problem at that time:

> ...if a ship is utterly unfit to go to sea and has been sent out to sea insured for as much money as would buy a new one, to bring a positive gain to her owner by being wrecked...the Insurance people ought to prove this, and if they did not bring the guilty to justice, at least prevent them from making a profit by their wrong-doing.

Every Master knows that excess time spent at loading/unloading terminals detracts from annual cargo-carrying (cost per ton-mile) productivity, and performance rating. Vessel-owner demands have historically been accommodated as evidenced by regulatory body deferral of repairs until a layup season.

This situation did not go unnoticed by certain classification societies, and in November 1990 the Lloyd's Register commenced a special bulk-carrier study for hull corrosion and cracking damage. It was reported that they held 17,000 sets of data for various vessels built since 1960, with many related to bulk-cargo vessels, including the *Derbyshire* and sisters of her Bridge class. The study results were discussed by Lloyd's Register Journal in 1991. Subsequently Lloyd's List gathered further information enabling some action to be taken for what they described (in their paper) as "vanishing" bulk-carriers, and made a statement that:

> "Commercial pressures dictating the growth of ship size for the carriage of low-value commodities such as ore, have also dictated that cargoes be handled at ever-increasing speeds." Their paper also pointed out that "many operators, acting under these basic pressure, were less than circumspect, not only about the speed at which they allowed their vessels to be loaded to their deadweight, but also as regards the pattern of loading."

Without question, Lloyd's did have necessary insight on a par with that of seafarers and, in essence, both parties had formulated a wholesome "wherefore" but lacked the executive "therefore." There was no admission of potential weakness in classification society design and construction standards; the absence of published and directly-applicable classification society rules for initial use by the Bridge Class (O.B.O.) shipbuilder; the paucity of scientific research for bulk-cargo vessel hydroelasticity assessment; the need for assigning an international Figure of Merit (FOM) to ensure a uniform standard for seaworthiness; and a requirement to more fully assess the life-cycle circumstantial background of casualties with and without survivors or witnesses.

Within the documented casualty and repair history of oceangoing bulk-cargo carriers, the six vessels of the Bridge Class embodied technical and operational ramifications on a global scale. The loss circumstances also provided an excellent focal point for classification society (Lloyd's) intervention. Of the six vessels, only the first vessel *M.V. Furness Bridge* was built to original design, the remainder received significant later reinforcement and modification in way of Bulkhead 65 in attempts (by other shipyards) to compensate for structural discontinuities and welded joint inadequacies.

No formal investigation was initiated by the British Government until six years after the *Derbyshire* sinking. However on, March 11, 1982, a surveyor representing the Regisro Italiano Navale Ship Classification Society inspected serious deck cracking in way of Bulkhead 65 on the (Italian-flagged) almost-sister *M.V. Tyne Bridge* after her towing to Hamburg, Germany. The surveyor did issue unsolicited warnings (with Lloyd's surveyor agreement) to effect significant structural strengthening modifications in way of Bulkhead 65 on the ten-year-old *Tyne Bridge* and her sister vessels based on their inspection findings.

Parliamentary Debate

During Parliamentary debate, some members with prior hands-on shipbuilding experience were extremely forthright in their practical points of view by making knowledgeable statements regarding structural misalignments and welded joint design details being contributory to defects. Doubts were also raised regarding hull unit fabrications using Grade 'A' steel when post-delivery repairs used plating of greater thickness and higher grade steel approved by Lloyd's surveyors. There was considerable consternation regarding Lloyd's Ship Classification Society and shipbuilder claims that *Derbyshire*'s original hull was designed and built in full compliance with specifications (which were hybrid and deemed by some to be inadequate).

Such assertions appeared invalid because of a failure to reconcile with the extensive costly repairs and strengthening materials that were required in way of Bulkhead 65 on other vessels of the Bridge Class. In view of the factual history, there appears to be sufficient circumstantial evidence to support an admission of design and/or construction deficiency in *Derbyshire* and all other vessels of the Bridge

Class. Partly based on this background, there was a certain degree of disbelief throughout the Parliamentary debate, and with intimation that an amount of *cover-up* was present by responsible parties desirous of avoiding claim liabilities. This position was also fueled by responsible parties being unable to:

(1) determine the location of evidentiary structural modification drawings in way of Bulkhead 65;
(2) determine the location of photographs of wreckage, specifically lifeboats, taken by a passing Japanese tanker;
(3) address the debarring of the on-site shipyard Lloyd's survey or (Mr. D.H. Swift) C.Eng. from giving evidence at hearings; and
(4) acknowledge the involuntary transfer of the Lloyd's surveyor from the shipyard.

While the Parliamentary debate did make passing reference to the plight of seafarers, stating that "...statistics prove that life is cheap at sea..." any heartfelt empathy for those who voyage in harm's way and their survivors appeared to be lost in technical conjecture and suppressed concern over financial liabilities for faulty design and/or construction. It was abundantly clear that if a Formal Inquiry could not assign liability to Lloyd's, it would be extremely difficult for damage claims to be made against the shipbuilder. Such a claim was reported to be estimated in the range of eighty to ninety-six million U.S. dollars. The purpose of any accident inquiry is to ascertain the truth so that curative and/or preventative measures can be taken in potentially parallel future cases, and there is a clear distinction between the purposes of an "inquisitorial" and an "accusatorial" inquiry, the former being concerned with what *actually* happened or what, given the known circumstances, most *likely* happened; and the latter being concerned with apportionment of culpability and liability.

M.V. Derbyshire Final Cargo Loading

As an important adjunct to the *Derbyshire* loss, a review was made of Canadian Loading Certificate information issued at the ore-cargo loading port of Sept Iles (Seven Islands), Province of Quebec, for her final load-out. A credible verification of safely loading 154,960 tons of iron ore (Carol Concentrates) at No. 2 Loading Terminal of the Iron Ore Company the following information was provided (Fig. 30):

Hold Number	Cargo (Tons)
1	22620
2	empty
3	28310
4	12790
5	27500
6	empty
7	26350
8	9840
9	27550
Total	154960

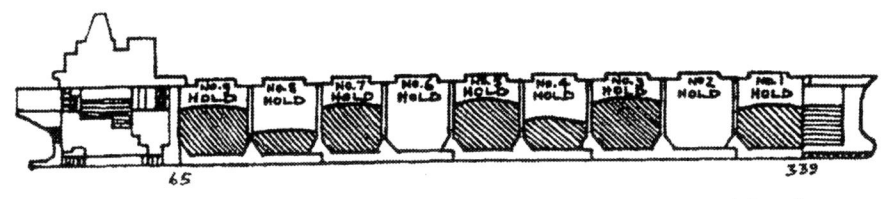

Note:- Cargo centroids assume level cargo within confines of hatchway opening with 33° angle of repose beyond hatch boundaries.

Fig. 30 – Last known loading condition of M.V. Derbyshire

Upon completion of loading, the cargo stow would have been reasonably level over the area immediately below each hatchway and would have sloped away from the area to the outboard sides of a cargo hold.

The distribution of cargo upon loading completion was as follows:

- In Hold Nos. 1, 3, 5, 7, and 9 the average depth of cargo under hatchways would have been in the 33 to 39-foot range sloping away to the vicinity of the top of the sloping sides of the lower wing ballast tanks. Also, cargo in Hold Nos. 1, 3, 5, 7 and 9 received passive support from the vertical sides of the holds, especially in No. 1 and No. 9 due to hull shaping in towards the bow and stern.
- Hold Nos. 2 and 6 were empty.
- In Hold No. 4 the average depth of cargo under the hatchway would have been about 20 feet, sloping away to about 10-feet up the sides of the lower wing ballast tanks.
- In Hold No. 8 the average depth of cargo under the hatchway would have been about 16-feet, sloping away to about 7-feet up the sloping sides of lower wing ballast tanks.
- In Hold Nos. 4 and 8 the cargo only received support from sloping sides of the lower wing ballast tanks, and therefore had less resistance to shifting should it be subjected to sufficient inducement to move.

On July 10 and 11, 1980, ore cargo was loaded from open stockpiles near the dock by using bucket wheel reclaimers and two Shiploader elevators. The concentrate was picked up from the stockpile by means of a revolving bucket, which delivered its load to traveling conveyor belts supplying the Shiploaders. The Shiploaders were able to travel along the loading berth when delivering the desired quantity of cargo into any *Derbyshire* hold and without a requirement to move the vessel. The loading equipment also enabled the cargo to be delivered in such a way as to achieve a reasonable level stow in the hold under the hatchway, as distinct from a free-fall cone. At the completion of loading each hold, the cargo would slope away at the edges outside of the hatch opening, and no manual or mechanical trimming of cargo was made in the outboard wings or the fore and after ends of the holds. Loading safety was creditable to careful management practices when using the foregoing equipment having long-reach capability to service generous hatch openings that facilitated broad spreading of iron-ore cargo and the negation of asymmetric stowage.

The master of every bulk-cargo vessel recognizes that there will always be significant variations in hull flexure during dockside loading operations as illustrated in Fig. 31. Such structural flexure is considerable and a vessel's final altitude cannot be determined until a vessel is underway and settled. These conditions clearly indicate that jumbo-sized bulk-cargo vessels, such as *Derbyshire*, have hydroelastic structures that are far from rigid, especially when masters can cite oceangoing experiences when *twelve feet* of vertical hull flexing were observed while in a seaway. With such observations there appears to be justifiable cause to reassess traditional naval architectural theories and stress analyses methodologies having a variety of self-evident shortfalls, since multi-axial strength and loading should really be examined in terms of hydroelastic vice non-dynamic still-water conditions.

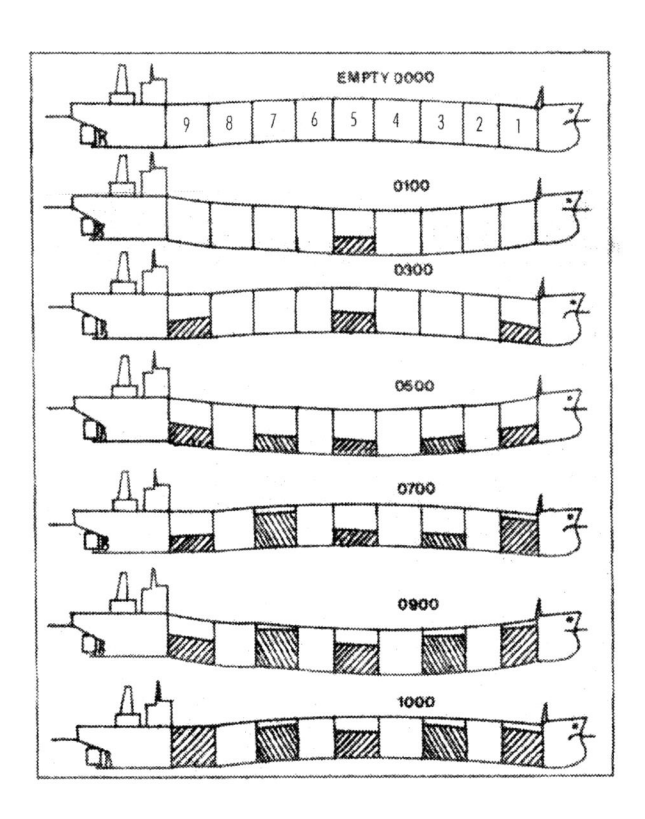

Fig. 31 – Schematic bulk loading sequence and hull deflections.

From a financial risk assessment point of view, one need only refer to underwriter reports, which fully recognize that aging vessels have relatively modest value, pose liability risk, but are *still* insurable, especially if subject to the dubious requirements of a lax classification society. Apart from these considerations, the high rate of bulk-cargo vessel losses also casts a measure of doubt on the technical adequacy of the design parameters provided by classification societies and traditional design-room practices for constantly enlarging vessels.

It would appear that the overall bulk-cargo vessel sinking pandemic is rooted in systemic inadequacies spanning a wide range of shortfalls, inclusive of deficiencies in scientific baselines, design and production practices, inspection, maintenance, and operational management. While the "business of business is business" in the maximization of commercial profit, it has proven to be at the expense of vessels and seafarer losses on an international scale. Regrettably the multiplicity of world-wide losses is not widely publicized, and each receives short-term media coverage and public interest—except for the *Derbyshire* Family Association (DFA) activities, which succeeded in gaining support from the unions and the All-Party *M.V. Derbyshire* Parliamentary Group to seek justice for the survivor families by re-opening investigative enquiry in the British High Court of Justice (Admiralty Court).

The Honorable Mr. Justice Colman made many recommendations for improving the safety of bulk-cargo carrier vessels, albeit implementation support appears to be minimal by shipowners, shipbuilders, the International Association of Classification Societies (IACS), the International Maritime Organizations (IMO), Lloyd's Register of Shipping (L.R.)., *et al*. The trend toward incrementalism to avoid cost escalation, while understandable, appears tantamount to "moving deckchairs around on the *Titanic*" on matters affecting vessel and crew safety in a high risk specialized marine transportation media.

Samuel Plimsoll Revisited

Parliamentary involvement is not new. For example, when one reviews notable earlier achievements of Samuel Plimsoll M.P. from the constituency of Derbyshire, it is evident that he was an early crusader for government load-line regulation to outlaw the overloading of British merchant vessels. At that point in time, the number of casualties was great for unsafe "coffin" vessels and their crews when operated by unscrupulous owners. His initiative was persuasive in having Parliament set up a Royal Commission to investigate merchant marine practices and conditions, and as a dedicated crusader, he initiated the Merchant Marine Act of 1875 to require load-line marking on British merchant vessels. As expected there was volatile resistance from shipowners *et al,* some of whom started a series of legal suits against him. The Plimsoll Mark prevailed, however, and was eventually adopted by maritime nations throughout the world.

At that time, and in the absence of modern communications, the fates of merchant sailing vessels and seafarers, were not made public until Lloyd's postings signaled "missing presumed lost—fates unknown." For other than communication reasons, today's international bulk-cargo vessel causalities (pre- and post-*M.V. Derbyshire* loss) appear reminiscent of an earlier sailing vessel era, as a considerable number receive *ex post facto* findings of "lost without distress signals, survivors, or witnesses." Although bulk-cargo vessels of American and British registry are now seriously diminished, appropriate "Samuel Plimsoll-type" Parliamentary, Congressional, and International Commission leadership appears to have merit, since there is little evidence that the global maritime industry is inclined toward responsible self-regulation.

The time for change is long overdue when taking into account universal losses in the ore-carrying trade for vessels and seafarers and the moderate indemnification and compensation for mariners when working in a hazardous environment; their difficult insurability in an occupation considered to be high risk; and the meager survivor family compensation after a loss.

Even though bulk-cargo vessel and operating crew losses continue apace, there appears to be reluctance to accept premising that extrapolation of Ship Classification Society Rules were exceeded for *Fitzgerald* and *Derbyshire* designs and based on precedent-questionable technical grounds. In all good conscience, I find it incongruous that the *Derbyshire* investigatory reports concluded that "there were *no* design deficiencies" when there were *no* directly applicable OBO-specific rules initially available from Lloyd's for this vessel having unique design requirements.

The situation requires a meaningful commitment for breakthrough technological change, modified shipbuilding design and construction practices, and systemic mental adjustments (at all echelons) in a similar manner to the maritime evolution when sails and wooden structure gave way to steel. In the aeronautical field, when new aircraft development practices were constantly evolving and many were found to have limitations for space craft applications, international commitment to *investment* in science and technology did facilitate successful transitions as programs progressed. If the hands of time could be turned back abut one hundred years, when Great Britain was the major producer of oceangoing, steel steam-powered merchantmen, a preparation for transition to a higher bulk-cargo vessel design and safety threshold would probably have befallen *their* shipbuilding industry, with Lloyd's as the dominant maritime technical authority.

Merchant Shipbuilding Paradigm Shift
With the passage of time, there has been an indisputable paradigm shift to the ascension of Far Eastern shipbuilding industries. They are now leaders in securing orders for merchant vessels to exploit the trade globalization of most products and commodities, including bulk-cargo vessels carrying ore, coal, grain, etc. Because of their lower labor rates and governmental support commercial shipbuilding industrial bases of America, Great Britain, Scandinavia, and Europe have become devastated, but the multi-disciplined intellectual capital and experience have not. They should be harnessed and marketed for formulating and prosecuting a global strategy to advance the status quo. The strategy should be novel and internationally funded, and it is suggested that *multi-disciplined* teams could develop a universal Circular of Requirements that provide *written* performance and operational requirements for "notional" bulk-cargo vessels (without conceptual drawings) for bulk-cargo vessels and their systemic operational scenarios. Upon reaching consensus, world-wide development teams could competitively form consortia to convert approved Circular of Requirements into "notional" conceptual designs for assessment by a designated central body. None of the foregoing evolutions need necessarily be headed by naval architects, and by process of elimination, a parent bulk-cargo vessel(s) could be subsequently selected for customization by specific shipowners without compromise of safety.

There is no doubt that such a suggestion will be met with resistance because (a) it disturbs the status quo; and (b) it has significant economic implication; and (c) it reflects ship system design by committee—which it is. This approach is selectively practiced on an international basis by military establishments in various nations.

Part Seven:
Plying the Great Lakes Trading Routes

Load Lines
Over the years the *Fitzgerald* plied her trading routes from Duluth, across Lake Superior, and to lower lake terminals via the Soo Locks. Her maximum full-load draft was dictated by the shallowest waterways and dredged channels connecting the five Great Lakes. Additionally, Load Line Regulations enforced freeboard limitations at various seasons of the year, and these resulted in decreases or increases in reserve buoyancy and cargo-carrying capacity. In 1967, a joint U.S.-Canadian committee undertook a reevaluation of requirements for operation on the Great Lakes. This study resulted in extensive changes to the Load Line Regulations, with the effect that *Fitzgerald* was considered to be "A steamer having superior design and operational features engaged on Great Lakes voyages." Subsequent amendments to the regulations in 1969, 1971, and 1973 resulted in progressive reductions of the minimum freeboards as assigned in accordance with 46 CFR Part 45 as follows:

Minimum Assigned Freeboard

Freeboard on the Fitzgerald was the vertical distance from the permitted full-load waterline to the spar deck at side during various seasons.

Date	Midsummer	Summer	Intermediate	Winter*
Originally assigned when vessel was built (1958)	11' 10-3/4"	12' 6-3/4"	13' 6-3/4"	14' 9-1/4"
July 03, 1969	11' 4-1/2"	12' 0-1/2"	13' 0-3/4"	14' 3-1/2"
Sept 17, 1971	11' 4-1/2"	12' 0-1/2"	13' 0-3/4"	13' 2"
Sept 13, 1973	10' 5-1/2"	11' 2"	11' 2"	11' 6"

*Most significant reduction in freeboard 3' 3-1/4"

Under the 1973 Load Line Regulations, the following effective dates applied for the above freeboards:

Midsummer	-	May 01 through September 15
Summer and Intermediate	-	April 16 through April 30
	-	Sept. 16 through Sept. 30
	-	Oct. 01 through Oct. 31
and	-	April 01 through April 15
*Winter	-	Nov. 01 through March 31

*Thus, the *Winter* load line applied to Fitzgerald at the time of her last loading.

Before the 1973 load line was assigned, minor modifications of the vessel were required. These included safety modifications of watertight doors for added stiffness; installation of deadlight covers; installation of covers on windless room chocks; addition of an extra course of railing; increasing the freeing port area aft, and extending the height of outboard tunnel vents to thirty inches above the spar deck. The steel vent pipes to side water ballast tanks were fitted with mushroom-shaped threaded caps for opening and closing purposes. Caps required manual turning to an open position for the release of air pressure during ballast tank filling operations, and the elimination of air vacuum when pumping out. It is noted that whenever a vessel was fully loaded with dense taconite cargo and ballast tanks were normally dewatered, it would have been technically correct for vent caps to be in a closed position for the preservation of watertight integrity and reserve buoyancy capabilities. It is known, however, that ballast tank vents on many Great

Lakes vessels are customarily left open during all conditions of operation in the belief that (with vents closed), it would *not* be possible to obtain pump suction to dewater a ballast tank if found necessary when deck access is hazardous.

In the case of *Fitzgerald*, it appears that her ballast tank vent caps were in an open position, since the Master *did* report that water ballast pumps were on-line in attempts to correct a listing condition. Hazardous boarding seas would have denied exposed spar deck access for the opening of vent caps while in transit.

Two eight-inch diameter vent pipes were installed at each end of sixteen side ballast tank compartments, with vertical extension to eighteen inches above the spar deck. By 46 CFR 45.133(b), these vent pipes were reduced from a required height of thirty inches because of interference with cargo handling operations. During the vessel's final transit it is possible that damage could have been sustained by a vent pipe servicing No. 1 ballast tank on one side of the vessel.

The height of single eight-inch diameter vent pipes, located at the forward and after ends of each 530-foot long underdeck side tunnel, was retained at thirty inches. During the vessel's final transit, it is possible that one tunnel vent pipe was sheared off by an Unidentified Floating Object, "UFO," that temporarily boarded the spar deck. No pump suctions were installed in either tunnel, since they were reliant upon manually-operated gravity drains (at the after end of the tunnel) connected to the No. 8 Ballast Tank below. In the event that a gravity drain was in the closed position and the steel watertight doors at the forward and after ends of a tunnel were dogged shut to preserve watertight compartmentation, significant water containment would be made possible should tunnel vent pipe(s) become broken-off, as in the case of *Fitzgerald*. For an order of magnitude perspective, with boarding seas assumed to have a constant height of about six feet, a broken-off eight-inch diameter tunnel vent would enable lake water ingress at a rate of about one thousand nine hundred gallons (8-tons) per minute to *one* sealed tunnel space capable of holding about one thousand six hundred tons of lake water and having a destabilizing free-surface (swashing) effect. This estimation is believed to be congruent with a reportedly increasing list condition deteriorating from an initially "slight" list at about 1530 hrs., before subsequently terminating in a "bad" list condition about two hours later.

During the voyage, when the Master ordered "Don't allow nobody on deck" at about 17.15 hrs., it is doubtful that his intent was to avoid obvious crew exposure to waves boarding the spar deck. The order more likely would have meant that he was countermanding any consideration for entering the flooded tunnel (passageway) deck to manually open gravity deck drain valve to No. 8 Ballast Tank. The experienced Master was evidently aware that opening of a dogged-shut watertight door would have released entrapped water from the tunnel and compromised flooding control for other internal spaces.

In retrospect, the progressive decreases in freeboard assignments to permit deeper loading of Great Lakes bulk-cargo vessels were accompanied by some vessel modifications of merit. However, it was *not* readily evident that appropriate technical consideration had been given to:

(1) Increasing the vessel's original structural scantlings to compensate for increases in the full-load drafts. This apparent oversight could be recognized as a small longitudinal strength deficit for *Fitzgerald*, since the midship section modulus shown on Great Lakes Engineering Works Drawing No. 113-1183 remained unchanged.

(2) Reinforcement of cargo hatch covers in recognition of the vessel's deeper loading, which would have increased the waterhead height of boarding waves and resulted in higher stresses in the stiffened steel plate (5/16" thick) hatch covers, albeit it may be expected that such wave loadings would have grossly exceeded hatch cover bearing load capabilities when under catastrophic "Constructive Interference Wave" pressure.

Each cargo hatchway (twenty-one) was made weathertight by a gasketed, single piece (11' 7" x 54' 0") 5/16" stiffened steel cover, with each secured by sixty-eight pivoting and adjustable Kestener clamps (Fig. 32) arranged on approximately two feet centers around the perimeter. The hatch cover perimeters each had concave "button" recesses (sixty-eight) for clamp positioning and clamping of the hatch cover gasket. It should be noted that weathertightness per 46 CFR 42.09–40 (versus watertightness) testing was expected and requiring criteria for waterspray testing (versus prolonged immersion and pressure).

Fig. 32 – Pivoting Kestener Clamps
68 per hatch (Total 1,428)

The U.S. Coast Guard's Official Report theorized that faulty hatch covers (i.e. ineffectively clamped) were attributable to the *Fitzgerald*'s catastrophic flooding, but this was unanimously rejected by the National Transportation Safety Board (NTSB) on March 23, 1978. While the original cargo hatch covers (circa 1958) were designed in accordance with 46 CFR.145, requiring structural design for a minimum waterhead height of four feet, it is not known if any pre-production hydrostatic pressure testing on simulation mockups was ever undertaken, even though there is strong evidence that the hatch covers collapsed when excessive waterhead loading would have induced elastic instability (implosive buckling). Kestener clamps were never intended to protect against such a catastrophic event. The CFR 45.145 design criteria were subsequently revised effective October 1, 2002, as shown in Appendix.
(3) The likelihood of bottom hull damage when "grounding" at terminals, due to the deeper draft allowance and/or shallower lake depths, necessitated dockside standoff or bottom ploughing. Such damage may be relatable to videotape evidence showing bottom shell plate scraping, which some observers are believed to erroneously have attributed to striking of the lake bottom while underway.

The Operating Environment
From the beginning of maritime activity on the Great Lakes the severity and unpredictability of storm ferocity unique to each fresh water mass, became fully recognized by the operating crews of laker vessels, as they plied their trading routes from Lake Superior to Lake Ontario. The laker crew experiences were later shared by large oceangoing vessel ("saltie") mariners subsequent to the St. Lawrence Seaway System opening in 1959 and, in most instances, respect for the natural forces of the Great Lakes as potentially hazardous (versus sheltered and tranquil) mini-seas has been earned. It does seem befitting that these deceptive waters are often referred to as "The Eighth Sea."

Each of the five Great Lakes has its own exposure and temperament with surface area, depth, shape, bottom topography, and geographic placements having major interplay with atmospheric variations endemic to the natural environment. Meteorologists and experienced masters of vessels are very aware and extremely respectful of those influences that are responsible for rapidly deteriorating seasonal weather conditions—and most significantly the recurring November storms of Lake Superior that have taken their toll of vessels and the lives of many mariners. While this lake does provide more sea room, its greater dimensions have demonstrated a powerful negative attribute that enables strong northwest winds to generate boundary-restricted destructive waves as they travel over a long wave fetch distance from deep to shallower water depths. The wind-generated and unimpeded wave fetches of Lake Superior are able to reach lengths of over three hundred miles, especially when driven by strong northwest storms, which have created a "graveyard of vessels."

At the eastern extremity of Lake Superior, the bottom topography is characterized by a series of long troughs, having depths ranging from 660 feet to 1310 feet, while the remainder of the lake is primarily large deep basins. Water depths of less than 330 feet are mainly found in a three to twenty-two mile band paralleling the shoreline, with rapid dropoff and often having underwater cliffs contiguous with convergent American and Canadian land masses.

Clapotic Wave Formation

Whenever high-energy trans-lake waves are produced under severe northwest storm conditions and are eventually bounded by rapidly convergent shorelines (Fig. 33) close to Whitefish Bay, Michigan, the marine environment is conducive to the random formation of standing

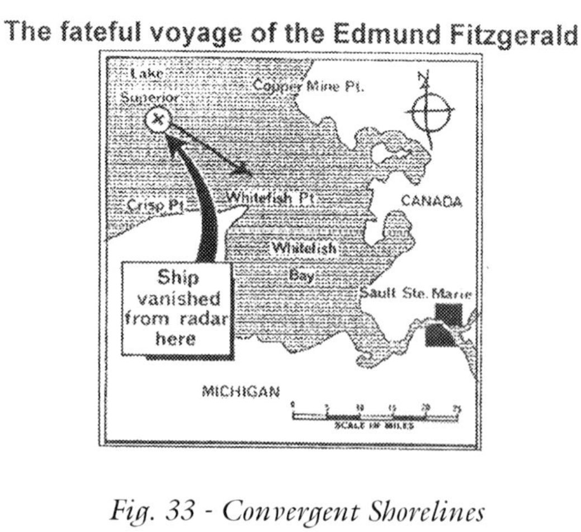

Fig. 33 - Convergent Shorelines

(clapotic) waves. These formations convert boundary-reflected wave energy into towering "walls of water" having a propensity to encounter and augment large incoming trans-lake wave formations.

Clapotic waves are unusually large waves having episodic periodicity and are known to have destructive effects. Their generation can be hazardous to mariners when in the proximity of land masses capable of storm wave reversal, reflection, and magnifications, as exemplified by the marine environment of Whitefish Bay, Michigan.

These waves belong in the episodic "Constructive Interference Wave" category in that they unpredictably appear and are hazardous because of their large size as a "Wall of Water." Available measurement and analysis have been extremely rare.

In a mature condition of clapotis, crests and troughs of grossly-heightened wave formations can double the height of "significant" waves, and they generally occur at approximately the same fixed positions under steady state conditions while producing momentary surface flatness twice in each wave period. "Significant waves" in themselves theoretically represent the averaged height of the one-third highest waves. While such estimations do have academic significance and are used for computerized simulations and hydrodynamic test tank experiments, they have little or no relevance to "real-world" storm conditions when episodic "Constructive Interference Waves," are generated by destructive "wall of water" interactions within the confines of Great Lakes basin land mass boundaries…in contrast to open-ocean storm conditions having infinitely-distant shorelines not conducive to mid-ocean clapotic wave formation.

To fully appreciate the destructive natural synergy that enveloped *Fitzgerald*, one is required to juxtapose dynamic vessel motions upon the overwhelming storm wave formations advancing from astern with a speed of advance greater than that of the vessel itself. For purposes of this brief treatise, the confluence of forces could include, but not be restricted to observations of Captain Cooper *et al*:

- Storm Speed of Advance: 40 mph   (Est).
- Vessel Speed of Advance: 16.3 mph   (max).
- Vessel Course (Downbound):   141° T.
- Storm Vector (from Astern):   135° T
- Wind Speed: 80 mph   (min).

-Wave Crest Spacing: 250 ft. (Est).
-Trans- Lake ("pooping") Wave Heights*: 40 ft. (min).
-"Constructive Interference Wave" Heights: 70 ft. (Est).

It is postulated that "Constructive Interference Waves" (reflected from U.S./Canada shorelines) could have caused abnormal crest and trough magnification during "clapping" augmentation with down-bound storm waves having capability to overwhelm *Fitzgerald* from astern. The finer-lined stern sections (Fig. 33) would have contributed lesser buoyancy than fuller hull sections in way of the cargo holds, as in most vessels.

The stern would have therefore become prone to deep plunging, with shipping of lake water, when dynamically transitting abnormal wave troughs in a fully loaded condition.

Follow-through abnormally-high wave crests breaking over the

Fig. 33 – Fitzgerald's Fine-Lined (vice Full-Lined) Stern Sections. Photo - Center for Archival Collections Bowling Green State University

stern should have produced an overwhelming "pooping" wave cascade, which would have induced dynamic waterloading exceeding the structural capabilities of (initially) the aftermost cargo hatch covers serving No. 3 Cargo Hold. Under such conditions, the hatch cover failure mode would be expected to be one of elastic instability (implosive "buckling") *without* negative attribution to Kestener Clamps (Fig. 32) used for the maintenance of hatch cover weathertightness and security.

The episodic and localized Lake Superior phenomena could have been accountable for the creation of abnormally steep and lethal "Constructive Interference Wave" development that contributed to the difficulties and loss of the *Fitzgerald* laker and, to a lesser extent, of other vessels transiting in the proximity of Whitefish Bay at a slightly different time and location.

M.V. Avafors
The following observations by Captain Cedric C. Woodward, an experienced Great Lakes registered pilot on board the upbound Swedish "saltie" vessel *M.V. Avafors*, were stated very well at an investigatory hearing when he said: "The sea was *straight up and down*, and a lot of them were coming at you. It was *not* like big rollers," and "It was one of the biggest and wildest seas I have ever been in, I mean fast." These descriptions appear to fully correlate with "Constructive Interference Wave" conditions that are frequently referred to as "walls-of-water" and can unpredictably emerge on the Great Lakes.

In retrospect it would appear that the *Avafors* had unknowingly contended with a similar environmental situation to (downbound) *Fitzgerald*, thereby placing both vessels within a comparable risk spectrum and bringing into question why the *Avafors* survived and the *Fitzgerald* foundered. Apart from considerations of advantageous seagoing (versus laker) vessel technical features, the key explanation could primarily lie in the operational decisions and actions of the *Avafors'* pilot and her Master, as discussed during a post-sinking meeting at Duluth between company representatives and the pilot, when it was determined that:

> "...the *Avafors* did make an attempt to proceed

(upbound) *into* the raging storm from the sheltered waters of Whitefish Bay because the Master was of the opinion that waves on the inland Lake Superior would *not* be a problem to his deep-sea vessel...in spite of warning relayed to him by his American pilot. As a result, the *Avafors* reached a point a few miles north and west of Whitefish Point where she wallowed in seas for a considerable time with her engines at full-speed ahead, but was *unable* to make any headway whatsoever with the result that she ultimately withdrew into Whitefish Bay and rode out the storm..." (where other vessels were anchored in safe haven).

The pilot's account of storm force magnitude, from ahead, allows another appreciation of storm forces when the *Fitzgerald* was "pooped" by episodic "Constructive Interference Waves" that overtook her from astern and left Master Captain McSorley with zero survival options—inclusive of beaching his vessel.

To exhaustively develop answers, it would be necessary to collect and review *all* elements of consideration within a "*circumstantial kaleidoscope*," which, upon each rotation (to enable viewing from alternative perspectives), would cause prisms to yield an infinite series of baseline combinations and permutations as necessary for analytic purposes.

Since the daunting task of accumulating all technical data input for each baseline would prove to be an insurmountable challenge, a high degree of objective and subjective rationalization would be necessary. As minimum, major factors to be used in contrasting and comparing analytical processes would be inclusive of such considerations as:

- The appearance of "Constructive Interference Waves" that are unpredictably episodic and usually localized, thereby qualifying for cause majeure (unexplainable acts of God) attribution, with the *downbound Fitzgerald* at a wave force epicenter—in essence, being at the "wrong place at the wrong time" without any implications of seamanship negligence by the vessel's Master, his officers, or his crewmen.
- The upbound *M.V. Avafors* had the advantage of riding *into* the storm with dynamic vessel motions responding to *head*

seas. This situation was the reverse of *Fitzgerald*, which was in downbound transit and violently subjected to storm waves overtaking from almost directly *astern*, thereby exposing the vulnerable vessel to highly probable "pooping" conditions, which would have exacerbated downward plunging of her stern. This was considered to be the initial onset of an uncontrolled and excessive weight of boarding water fully enveloping the stern section, with immediate buckling damage to certain cargo hatch covers and water ingress to No. 3 Cargo Hold.

M.V. Benfri and M.V. Nanfri

As "salties," these less-familiar foreign-flagged vessels were probably piloted with extreme caution and at reduced speed in a Seaway System, having more restrictive navigational constraints than for oceangoing operations.

Both large vessels were heading into the storm on *upbound* navigational tracks and were either almost in or outside the unique turbulent zone in which (downbound) *Fitzgerald* was lost. Their geographic locations in the rapidly-moving transitory storm required decisions whether they should proceed and make later course reversals with risk of broaching or capsizing from temporary exposure to beam or quartering seas. Their caution resulted in decisions to seek safe haven near Whitefish Bay, as in the case of *Avafors* and other vessels.

Some favorable "saltie" features, having technical importance, were considered to be oceangoing (versus Great Lakes) design characteristics, inclusive of:

- a lower block coefficient (finer-lined) hull form than that of the (full-form) *Fitzgerald* and *Anderson* bulk-cargo laker vessels. Such a "saltie" hull form is considered to have a favorable influence on seakindliness and dynamic stability response;
- higher strength cargo hatch covers for open-ocean wave pressure loading;
- greater longitudinal strength capability as an outcome of having an *unreduced* midship section modulus meeting classification society standards for oceangoing (versus Great Lakes) vessels; and
- controlled cargo loading distribution and watertight hold

compartmentation, which, although not specifically known (to the author) would have enabled:
(a) survivability in the event of a flooding casualty; and
(b) secure cargo containment resistant to shifting.

Conversely the *Fitzgerald* design had three cavernous cargo holds of 860,950 cubic feet capacity extending over about 70 percent of the vessel's length, wherein bulk cargoes were separated by two non-watertight "screen" bulkheads. This cargo hold arrangement was congruent with extant laker design practices at that time, and was expected to be incapable of preventing progressive flooding should the cargo-hold watertight envelope or spar deck cargo hatches be breached.

S.S. Arthur M. Anderson
The trailing *Anderson* laker was reported to be finally on the same downbound 141° T track, and about ten miles astern of *Fitzgerald* (Fig. 33-1). Since the vessel was underway at a greater range from the USA/Canada shorelines than *Fitzgerald*, she appeared to be less affected by the perilous wedge-shaped zone of reflected clapotic wave influence, albeit the extant overtaking trans-lake wave conditions were severe. From the hearing testimony and other statements by her Master (the late Captain Jessie B. Cooper), it was observed that *Anderson* had taken large waves over the stern before they rolled forward with a crest-to-crest spacing of about 250 feet. It was also reported that (at times) the vessel felt suspended on three wave crests when in the vicinity of Caribou Island, which gave added credibility to the preceding statement.

These observational patterns therefore made it apparent that the *Anderson* was never subjected to *exactly* the same trans-lake "pooping" wave severity coupled to localized clapotic "wall of water" wave conditions, as in the *Fitzgerald* circumstances.

Waves and Wedges
Re: Constructive Interference Waves
At the instant of *Fitzgerald* sinking, the transient northwest storm conditions advancing from almost directly astern had a generalized speed of advance (SOA) approaching 40 m.p.h. with minimum wind speeds of about 80 m.p.h. and trans-lake wave heights of at least forty

feet immediately prior to encountering an unpredictable confluence of trans-lake and magnified clapotic waves when within seventeen miles of safe-harbor at Whitefish Bay. The trans-lake waves which overtook both *Fitzgerald* and *Anderson* from directly astern would have developed energy over an unimpeded linear fetch distance of over three hundred miles with a maximum Lake Superior water depth condition shallowing from 1,333 feet to about 500 feet slightly west of Whitefish Bay.

On the final approach to Lake Superior's eastern terminus, it is

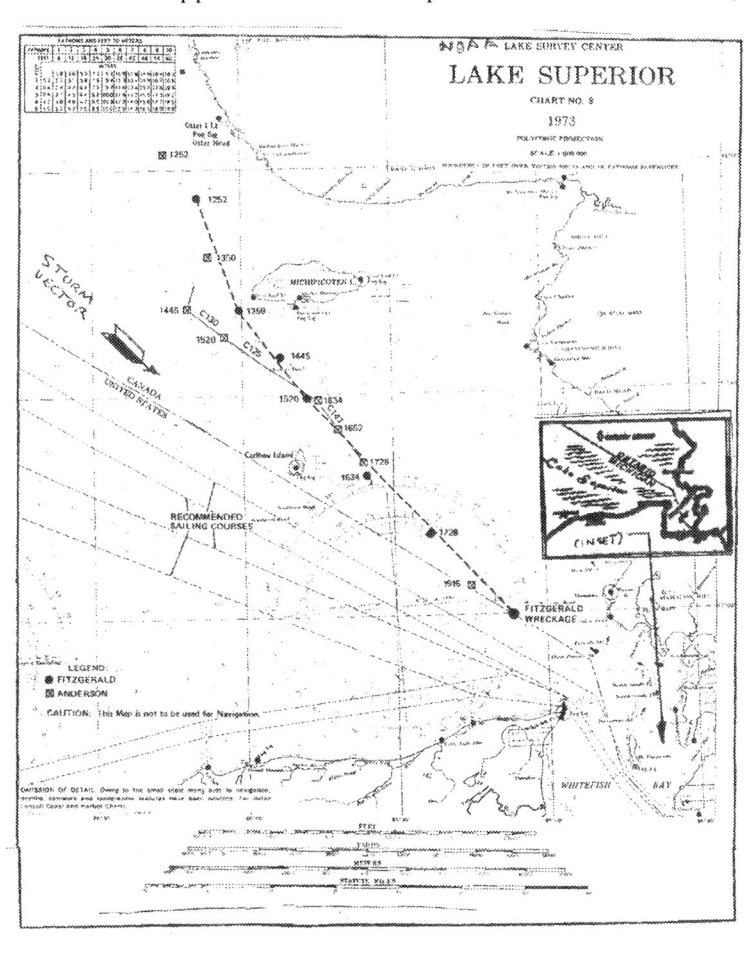

Fig. 33-1 – Probable tracklines of SS Edmund Fitzgerald and SS Arthur M. Anderson on November 10, 1975.

evident that *Fitzgerald* was entering a narrowing three-dimensional wedge-shaped zone (Fig. 33-1, inset) characterized by reducing water depth (530 feet at the sinking site) and bounded by convergent American and Canadian shorelines. This geographic and topographic scenario appears to have been readily conducive to accumulative *clapotic* wave formations capable of creating turbulent "wall-of-water" conditions when downbound magnified waves, traversing Lake Superior, could collide with waves reflected from cliff-like land masses on each land mass. For such situations, mariners have developed a lexicon of their own to describe such waves, including such expressions as "freak waves," "rogue waves," "walls of water," and even "holes in the sea," as coins of their nautical realm. Other descriptors, such as "Constructive Interference Waves" and "episodic waves" have had general acceptance within the scientific community.

From the theoretician's point of view, waves are generally looked upon as having regular or irregular characteristics with a "significant" wave height being the average of the one-third (1/3) highest waves, as stated earlier. The vertical distance from crest to trough of the highest waves can be increased to at least two times the "significant" wave height when there is severe "Constructive Interference Wave" interaction with multi-directional storm-generated phenomena having seiche, surge and clapotic wave augmentation. Also, it is generally appreciated that the spacing, height, and lake wave periods of encounter are *not* the same as for the almost limitless open-ocean operational environment. All of these factors can contribute to structural fatigue, cracking, hull vibration, cargo shifting, and a shortened life for flexible laker hulls.

In simplified form, the foregoing may be influenced by:

- The wind speed.
  The higher the wind speed, the larger the force and thus the bigger the wave. The wind would also be steady and of constant speed.

- The wind duration.
  The longer the wind blows over open water, the larger the waves could become.
- The fetch.

Wind fetch is the length of unobstructed open-water across which the wind has an opportunity to generate waves. The fetch is mostly a function of lake size but also relates to shape and orientation of the long axis relative to prevailing winds. During the northwest storm, the wind *did* generate waves of ever-increasing height across a fetch distance of over 300 miles, with reflective termination at the eastern boundary of Lake Superior.

- Clapotic waves.
  The steep and dangerous waves generated by directional reversal and turbulence, when reflected off buffering shore-lines, harbor walls, or shallowing lake floor topography, can result in the destructive formation of "walls of water."

- The wave period of encounter.
  In the *Fitzgerald* situation, with storm waves almost from directly abaft the stern and having a greater forward speed of advance (S.O.A.) than the vessel, the wave period of encounter would become increased. Under such overtaking wave conditions, forced pitching or rolling, just above the natural period, could have occurred with risk of synchronism for such a large vessel. Also, the vessel's rolling motion could have become increased and asymmetrical due to a damaged listing condition induced by forward compartment and one tunnel flooding casualties.

With hindsight it would appear that Captain McSorley *may* have increased his speed to a full-power setting in his final moments when attempting to change the *Fitzgerald*'s period of wave encounter for improved control and attempting to outrun the waves overtaking his vessel from astern. The final engineroom telegraph full-power setting was recorded by a videographer on board the Harbor Branch Oceanographic Institution's submersible *Clelia* (Fig. 34) in July 1994, when positioned on a bulwark directly forward of the *Fitzgerald*'s pilothouse. In everyday operations, however, it is known to be frequent practice for the engineroom to make speed changes in response to bridge telephone orders, and the mechanical indication on the engineroom telegraph *may not* always visually reflect every order. (i.e., In her final moments, there is a possibility that *Fitzgerald* may *not* have been proceeding at full power.) Based on the *Fitzgerald* loss and probably other unexplained prior sinkings close to the Whitefish Bay area, the described destructive waves appear to have had capability for the generation of "Constructive Interference Wave" force(s) exceeding the structural capabilities of Great Lakes vessels...whenever there were others having the misfortune to be "at the wrong place at the wrong time," while underway and exposed to severe storm conditions.

Experience and Judgement

Of operational necessity, the masters of laker vessels have strong dependency on inter-ship communications, shipboard and shoreside navigation aids, weather forecasts, and past experience. All of which come into play when exercising experienced judgement in weighing their primary options of selecting alternative routing, becoming hove-to until storm abatement, or emergency beaching.

It is apparent that the experienced master of *Edmund Fitzgerald* (the late Captain Ernest M. McSorley) was not alone in making the choice of proceeding with the initial alternative routing, since the veteran master of *Arthur M. Anderson* (Captain Jessie B. Cooper) was following a similar track on full power and in frequent radiotelephone communication before the sudden catastrophic loss of *Fitzgerald*. Their combined judgment had resulted in mutual selection of a northerly track, providing a sheltered lee parallel with the Canadian shoreline, when weather forecasters were initially addressing northeast gales and before the storm direction shifted and later hauled to the northwest with increasing force. Subsequently both vessels appear to have followed a less-frequently used 141° T downbound track after changing courses at Michipicoten Island and passing to the east of Caribou Island while in Canadian waters.

The possibility of other vessel usage of the latter track, on an established basis, remains as a point of contention in that there was no known passage of any downbound laker through that area of Canadian waters in the recent memory of anyone having knowledge of the casualty timeframe. During a speech by Captain Cooper on November 7, 1986, he stated that "The *Fitzgerald* and I, by the way,

Fig. 34 The three person submersible *Clelia* is launched from the A-frame crane.
Photo *Harbor Branch Oceanographic Institution.*

Clelia

Owned and operated by HARBOR BRANCH Oceanographic Institution, Clelia is a PC 1204 submersible built by Perry Oceanographics in 1976 and refitted in 1992 by HARBOR BRANCH to address the needs of the shallow water scientific community. At 23 ft long, 8 ft 3 in wide and 9 ft 7 in high, the *Clelia* travels at a maximum speed of 3 knots and is classed and certified to a maximum operating depth of 1,000 feet by the American Bureau of Shipping (ABS).

The vehicle can accommodate two scientists/observers and a pilot allowing excellent visibility through the forward acrylic hemisphere. The proximity of the occupants to the bottom (approximately 18") allows tasks to be completed in areas of low visibility. Researchers are afforded an excellent view of the ocean environment through 10 view ports. A hemispheric, 3-ft-diameter window is located at the front end of the sub. Eight 8-in diameter ports are equally spaced around the conning tower of the sub, and one upward view port is in the center of the overhead hatch.

were the only two ships in the area for quite a long time." The NTSB report stated that "Information from other Great Lakes mariners indicated that 141° T is a usual course from West End Light (Michipicoten) to Whitefish Bay, and this trackline is well clear of shoals."

Be that as it may, the practical reasoning appears to have been one of selecting the shortest protective routing to reach safe haven at Whitefish Bay.

The caution of Captain Cooper was also recognized as *Anderson* made a wide haul (turn) around the westerly tip of Michipicoten Island, when her master conservatively allowed more sea room, relative to the land mass, at a lesser speed than *Fitzgerald* who was about sixteen miles ahead. Even then, the *Anderson* was already experiencing "...a beating with a huge amount of water coming aboard with waves advancing from astern, and exceeding the vessel's forward speed when they were observed to be surging past." His recollection of "...two huge passing waves flooding out his poop deck and filling a lifeboat to a point where the wave pressure pushed the lifeboat downward into its saddle," was clearly indicative of abnormal ("pooping") waves of at least thirty to thirty-five feet in height and a precursor for magnification as they rolled forward toward the *Fitzgerald*'s stern. These conditions did not bode well for the listing *Fitzgerald*, which was entering a shallower water regime having converging shorelines.

In-service Operation

The *Fitzgerald* ("Big Fitz") gained early recognition as the "Pride Of The American Flag" and held a leadership position as the largest laker, credited with many cargo-hauling records for about eleven years after delivery to her owners. In the course of her seventeen-year working life, the record shows that she experienced her share of operating damage in the Seaway System with its unique locking and navigational hazards.

By reviewing historical records, it is evident that experienced masters of all laker vessels are required to be always on the alert to expect unexpected events, such as:

- the freighter S.S. Buffalo colliding, under perfect weather

conditions, in daylight, with a Detroit River lighthouse located in Lake Erie;
- a vessel approaching a dangerously delayed opening of a bridge when signaled;
- capsizing of the 444-foot "saltie" *M.V. Montrose* to a forty-five-foot depth, in the swift-current Detroit River, which swept the vessel below the *Ambassador Bridge*. The freighter was rammed by a tugboat B.H. *Becker* without red/green running lights and pushing a 200-foot barge with cement cargo (Fig. 35).
- the head-on collision between *S.S. Arthur B. Homer* with "saltie" *M.V. Navshipper* which failed to have a licensed pilot on board.

All of these events involved human error *without* any design deficiency implications. Incidents of grounding and collision with lock walls or other vessels are ever-evident, thereby necessitating that all shipboard operating systems are in working order with crewmen alert and fully trained.

Such a new and large higher-speed vessel placed extraordinary responsibilities and pressures on successive masters of the *Fitzgerald*, as ever-higher records were achieved for iron-ore transportation. Under these operating conditions, it was not surprising that, in the short lifetime of "Big Fitz" she sustained her share of groundings, striking of dock walls, the *S.S. Hochelaga* collision on May 1, 1970, and the emergence of structural cracking in later years.

As a matter of personal interest, I reviewed information related to the *Fitzgerald*'s in-service hull damage and repair history to determine whether there may be any correlation between reported damage and repair zone locations, and the identified hull separation points on the sunken vessel. In the course of this review, dimensional inconsistencies were discovered in the reported (1975–76) site survey data, which were obtained by the USCG, who made a series of three side-scan sonar surveys with assistance from private contractor *Seaward*, Inc. These sonar traces recorded slightly different hull separation locations but were translatable into stern section lengths of 228 feet (0.32L) and 253 feet (0.36L) per NTSB and USCG reports respectively. The stern separation point approximated the mid-point of No. 3 Cargo Hold. The review also confirmed that significant

The British freighter Montrose *became the first major ship to sink in the Detroit River since the opening of the St. Lawrence Seaway. July 30, 1962*

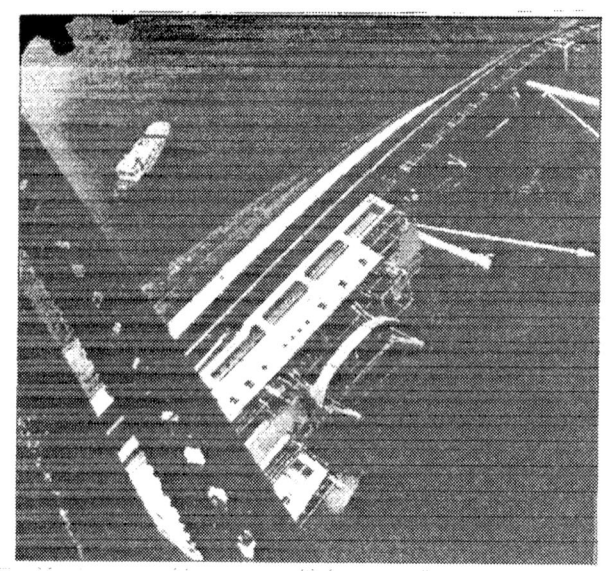

The Montrose, *unable to steer with her propeller and rudder out of the water, was dragged downriver by the strong Detroit River currents until it went aground under the Ambassador Bridge between Detroit and Windsor, Ont.*

Fig. 35 – The night the Montrose *sank in the Detroit River. Courtesy* – The Detroit News.

prior damage had been repaired during the vessel's lifetime in the hull separation proximity (viz: September 6, 1969, during grounding; April 30, 1970, collision with *S.S. Hochelaga,* May 1, 1970; and September 4, 1970, striking a lock wall).

The *Fitzgerald* was reportedly repaired following accepted laker shipyard practices and under difficult working conditions when accomplishing repair work within the confines of an existing hull envelope, having limited access and most probably without the benefits of off-hull prefabrication and fixturing. While the repair work was expected to be cosmetically acceptable, the investigatory hearings do not appear to have made any inquiry pertaining to the restoration processes and the quality control measures taken, all of which could have had influence on the hull fracturing under abnormal loading conditions.

Hull Separation

In May 1976, as surveying follow-on, the USCG contracted to use the U.S. Navy's Cable Controlled Underwater Recovery (CURV) system with private contractor assistance. This system (Fig. 36) was capable of facilitating televised feedback and photographic recordings. Twelve dives were made, and over fifty-six hours of bottom time were logged. The summary report stated that the stern separation was "at approximately Frame 178." This corresponded to a shorter separated stern length of 162 feet (0.23L), which was considerably at variance with the prior cited points of points of separation shown in Fig. 37.

In August 2004, I received valuable assistance from Mr. Tom Farnquist, director of the Great Lakes Shipwreck Museum at Whitefish Bay, Michigan, who shared compelling sonar imaging evidence (Fig. 38). This evidence conclusively eliminated any further consideration of a stern section separation point at Frame 178 immediately forward of the propulsion machinery space transverse watertight bulkhead. The sonar imaging was obtained using Marine Sonics Digital Side-Scan Sonar and yielded good correlation with the USCG surveys. Since the new forensic information established a median stern separation location between the estimate 228-foot (NTSB) and 253-foot (USCG) lengths, the separation point will henceforth be identified as "the mid-point of No. 3 Cargo Hold" at 0.34L from the stern.

Since other new supercarriers and lengthened vessels were entering

Fig. 36 – Cable Controlled Underwater Recovery Vehicle (CURV)
Photo – U.S. Navy

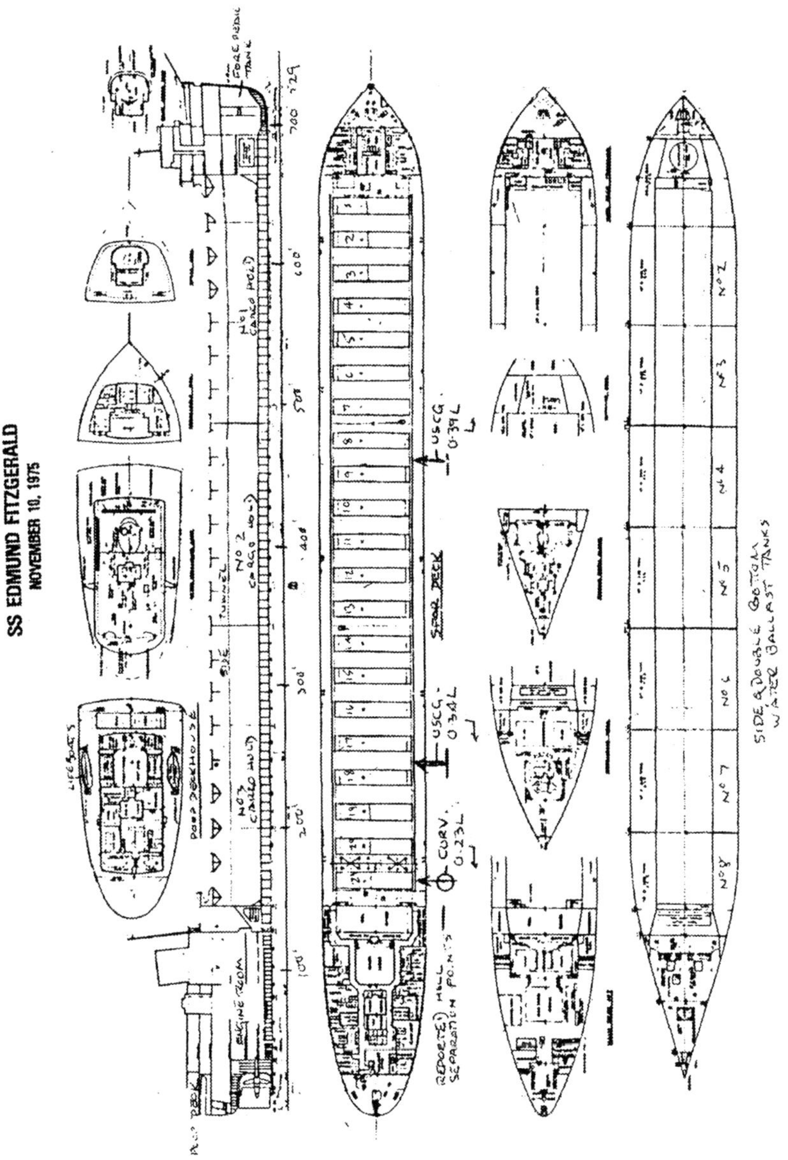

Fig. 37 – Estimated Hull Separation Points

*Fig. 38 – Sonar Imaging of S.S. Edmund Fitzgerald At 530-foot Depth
Courtesy of: Great Lakes Shipwreck Museum, Whitefish Point, Michigan*

Great Lakes service, a considerable number of older and smaller lakers were withdrawn to balance the bulk-cargo supply-demand business profile. This made it essential that each active vessel be maintained in a high state of material readiness and utilization.

Prior to her loss, the inspections of *Fitzgerald* revealed an expected amount of wear and tear for a Great Lakes vessel of her age. A periodic (five-year) out-of-the-water inspection was completed in April 1974 at Cleveland, Ohio, and a regulatory annual inspection was completed in the spring of 1975 with certification, on April 19, 1975, as being seaworthy and safe for operation.

A final spar deck inspection was satisfactorily completed by the United States Coast Guard (USCG) and the American Bureau of Shipping (ABS) on October 31, 1975, less than two weeks before her untimely loss.

PART EIGHT:
THE FINAL VOYAGE OF FITZGERALD

Before Michipicoten Island

When the *S.S. Edmund Fitzgerald* departed from the Burlington Northern Railroad Dock No. 1 East in Superior, Wisconsin, on November 9, 1975, at approximately 14.15 hrs., under the command of her experienced Master Captain Ernest M. McSorley, she was downbound for Zug Island on the Detroit River. On the same day, the *S.S. Arthur M. Anderson* departed from the loading terminal at Two Harbors, Minnesota, at 16.30 hrs., under the command of another Great Lakes veteran, Master Captain "Bernie" Cooper, who was downbound for Gary, Indiana. Both vessels were on similar tracks and were initially separated by about ten to twenty miles, with each carrying a cargo of taconite (iron ore pellets). Because of the late navigating season, they were fully prepared for anticipated harsh November weather conditions forecasted by the NOAA/National Weather Service (N.W.S.).

The masters were understandably concerned about the deteriorating weather forecasts, and when the *Anderson* was abeam Knife River and proceeding at 14.6 m.p.h., she made radiotelephone contact with the *Fitzgerald*, which was overtaking from astern at approximately full speed (16.3 m.p.h.). Gale warnings and changing wind directions were central to their communication, and they made a mutual decision to avoid the more exposed and weather-vulnerable sailing courses to the south in American waters. The vessels subsequently followed a northerly track, abeam Isle Royale, which enabled the Canadian shoreline lee to provide a more sheltered easterly transit,

Sometime shortly after 03.00 hrs. on November 10, 1975, the faster *Fitzgerald* overtook the *Anderson*, at a time when weather conditions were further deteriorating, with increasing wind speeds of thirty-five knots and waves having a height of about ten feet. In the early morning report to his parent company, Captain McSorley advised that the *Fitzgerald*'s estimated time of arrival at Sault Ste. Marie would be indefinite because of bad weather conditions. Later, at 13.40 hrs., and after changing course to follow a southeasterly track for Michipicoten Island, Captain Cooper again radiotelephoned Captain McSorley and informed him that "I'm going to haul (turn) to the West for a while, in order to ensure that the seas will be astern." This course adjustment judiciously allowed more sea-room and increased offshore clearance to about 7.7 miles between the *Anderson* and the western tip of the Island.

Captain McSorley apparently thought otherwise and decided to hold his original course before turning eastward, with a lesser distance (about 2.5 miles) between his vessel and the Michipicoten West End Light, immediately prior to following his final course of 141° T en route to Whitefish Bay via Caribou Island. He appeared to be cutting corners and proceeding at maximum speed to either follow his (reputed) hard-driving operating practice or to compensate for a delayed schedule, although there may have been other reasons.

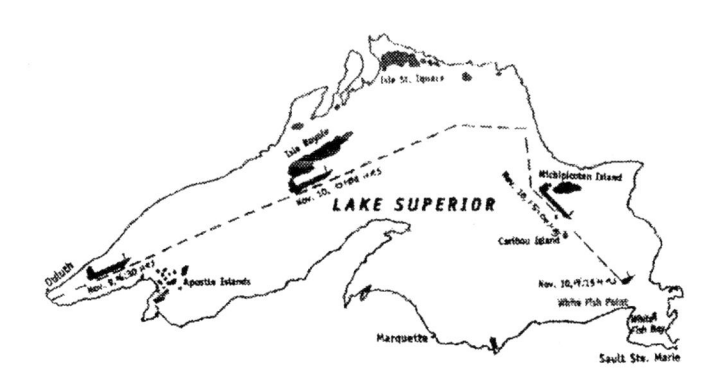

The final track of Edmund Fitzgerald.

At this juncture, some are aware that there has been commentary regarding Captain McSorley pushing the "Big Fitz" to her limits in any weather condition, and this may have fueled controversial opinion when such expression was made with "high risk" connotation. From my research, it appears that the command selection made by his employer, Columbia Transportation Division of Ogelebay Norton Company, was judiciously correct. They evidently matched this capable mariner, with a relatively unblemished record, and the most capable straight-decker ore carrier on the Great Lakes.

His predecessors had set a standard for record-breaking achievement, and it must have been a prerequisite that he accept similar business pressures requiring him to perform without allowing costs and delays to get out of hand—or to get relieved. His man-machine relationship surely must have attuned him to the fact that, when a full-form (box-like), deep-draft, vessel is driven hard by a 7,500 shaft horsepower steam turbine propulsion plant under severe weather conditions, there would inevitably be a hull structural price to pay during near-future operations. It is indisputable that every ship master develops a symbiotic understanding for his command as a "tight" of "loose" cargo transportation platform. Captain McSorley's awareness and concern for "the wiggling thing," when observing hull bending and springing, is considered notable and a worthy cause for technical concern that should have been thoroughly investigated.

His estimated course was plotted on Canadian Hydrographic Service Chart No. 2310 dated 1916, 1919. An updated version was used for reference (by the author) to develop a probable time/event analytic baseline based on the coordination of recorded "fixes."

During the radiotelephone interchange, Captain McSorley made a general comment that *Fitzgerald* "was rolling some," but this was not made with alarm. The rolling motion may have been attributable to his vessel's normal response to a turning maneuver and to the increasing northwest storm force vector changing to an almost full-astern position.

Storm Warning

At that time, the N.W.S. forecasts were downgrading from gale warning to storm warning status, with a major direction shift (Map A and Map B) from northeast to northwest. It is important to note that during the *Fitzgerald* inquiry proceedings, a N.W.S. meteorologist testified that:

"There are four to five intense storms on the Great Lakes during the fall to spring shipping season. The storm intensity of November 10, 1975, would not occur every year..[and] more intense storms than November 10, 1975, have been recorded."

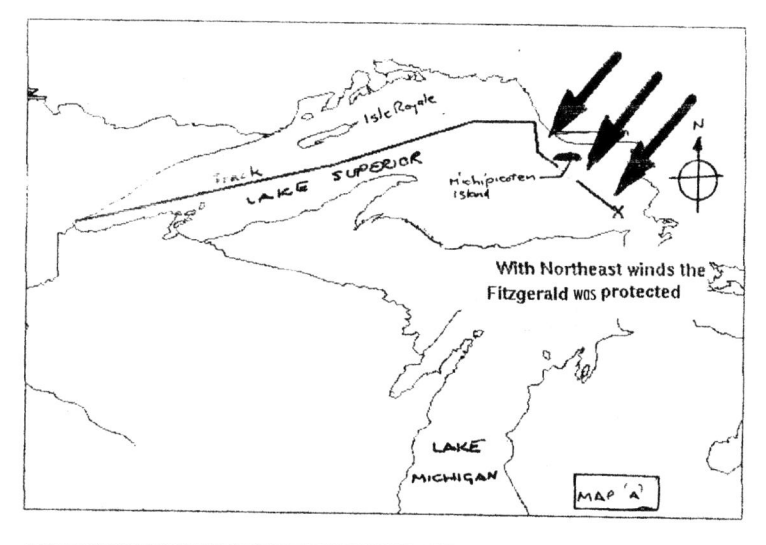

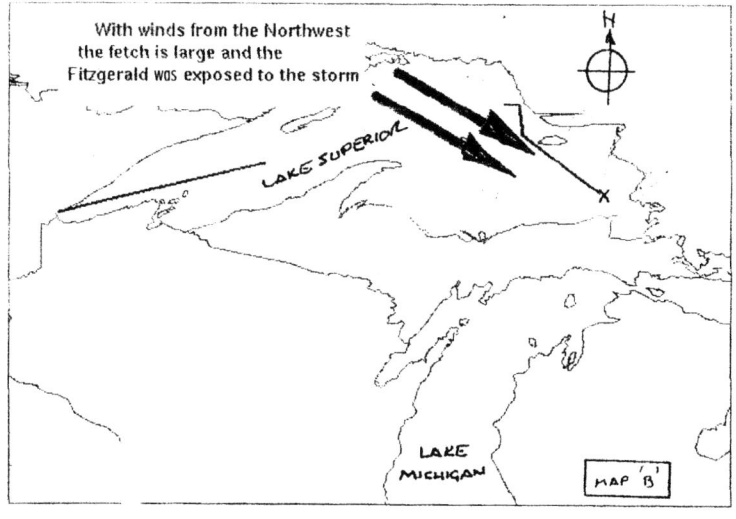

It would appear that such precedent information should have given the N.W.S. valid indicators for a "Seek Safe Anchorage" announcement to be communicated to the U.S. Coast Guard earlier than about 1540 hrs., midway through a snowstorm, and when *Anderson* and *Fitzgerald* were already experiencing weather conditions approaching operational extremus.

Visibility decreased when it started to snow at 14.45 hrs. It was still snowing at 15.20 hrs., when winds were steady at 43 m.p.h. from the northwest and waves were twelve to sixteen feet in height. At that time *Anderson* was shipping a considerable amount of water on deck, and Captain Cooper executed a course change to 125° T before following *Fitzgerald*, then about sixteen miles ahead and already proceeding on her final 141° T heading toward Whitefish Bay.

The final common course for both vessels required them to pass safely between four shoaling areas. With commendable seamanship the "Hummock" and "Chummy Bank" shoals would have been simultaneously passed on the port and starboard sides, respectively, then the "McMillan Bank" and "North Bank" shoals subsequently passed on the starboard side. Assuming that the Canadian Hydrographic Service Chart No. 2310 is (now) accurate, and accepting that both vessels actually followed common 141° T tracklines, it would appear that *no* disabling lake bottom contact could have occurred since there was generally adequate water depth and lateral clearance between underwater topographical formations. The minimum sounding was twenty-three fathoms—extremely close to the location where Captain McSorley coincidentally reported that he was "reducing speed, and had a fence rail down, lost two vents and had a small list" between 1520 and 1535 hrs.

As a conjunctive observation, the Venturi-effect phenomena known to mariners as "smelling the land" may have been detectable, albeit without negative consequences, if either vessel experienced sinkage (squatting) in shallower water depth or the stern tended to veer toward lake floor shoaling formations because of their closeness.

U.F.O. Encounter

Sometime between 15.30 hrs. and 15.35 hrs., *Fitzgerald* called *Anderson* to report a fence rail down, two vents lost or damaged, and a (small) list with two pumps going, and that he would check down (i.e., reduce speed) to close the distance between their vessels. Captain Cooper agreed to keep track of *Fitzgerald*, then about seventeen miles ahead. This transmission was not considered to reflect any real concern about safety of the *Fitzgerald*.

From the brief information at that time, it could be premised that an Unidentified Floating Object (U.F.O.) was struck when the vessel was proceeding at full power under extreme weather conditions. Credibility to this premising may be gained by considering that, in July 1994, observers on the Harbor Branch Oceanographic Institute's submersible *Clelia* discovered that a visible length of four-inch wide steel stem bar (the foremost structural member of the vessel rising vertically from the forefoot of the keel throughout full bow height) was distorted almost ninety degrees to starboard. The observers attributed the stem bar distortion to final impact of the bow forefoot with the lake floor.

The lake bottom impact force must have been undeniably large, based on the U.S. Navy's earlier unmanned CURV vehicle survey results, showing a twenty-seven-foot depth of lake floor glacial mud penetration and the 276-foot-long bow section that had about a fifteen degree inclination to one side. However, full attribution of ninety degree stem bar distortion *in response to lake floor impact* may be questionable, albeit still of analytic value. It could be expected that high-impact bow contact with the lake floor could have fractured welds and partly detached the stem bar from abutting shell plating through vertical displacement, but this does not explain the origin of a direct or oblique force vector having capability to deflect the stem bar ninety degrees to starboard while in transit. I feel confident in assigning a high probability that a large adrift U.F.O. (such as a "saltie" sea container), as occurs during some oceangoing voyages, or another large buoyant mass may have been encountered by the bow. I also consider that the U.F.O. impacting force could have caused ninety degree stem bar deflection and the fracture of welds attaching the bar to bow and side-shell plating while in transit. A propagative "unzippering" of this welding would have resulted, allowing shell plating detachment and water incursion into (a) the Fore Peak Tank and (b) possibly No. 1 Ballast Tank on one side of the vessel. Under the turbulent conditions, a bow-to-stern trajectory of the U.F.O. could have followed, with strong potential for upwardly riding a strong bow wave crest and with sufficient momentum to temporarily board the spar deck. The resultant tankage flooding would have caused an increase in bow draft. This change in bow attitude, when coupled with the reported listing condition, would have exacerbated vessel control under severe storm conditions.

Hull breaching casualties would have also caused a permanent loss in hull buoyancy when these bow compartments were given direct lake water access, thereby requiring shipboard pumps to drain *Lake Superior* (rather than vessel compartments). Further, the U.F.O. trajectory could have also accounted for a downed section of spar deck fence rail and caused two eight-inch diameter (tunnel and/or ballast tank) vents to be lost or damaged before final U.F.O. expulsion outboard and clear of the hull, as the vessel continued ahead.

Seek Safe Anchorage
At about 15.40 hrs., the *Anderson* received a Coast Guard broadcast that the Sault Ste. Marie locks had been closed and that all vessels should seek a safe anchorage. Between 16.10 hrs. and 16.15 hrs., *Fitzgerald*'s two surface-scan radar sets, mounted on a single mast above the pilot house, were reported inoperable, and *Anderson* agreed to provide navigational assistance by radiotelephone.

In this predicament, it should also be recognized that no fathometer equipment was installed or *required,* for the tracking of lake floor topography. The absence of a fathometer may be attributed to an overconfident viewpoint regarding the infallibility of radar installations and the perceived routine nature of lake transits by experienced vessel masters. The *Fitzgerald* navigational handicaps, under extreme conditions with inoperative surface-scan radar equipments serve to demonstrate the vital need for installation of a fathometer backup system.

The *Fitzgerald* was further handicapped after being advised that the unmanned/automated Coast Guard-maintained Whitefish Point Light radio beacon was inoperable due to power failure. Even if operable, the battery-powered nine-and-one-half mile range auxiliary light could not have been seen by *Fitzgerald* at a seventeen-plus miles distance—especially in a snowstorm.

It was fortuitous that the *Anderson* was available to keep the *Fitzgerald* under surveillance to provide Captain McSorley with course verifications when he was "sailing blind" in a snowstorm and without vital shipboard or shoreside navigation aids.

Without the *Anderson*'s dedicated support, the only visual shoreside checkpoint for the *Fitzgerald* would have been the automated/unmanned USCG light and radio beacon at Whitefish Point. The inoperative condition of this navigational aid further increased Captain McSorley's sailing blindness and operating area.

At maximum speed (16.3 m.p.h.), it may appear that Captain McSorley was "making a run for it" to reach safe harbor only a small distance away, with full knowledge that his vessel of over 30,000 tons displacement would require a stopping distance of over two miles (about fifteen ship lengths) if on a collision course. The USCG Conclusion No. 13 that "..the outages of Whitefish Point light and radio beacon (Fig. 39) did *not* contribute to the casualty.." is reprehensible. While the outage did not *directly* contribute to the sinking, it *did* fail (again) to provide reassurances to a mariner in a severe state of extremis and others requiring navigational guidance when seeking safe harbor in a high-traffic area.

Fig. 39 - The beacon and light on the Whitefish Bay lighthouse failed during the storm. Photo – U.S. Coast Guard

The 767-foot S.S. Arthur M. Anderson
Captain Jessie B. Cooper, Master

Photos – The Kenneth E. Thro Collection

The 729-foot S.S. Edmund Fitzgerald
Captain Ernest M. McSorley, Master

Equipment failures could have been due to unreliability or deferred maintenance and may be reflective of the government's over-commitment of USCG national resources without commensurate funding and adequate personnel staffing. Such overcommitment and underfunding of USCG resources has significantly increased over the intervening years, and does not bode well for the future.

Gran Marais Coast Guard station was contacted on emergency radio Channel 16, then was switched to Channel 22.

The *Fitzgerald* was not equipped with an Emergency Position Indicating Radio Beacon (EPIRB), which could have been released, floated-free, and autonomously operated on battery power in the event of sinking. At the time there were *no* regulatory requirements for EPIRB or crew survival module installations which could be activated under "abandon-ship" circumstances. In the same year (1975), I observed North Sea industry marine operations aboard the Norwegian offshore workboat *M.V. Seaway Falcon* and found that *jettisonable* autonomous survival modules were fairly common installations for that hazardous service environment. (*ergo*: Crew survival modules were already state-of-the-art, and they reflected vessel owner concern for crew survival in a very basic form.) Even though wintertime survival under casualty conditions on the Great Lakes is known to quickly exhaust human endurance, *no* exposure suits were required or on board the vessel.

Between 1700 hrs. and 1730 hrs., Captain McSorley communicated with upbound "saltie" *M.V. Avafors* and advised "I have a *bad* list, I have lost two radars, and am taking on heavy seas over the deck in one of the worst seas I have ever been in." This admission exuded controlled concern and signified that shipboard and weather conditions had definitely worsened since his previous radiotelephone communications, less than two hours earlier.

At about 19.10 hrs., the snowing stopped, almost five minutes before the sinking occurrence. With unimpaired visual capability, this may have been the point (or sooner) when Captain McSorley *perhaps* made a decision to "make a run for it" by setting the engine room telegraph to a full-ahead position. This proposition would be nullified if the engineroom was responding to other power-setting changes ordered from the bridge via telephone and *without* changes in engineroom telegraph indication.

Without the navigational assistance of *Anderson* in such a critical operating situation, having dangerous storm and snowing conditions, Captain McSorley would have been "sailing blind" and completely reliant upon experienced mariner skills and instinct, a compass, a radiotelephone, and radio direction finder (RDF), and most probably with crew lookouts positioned at (a) the port side pilothouse door when attempting to observe *Anderson* and any other vessels and/or (b) the starboard side pilothouse door when attempting to observe the proximity to Caribou Island.

Final Moments
Although the snowstorm had abated at about 19.10 hrs., allowing Captain McSorley to temporarily regain visual capability and full-power operation, he would have still been struggling to maintain control of his listing vessel, having boarding seas from astern and multiple degrees of freedom, namely rolling, pitching, heaving, yawing, surging, and swaying, with various force vector permutations and combinations. Moreover, none of these communication elements was considered to convey capsizing imminence, since adequate buoyancy reserve could be provided by the empty double-hull water ballast tanks; and intact cargo hatch covers. Adequate transverse stability was inherently available. Further, Captain McSorley's radiotelephone statements at 1910 hrs., made shortly before the sinking, gave positive assurance that his disabled condition was under control when he informed that "She was going like an old shoe" and "He was holding his own."

The destructive effects of the overtaking storm and the survivability of the fully-loaded *Fitzgerald* were of major concern to the masters of both vessels. The storm's advancing rapidity and wave generation turmoil no doubt contributed to considerable variance in the reporting of weather conditions. Such circumstances have been variously named "Witch of November" and "Old Treacherous." Even if the occurrences of such chaotic natural forces are reasonably predictable, their absolute quantification is not, and a cause majeure (unexplainable act of God) judgement appears to have (again) become a general outcome of investigations.

Some examples of weather variance reporting are presented as follows:

(1) A N.W.S. meteorologist testified that "before the *Fitzgerald* sank, the average sustained wind speed was forty-five knots (about fifty-two m.p.h.) from the northwest for a period of six to seven hours and could produce a significant peak-to-trough wave height of about fifteen feet."

(2) The master of the *Anderson* testified that "when South of Caribou Island, he observed seas running eighteen to twenty-five feet and that he had observed winds of seventy to seventy-five knots (about eighty-one to eighty-six m.p.h.)." Prior to that point, he had already experienced two huge (thirty-five foot) wave crests overtaking from astern when proceeding abeam of Caribou Island sometime after 18.30 hrs. One of these waves flooded *Anderson*'s poop deck, loaded water into her lifeboats and caused damage while in their saddles. Another forward-running overtaking wave subsequently covered the bridge deck, and both deck locations are measurable at about thirty to forty feet above the load waterline under static conditions.

Captain Cooper's voiced concern for overtaking stern wave effects on *Fitzgerald*, when heading toward a shallowing and convergent clapotic wave generation regime, proved to be well founded. His testimony that "I was riding on three wave crests at all times in the vicinity of Caribou Island," was valuable sensory feedback to the vessel's master and was used in the graphic reconstruction of *Fitzgerald*'s final moments.

When the *Anderson* became abeam of Whitefish Point at 20.59 hrs., wind speeds of forty-eight knots (fifty-five m.p.h.) were logged by Captain Cooper, reporting in-situ from his vessel's deck plates, and as a recognized weather buff, he should have been accorded high credibility. As an experienced God-fearing mariner, it is possible that he could have also prayed with thoughts of "There but for the Grace of God go I," when mindful of personal consequences that could have occurred had the locations and hazardous exposures of *Anderson* and *Fitzgerald* been reversed. With 20/20 hindsight, and with acknowledgement that both vessels were attempting to cope under extremely dangerous storm conditions in turbulent waters, becoming hove-to may *not* have been a viable option for the safe operation of either vessel.

(3) Subsequent to the USCG broadcast at 15.40 hrs. advising vessels to seek safe anchorage, the master at the Sault Ste. Marie locks recorded wind gusts over ninety m.p.h., with water sweeping regularly over the lock gates (as reported by: Sault Evening News, Sault Ste. Marie, Michigan, Nov. 11, 1975) and at one point, vessels below the locks were reporting winds of seventy knots gusting to eighty-two knots (ninety-five m.p.h.). The Mackinac Bridge was closed down when the wind reached eighty-five m.p.h. (As reported by *The Toledo Blade*, Ohio, Nov. 13, 1975).

(4) While all of these reported observations were at considerable variance with those of the NWS, this may be attributable to their statistical averaging of data over a greater geographical area, whereas those of *Anderson, et al*, were site-specific and considered more representative of the *Fitzgerald*'s environmental proximity.

With the utmost respect, it is very apparent that Captain Cooper's dedicated assistance prevented Captain McSorley from endangering the *Fitzgerald* and others by becoming an underway hazard while blindly proceeding in a snowstorm without operable shipboard and shoreside navigational aids.

The *Anderson* continued to follow in the waterway at a distance of about ten miles, with her master maintaining contact with *Fitzgerald* and upbound "saltie" vessels. His last radiotelephone contact with *Fitzgerald* was at 19.10 hrs., when his vessel was seeking safe haven at Whitefish Bay and still fighting the abating storm.

The *S.S. Edmund Fitzgerald* was lost without a distress signal, survivors, or witnesses at about 19.15 hrs.

M.V. Derbyshire Ex Post Facto Events
The 1975 sinking of *Fitzgerald* was followed by considerable speculation; critique of the vessel itself and the timeliness of search and

rescue operations. Similarly, in 1980, the short-lived British vessel *M.V. Derbyshire*, was lost, and again, there were neither survivors nor witnesses, and distress signals were not received.

While each vessel experienced widely different scopes and depths of respective government involvement and technical investigative testimony through public hearings, both tragedies *still* remain unresolved to the satisfaction of surviving families and other interested parties. For *Derbyshire*, a delayed forty-six day Formal Investigation (FI) was concluded in 1989, with much conjecture and a number of highly questionable conclusions in the absence of *prima facie* evidence since the wreck had *not* been located for forensic examination.

At 01.23 hrs. on June 3, 1994, Oceaneering Technologies of Maryland USA, under contract to the International Transport-workers' Federation (ITF), initially located the wreckage (Fig. 40). The search system teamed their Ocean Explorer 6000 side-scan sonar and Magellan 725 Remote Operating Vehicle (ROV), with the Japanese survey vessel *Shin Kai Maru* as the mission support platform.

The letters "SHIRE" on *Derbyshire* wreckage were located at a depth of 13,812 feet (2.6 miles), within a scattered debris field of immense destruction and fragmentation, inclusive of a very large hull section in an upright position but deeply buried within an impact crater. The bulk of the wreckage was found to be concentrated within a relatively small area by comparison with the depth at which she lay.

Further surveys were conducted in 1997 and 1998 with support from the Wood's Hole Oceanographic Institution, Massachusetts, using the United States Research Vessel *Thomas G. Thompson*. This vessel was used as a platform for deployment and control of the DSL 120 deep towed side-scan sonar, to delimit the wreckage field, and anARGO 11 visual search unit. High-definition filming was carried out by the JASON system (Fig. 41). The gathering of such evidence was expected to satisfy court evidentiary requirements, shipwreck insurance investigations, and many considerations for special salvage operations.

With this new forensic evidence in hand, on December 17, 1998, the Deputy Prime Minister, the Rt. Hon. John Prescott, MP, announced that there would be a full reopening of the Formal Investigation in the British High Court of Justice (Admiralty Court). It should be recognized, for the record, that without the dogged determination of the *Derbyshire* Family Association (DFA) in their search for justice, in collaboration with seafarer interests and bolstered by Parliamentary safety advocates, this high level of government attention could not have been attained, albeit the losses of oceangoing bulk-cargo carrier vessels continued to increase with great loss of life on a global scale, as exemplified by reports. While representing about 7 percent of the world fleet population, they were reported to be sustaining 57 percent of the casualties.

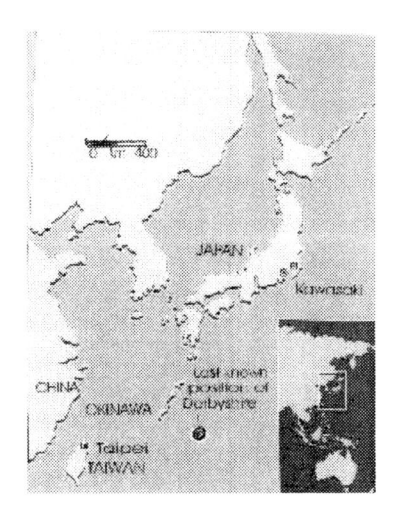

1. A tethered towfish is suspended from the surface support ship before sinking toward the seafloor.

2. Sonar pulses scan the seafloor as the towfish moves forward and provides data feedback to the support ship.

3. Magellan 725 (ROV) for mapping of wreckage field and photo/video recording via fiber-optic umbilical.

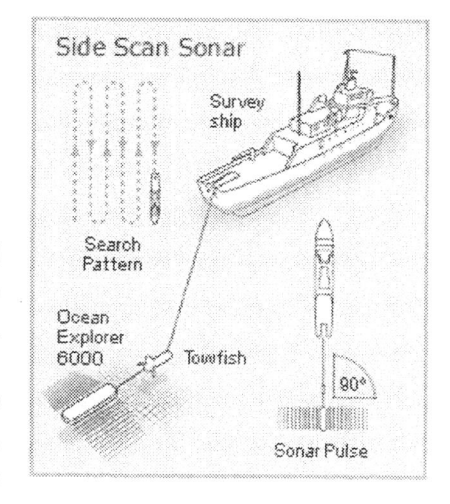

Fig. 40 - Teamed Ocean Explorer 6000
Side-Scan Sonar System
and
Magellan 725 ROV
Photo – Oceaneering Technologies (USA)

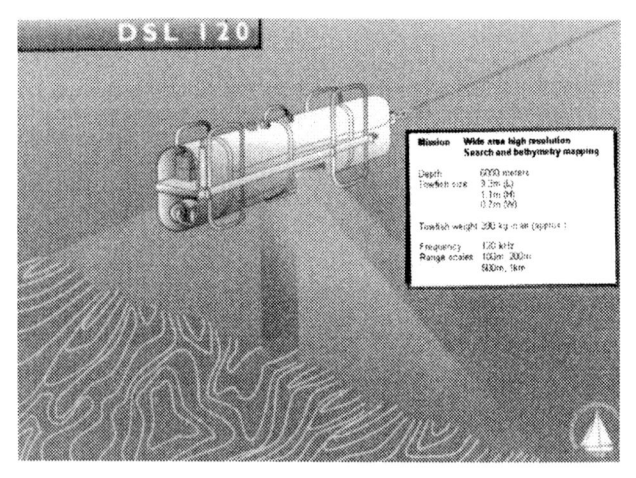

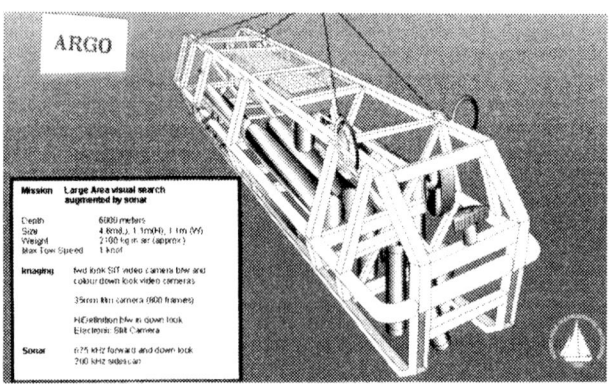

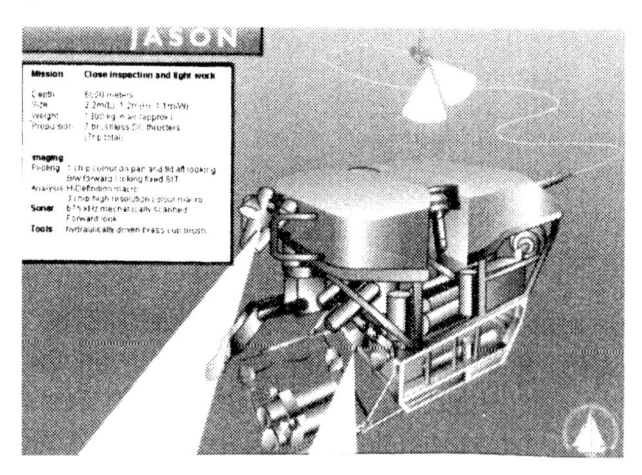

*Fig. 41 - Teamed DSL Towed Side-Scan Sonar and
ARGO Visual Search Unit and JASON High-Definition Filming
Photo – Wood's Hole Oceanographic Institution (USA)*

High Court of Justice (Admiralty Court) Hearing
Subsequent to the case reopening on April 5, 2000, the rehearing ran for fifty-four days, with conclusion on July 26, 2000, and was followed by publication of a final report on November 8, 2000—*twenty* years after the *Derbyshire* loss. Regrettably, the Court practiced selective admission and rejection of evidence available from worthy witnesses from academia, the shipbuilding trades, and a cognizant Lloyd's Classification Society surveyor. This caused severe limitations in the evidentiary data base, resulting in attribution of the vessel's loss to a master's failure to avoid Typhoon Orchid that caused progressive cargo-hold flooding through breached hatch covers. The master was later exonerated. (Cause majeure rides yet again!)

I have specifically singled out the court practice of selectively denying the admission of germane evidence because the chance of getting to the (technical and/or scientific) fallacies and truths of ship design and construction is generally lost or blurred, once legal processes become engaged. One of the key points at issue was the denied admission of a valuable naval architectural treatise by Professors Bishop, Price, and Temeral of the Brunel University, U.K. They had the necessary intestinal fortitude to disturb the status quo by providing bulk-cargo vessel structural treatise in terms of shortfalls in conventional stress analysis theories and assumptions. The *Derbyshire*, and others of the Bridge Class, were classic examples of vessel requirements that compelled designers to over-extend traditional semi-empiricism and heuristic reasoning in the absence of sound scientific baselines while endeavoring to bridge the design chasm created by vessels without direct precedent and technically "beyond the Rules."

Without doubt, the primary interest of the legal profession is the application of litigation after gathering sufficient evidence to sue a party. In the case of *Derbyshire* clientele, financial compensation was certainly present, but it did not predominate in the hearts and minds of surviving seafarer families. Unfortunately after twenty years of roller-coaster exasperation, with perplexity almost transmuting to apoplexy, some of the neutral parties were forced to take positions and started to refrain from saying too much—or worse, by declining to produce key documentation. In essence another speculative cause majeure (unexplainable act of God) outcome appeared to be the Court's core outcome, which could have similar applicability to the

Fitzgerald tragedy. It is acknowledged that cause majeure judgments will inevitably be made when appropriate and, in the absence of acceptable *prima facie* evidence. This is (perhaps) the only viable court ruling which may be expected.

As a naval architect with a judgmental disposition, but no *locus standi*, it is proffered that liability claims for most unexplained vessel losses *cannot* usually be amicably resolved through court proceedings when legal interest is mainly focused on gathering enough evidence to sue a guilty party(s). Not only do complex technical matters of shipbuilding and design confound the legal lexicon, causing communication difficulties in litigation processes, but some of the archaic ship design practices and incomplete data bases also are replete with their own shortfalls in specialized fields such as fatigue cracking; realistic and dynamic analysis of structure and ship motions; brittle fracture; material and welding quality control; etc.

In fairness to the Court and casualty investigators, their findings of fact, when weighing the limited completeness of technical and eyewitness evidence, negated any possibility of absolute comprehensiveness. Part of this "grey area" included determination of the structural adequacy for each vessel, which was designed *beyond* the empirically-developed limits of Lloyd's (and ABS) Ship Classification Society Rules. These Societies can claim long-term *primus inter pares* status but with historical reliance on empirical data extrapolation and their judicious adaptation of structural design criteria from lesser-sized bulk cargo vessels.

In both *Derbyshire* and *Fitzgerald* cases, analytical attempts to apply first-principle design approaches were not readily discernible since quantitative baseline data pertaining to force field magnitudes under dynamic conditions of wave loading were unavailable. When these vessels were designed, there was minimal attention paid to the need for hull strength calculations beyond traditional "rigid ship" still water stress analyses when, in actual fact, the structure was flexible and subject to dynamic loading, which required *hydroelastic* consideration. There was scant hydroelastic theory for merchant vessels available in the 1950–1960 timeframe, and, with the ever-increasing size of bulk-cargo vessels, there is still a need for design risk assessment if the past *modus operandi* of semi-empiricism is continued. While Finite Element Analysis (FEA) has proven to be an excellent stress analysis tool in many fields, its efficacy has absolute dependence on full knowledge of the conditional environment to which it is applied. For example:

(1) Correlation of complex and random interactions between wind and wave force fields, within a natural typhoon, are practically impossible to measure or express mathematically, and yet finite element calculations were undertaken by Lloyd's, the shipbuilder, and their consultants, based on idealizations of *Derbyshire*'s aft end structure when subjected to assumed bending and shearing forces. Neither of these calculations considered loading which represented warping constraint under torsional loadings in these flexible structures. The FEA 'operation' may have been considered a success (by some) but alas, the patient died.

(2) Since commercial vessels are not conceived, constructed, or operated under Utopian conditions using infallible design criteria, or zero defects in materials, workmanship during construction and perfect life-cycle maintenance, these variables can seriously undermine the credibility of finite element (FEA) or any other analyses that are seized upon as potential "silver bullet" technical solutions. To further make this point, a report by the U.S. Coast Guard of 1990 cited major causes of structural degradation as "...poorly designed details, poor weld workmanship and material failure..." but this critique was for commercial tankers and *not* bulk-cargo carriers—albeit one may expect that their design and construction environments would follow the shortfalls of similar industrial standards and practices.

While the naval architecture profession and ship classification societies are recognized as having a long and noble heritage, experienced practitioners do recognize that many scientific proofs can have broad-band application, but their limits must be identified and quantified considerably in advance of initial design processes—and certainly prior to prosecuting *ex post facto* casualty analyses. It is also appreciated that there are "different courses for different horses" when one is engaged in the design and construction of an array of specialized vessels within commercial and military nautical domains. In each situation, for advanced and specialized commercial vessel design and construction purposes, the "Rules" must have sound empirical and/or theoretical foundations supported by extensive research, development, and testing.

Fitzgerald Sinking Propositions
In attempting to develop cause-effect sequencing for the *Fitzgerald* sinking, I continually rotated my notional "*circumstantial kaleidoscope*," with subliminal awareness that not all prism elements could be present. The rationalized opinions of others also entered into many "prismatic" adjustments, but fault, civil or criminal liabilities were not addressed since, although of judicial mind, the author does not hold *locus standi* qualifications.

By subjectively correlating and selecting dominant prism patterns, and after considering many alternatives, the following propositions are believed to be worthy of inclusion in the extant repertoire of others seeking to unravel the *Fitzgerald* mystery:

*Lemma 1.
The *Fitzgerald*'s pre-sinking operating circumstances may be realistically represented by hull casualty impairment, dependency on remote navigational guidance, and the encountering of environmental chaos having abnormal natural forces seeking out the "Achilles Heel" of her marine system.

Lemma 2.
The fatal scenario clearly portrays the listing vessel, with lost buoyancy due to bow-damage and one breached side tunnel, in a condition of operational extremus while underway. She was subjected to a violent northwest (135° T) Lake Superior storm, which overtook the vessel from almost full-astern when on downbound course 141° T en route to Whitefish Bay. In nautical terms, the vessel would most certainly have been "pooped" by waves of enormous height, mass and energy, with troughs and crests collectively passing under and over

---

*Footnote: LEMMAS are propositions proved, or sometimes assumed, to be true and used in proving a theorum. (Webster)

her stern and across the starboard stern quarter superstructure. Additionally the vessel would have subsequently experienced the devastating effects of "Constructive Interference Waves" when entering a convergent land-mass zone conducive to the generation of clapotic waves and possibly the powerful Lake Superior seiche and storm surge effects driven by the storm.

Lemma 3.
The vessel was capably manned and held necessary seaworthiness certifications after recently passing USCG/ABS inspections, and she was under the command of an experienced master, with qualified officers and crew members aboard.

No shoaling damage is believed to have been sustained during transit.

Lemma 4.
It is highly probable that the wheelsman was able to compensate for any heading control difficulties caused by asymmetric buoyancy losses in the bow compartments and the added weight of water flooding the tunnel compartment on one side of the vessel following U.F.O. impact.

Underwater surveys of the inverted stern indicated an offset rudder angle of up to ten degrees, possibly reflecting the wheelsman's compensatory action to maintain a heading.

Lemma 5.
The vessel was experiencing extraordinary November storm conditions from the northwest when steaming toward the eastern terminus of Lake Superior and within seventeen miles of safe haven at Whitefish Bay, Michigan.

The rapidly converging American/Canadian shorelines, with steep underwater cliff frontage, were capable of reflecting incoming trans-lake waves. Ensuing wave generation could be expected to augment downbound, storm-driven trans-lake waves to form destructive and episodic "wall of water" conditions having abnormal height and energy. When combined with "pooping" waves and plunging of the stern, the vessel's stern would have become overwhelmed and certain cargo hatch covers immediately forward of the poop front would have been breached...prior to rapid flooding.

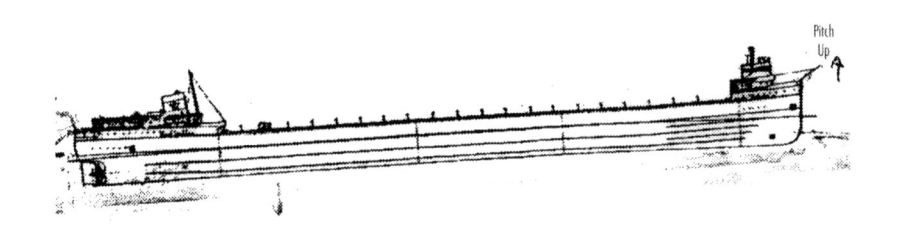

Lemma 6.

Wave troughs advancing below the stern and (seventy-foot) "Constructive Wave" crests periodically overtaking ("pooping") the vessel's stern would have induced significant stern sinkage and trim when experiencing dynamic plunging motions. Coupled with rapid water ingress through the aftermost breached cargo hatches, a permanent increase in stern immersion would have made the vessel "stern heavy." Progressively increasing water inundation of cargo holds would have immediately followed as the vessel began to sink *stern first*.

For example.
Estimated time to fill (159, 510 Cub. Ft.) *void space above* taconite in No. 3 Cargo Hold (only) subsequent to breaching of hatch cover(s).

Waterhead Height(Feet)	Water Ingress Rate (Tons/sec.)	Estimated Filling Time (seconds) Through:		
		Hatch No. 21	Hatch No. 21 20	Hatch No. 21 20 19
20	316	14.0	7.0	4.7
40	446	9.9	5.0	3.3
70	591	7.5	3.8	2.5

N.B.
Rapid vessel sinkage assumed to preempt consideration of lake water appreciably permeating the interstices of stowed taconite pellet cargo.

Lemma 7.
The vessel could have been expected to retain a small amount of residual forward momentum with multiple degrees of dynamic motion, as the vessel rapidly lost reserve buoyancy in a severely stern-trimmed condition due to progressively added lake water weight (est. 12,300 tons) in the void space above the stowed taconite ore in *all* cargo holds. Taconite ore shifting in a sternward direction within No. 3 Cargo Hold would have contributed to the vessel's increasing stern sinkage demise.

Upon flooding of the machinery space and cessation of propulsion power, the vessel's residual momentum would have continued to facilitate forward motion for a very limited distance (est. one-half mile/four ship lengths), before progressive filling of No. 1 and No. 2 Cargo Holds and simultaneous submergence.

Lemma 8.
While on the surface in an unrecoverable stern-heavy condition, and with pitching downward motion of the bow, the *Fitzgerald*'s hull girder would have experienced non-uniform distributive loading conditions as the after end of the vessel increased in weight due to flooding, boarding seas, and the sternward shifting of cargo. The dynamic motions of the vessel, and superimposed external loading, would have induced excessive hogging (bending upward), causing failure of the longitudinal hull girder as the bending, shearing and torsional strength capabilities were exceeded.

At this juncture a propagative spar deck rupture condition (but not total hull separation) would have developed at about the mid-length of No. 3 Cargo Hold, as recorded on videotape, and immediately prior to the onset of rapid hull submergence.

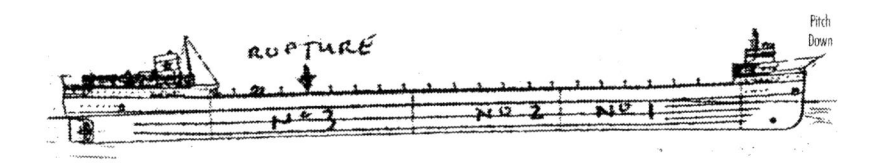

In the process:
- the shell and cargo hold plating boundaries of Ballast Tank No. 7 (See Fig. 37) would have also been ruptured, thereby causing localized flooding with a loss in reserve buoyancy;
- lake water entrapped in the tunnel would have been released; and
- uncontrolled flooding of No. 3 Cargo Hold, with taconite ore spillage and shifting, would have commenced.

Lemma 9.
On each side of the hull rupture, taconite would have been spilled, causing shifts in the longitudinal centers of gravity of the conjoined 240-foot stern and 489-foot bow section that was submerging with a slowing, forward bow-down trajectory.

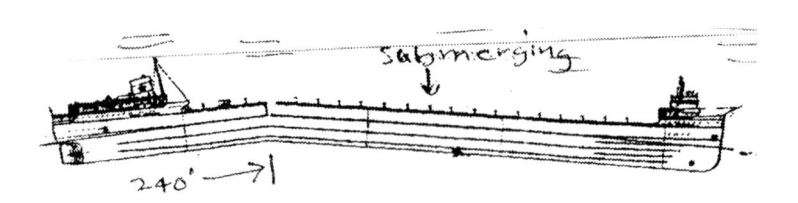

Lemma 10.
It is considered likely that the 240-foot stern section could have become separated and capsized during submergence within the water column as it became fully rotated to a final inverted position *before* the inclined bow plowed into the lake floor to a penetration depth of about twenty-seven feet, and with an inclination of about fifteen degrees. It is also possible that the stern section descent was at a *lesser* rate than the taconite-laden 489-foot bow section, because of hydrodynamic resistance (bluntness) at the stern hull separation facing forward.

A 213-foot cargo hold section appears to have separated *after* the 489-foot bow section forcefully penetrated the lake floor to a depth of about twenty-seven feet, with an inclination of about fifteen degrees.

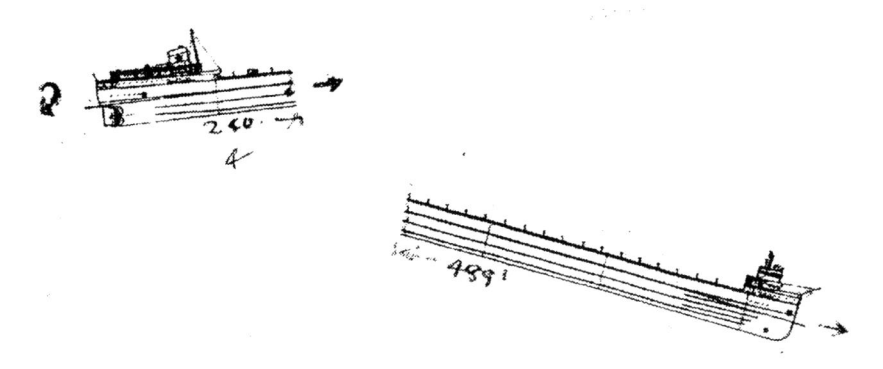

In this position, the bow was placed in a cantilevered loading condition vulnerable to separation into a forward 276-foot length and a dislocated 213-foot center section due to cargo shifting and bottom impact. This 213-foot section was later identified as "An area of distorted metal lying between the two (separated bow and stern) sections, and to both sides over a distance of some 200 feet." Part of the separated 213-foot center cargo hold section does rest between the sunken bow and stern, and a portion could be entrapped below the inverted stern.

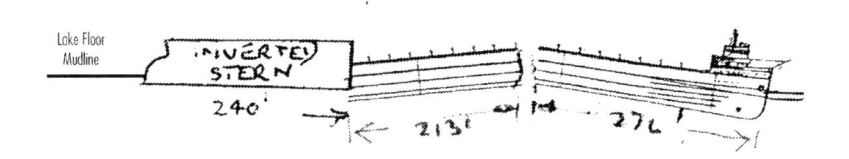

After the sinking, steel cargo-hold hatch covers were observed to be in many forms of implosion, explosion, dislodgment, and release, which may be attributable to external hydrostatic pressure instability (buckling) failures and internal air pressurization causing release.

Lemma 11.
With the increasing depth of submergence, hydrostatic pressure equalization would have progressively collapsed the boundaries of side ballast and other tankage (during pressure equalization), as recorded by videotape. A domino-effect of co-dependent structural failures would also be present during submergence to a maximum depth of 530 feet (230 psi).

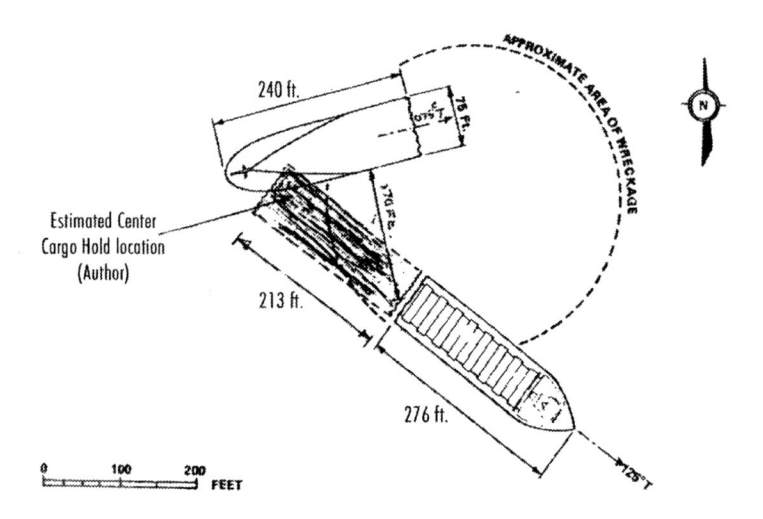

[Figure: Diagram showing wreckage layout with labels "240 ft.", "75 ft.", "Estimated Center Cargo Hold location (Author)", "213 ft.", "276 ft.", "APPROXIMATE AREA OF WRECKAGE", with scale 0–200 feet and north compass indicator]

Lemma 12.
If the structural and watertight integrity of *Fitzgerald*'s hull envelope and cargo hatches had remained intact, her stern should have subsequently risen in response to the dynamic redistribution of overall hull buoyancy and the attendant center of buoyancy adjustments.

Should such circumstances have prevailed, the author considers that, with adequate reserve buoyancy from her (empty) ballast tankage, survivability would have been viable over the final seventeen-mile transit.

Note: It was reported that it would require flooding of more than three adjacent ballast tanks, on the same side of the vessel, to be completely breached for capsizing to occur.

Lemma 13.
Crew members were unable to escape or survive due to:
- the vessel's catastrophic and rapid sinking mode;
- the inability to gain access to, or launch, lifeboats or liferafts when overtaken by boarding seas having abnormal "Constructive Interference Waves";
- the absence of an autonomous-ejectable survival module(s), which was neither specified nor available; and
- lack of exposure suit equipment, which was neither specified nor available.

- 240 ft -

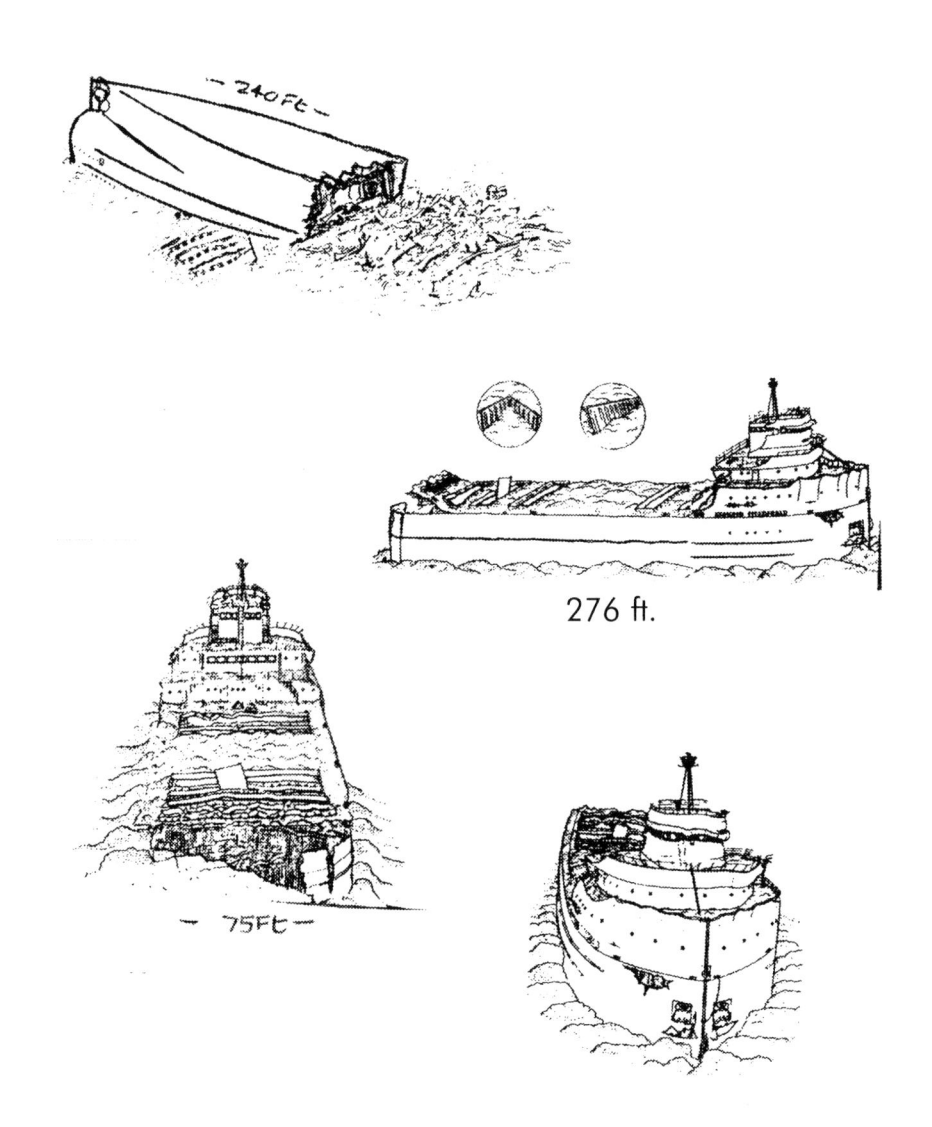

276 ft.

- 75 ft -

PART NINE:
SUMMARY

There is no doubt that rapid flooding events under abnormal storm conditions (while underway) could have caused the *Fitzgerald*'s longitudinal hull girder bending strength to be exceeded, as the outcome of an initial "stern-heavy" flooding circumstance which imposed serious imbalance of girder distributive loading under dynamic conditions. The stern also incurred excessive trim, unrecoverable sinkage, and problems of hydrolasticity (because the vessel's structural envelope was *not* rigid), and dynamic vessel motions were in effect. It may be rationalized that the onset of after cargo-hatch breaching and hold flooding were closely followed by ductile separation of the hull envelope during submergence, the separation being at about the mid-length of No. 3 Cargo Hold. Hence, it appears reasonable to attribute the vessel loss to catastrophic flooding through breached cargo hatch covers, and subsequent foundering, when the added weight of flooding water exceeded the reserve buoyancy margin as other cargo hold hatch covers failed.

Even though the foregoing propositions appear to be self-evident, they are made with full awareness that there are many areas of bulk-cargo vessel structural design and investigative loss reconstructions that qualify for the "we don't know what we don't know" mantle in the scientific and naval architectural fields of endeavor. Since 1958, the author has been "haunted" by the hogged (bent upward) still-water hull deflection as statically measured on the new vessel, and the hull flexibility and springing observed while underway on the *Fitzgerald* lake trials with relatively calm prevailing conditions. The observations were somewhat unnerving, when knowing full well that structural requirements for Great Lakes bulkers have a midship section modulus designed to a strength standard a little over 50 percent of that for an oceangoing vessel. Based on the testimony of a NWS meteorologist, that "...more intense storms have been recorded on the Great Lakes...," it would have appeared appropriate to seek an increased hull stiffness standard and analytical methodologies of the highest order to offset potential long-term fatigue and cracking. Without the onset of cause majeure circumstances, one could have expected this well-maintained seventeen-year-young vessel to have achieved a life expectancy of about forty-seven years, which was an average service life expectation for Great Lakes bulk-cargo vessels at that time. No one, however, could have accurately estimated *Fitzgerald*'s fatigue life if she continued to be hard-driven in bad weather conditions while under full-load, although a below-average lifespan would have had to be expected at some distant date. For a "given life" expressed as a given number of loading cycles, there is, for any given material, an upper-limit cyclic stress parameter.

Before the belated (1935) advent of the Great Lakes Load Line Regulations, laker ship draftsmen followed their conservative, esoteric design practices using semi-empirical data based on proven in-service experience, with a practical understanding of the physical constraints associated with lifting locks and cargo terminal loading/unloading facilities.

In the somewhat insulated industry of the Great Lakes, shipbuilders progressed with conservatism and at their own pace. Fortunately their industry introduced hull fabrication improvements benefiting from welding advances of World War II, when more attention was paid to fabrication details, quality control for the assurance of sound hull structure, and general awareness of advancing national shipbuilding standards and practices.

For the record, it is my belief that the profession is well aware that *no* "perfect" commercial vessels can be cost-effectively produced because of many production variables within a shipyard. These are inclusive of hull welding, which has a long and checkered history under exposed on-berth conditions, requiring high performance from welders susceptible to nomadic trends in their quest for incentivized and higher-paid employment opportunities, often in industries having stability and better/safer working conditions. Within this labor-intensive matrix, welder supervision is frequently dispersed thinly among inexperienced and/or inadequately-trained welders, who are subjected to random non-destructive testing (NDT) procedures for the welding quality control of commercial vessels.

In welding circles, it is known that "slugging" of welds is sometimes practiced to maximize production rates and piece-work earnings, as I observed during my apprenticeship and at other shipyards. This practice involves the placing of unfused welding electrodes and "slugs" of iron or steel in the welding root gap of abutting steel plates before covering them with deposited weld material both manually and by welding machines. A typical case in point, from the pages of Great Lakes Engineering Works (G.L.E.W.) history books, involved three of their welded vessels built during World War II at a time when "Kaiser Coffin" Liberty's and other vessels were gaining notoriety as casualties abounded, due primarily to welding failures. The G.L.E.W. vessels were *Leon Fraser*, *Enders M. Voorhees* and *A.H. Febert*, which were known as the "Supers" or "AAs" Class. Their welding deficiencies were not discovered until near the end of the 1976 sailing season (post-*Fitzgerald* loss) when their welded spar deck joints were subjected to U.S.C.G. inspections involving non-destructive testing (NDT) using X-ray and ultrasound. Defective joints were repaired after "slugging" was discovered in the form of unburned welding rod, wire, and other inclusions. Over the course of thirty-two years of typical Great Lakes service, it was interesting that these less-than-perfect welds had *not* failed. It was also significant that construction accept/reject standards for welding defects and anomalies had been minimal.

The passage of time probably negates use of the foregoing World War II welding quality yardstick for applicability to *Edmund Fitzgerald*, and it is reassuring that her almost-sister vessels, *Herbert C. Jackson* and *Arthur B. Homer* did not report similar defects. Without stringent non-destructive testing (NDT) and fabrication procedures (as in submarines), *selective* sampling of welded joints should have been practiced during *Fitzgerald* and *Derbyshire* construction and during post-casualty investigations of almost-sister vessels.

As the size and service requirements of bulk-cargo vessels continue to place increasing demands on all elements of the global maritime spectrum, it is reasonably predictable that the losses of *Fitzgerald*, *Derbyshire*, and many others, will be reported without survivors, witnesses, or distress signals. There will also be expectations that technical and legal communities should subsequently carry out investigations using indisputable marine principles and theorems of Archimedes, Bernoulli, and Froude, which are always alive and well, but with a paucity of commercial investment in much-needed original research associated with dynamic hull stressing and hydroelastic certitude, which are vital to a more realistic understanding of structural fatigue and brittle fracture mechanics. Without such research and/or technology transfers from other fields, barriers to comprehensive findings, conclusions, and legal judgements will continue to be handicapped and couched in "...from the *available* or *limited* evidence..." terms of reference.

Hence I have concern that *cause majeure* rulings may predominate as judicial mantra in consequence of:

(1) the absence of comprehensive naval architectural evidence having capability to provide scientific proof, which is acceptable to a Court, beyond a reasonable doubt; and
(2) Court reluctance to admit *all* evidence conducive to informed awareness of circumstantial support elements, as demonstrated in the *Derbyshire* case and enunciated in the British House of Commons debate of July 3, 1996 by:

The Honorable Frank Cook, M.P. (Stockton, North), quote:

> "...I am sorry to labor the point about the *M.V. Derbyshire* Family Association's (DFA) technical advisors, but who found the wreck? It was *their* technical advisors funded by the unions. Despite protestations to the effect that the Government had made various efforts in this respect, nothing was done other than to go through the motions of an investigation. Indeed it is on record that informed commentators such as, for example, the Lloyd's surveyor who was debarred from giving evidence. They were not invited to do so, despite their (technical advisors') consistent appeals

to be heard.
I suggest that this a clear indication that the pursuit of the truth was *less* than energetic..."

and

The Honorable Graham Allen, M.P. (Nottingham, North), quote:

"...The debate also shows our weakness, in that Parliament has been unable to hold the Government to account over the past sixteen years in order to get a serious and full investigation into what really happened to the *Derbyshire*..."

and

"...The (Derbyshire-type) vessels were built by private owners of Swan Hunter, but liability is now consequent upon the Government (British Shipbuilders) and Lloyd's. If the *Derbyshire* Family Association (DFA) make a breakthrough and the Government and Lloyd's become liable, how will that effect the dozens—indeed hundreds—of bulk-carrier losses since 1971?

That may provide a clue to why the Government has dodged and edged and not been clear, open and honest about what happened to the *Derbyshire*. When big money is at stake, *it seems that (seafarer) lives are cheap, but insurance is expensive....*"

Over the years I have read a considerable number of other investigatory reports and court opinions that attempt to objectively seek maritime casualty resolutions. Most have a cadre of expert witnesses who expertly "play their own instrument" with musical variations on familiar themes from *other* investigations in deference to "total system" perspectives embodying the vested interests of surviving families who appear to have minimal entitlement to justice and appropriate compensation.

An *ex post facto* technocratic approach is usually pursued in forensic explorations, and it cannot be ignored that political factors many times obtrude in a subliminal sense and may deflect investigators from their dedicated search for truth. There is no doubt that if the nationalized British Shipbuilders and Lloyd's were found to have culpability for the *M.V. Derbyshire* catastrophic sinking, there would have been a Tsunami-wave of investigation and claims associated with many other unresolved bulk-cargo vessel losses as follow-on challenges to the *M.V. Derbyshire* Family Association initiative. An initiative which sought justice, compensation, and awareness that seafarers and their families' lives *should not be randomly expendable resources in the maritime world regardless of nationality.*

For those who question the cost-effectiveness of sea-bed surveys: it would appear that a primary principle is definitely served by providing *prima facie* court evidence that a vessel is indeed sunk and not a victim of high seas piracy. Secondary, post-mortem and video-enhanced, sea-bed surveys should be a prelude to the unleashing of theorizing along various forensic investigatory pathways of inquiry, such as Failure Mode and Effects Analysis (FMEA), when seeking elusive "truths" about what actually happened during a prior event. In the real world, investigators should also be ever-vigilant to recognize that subsequent conclusions and recommendations can be influenced by the use of hackneyed "solutions-looking-for-problems" mantras that, in the absence of irrefutable scientific proof inputs, obstruct the derivation of *absolute* truth. Under such circumstances, truth or opinions could become unfavorably influenced by unquantifiable subjective factors.

While my original education and training facilitated a thorough understanding of merchant vessel design and construction evolutions, my main career was dedicated to the military *modus operandi* which is 100 percent subsidized by the U.S. taxpayers. This experience contributed to an understanding that military vessels and designers have a higher affordability index and are able to exercise more planning and technical exactitude for combatant and auxiliary vessels that conduct their operations in harm's way.

Such a bifurcated background also provided philosophical enlightenment by augmenting the "we don't know what we don't know" dilemmas of merchant vessel technical concerns with the mantle of "we cannot finance what we can't afford"—but this must change for the future safety of *all* merchant vessels and seafarers who globally voyage in harm's way of the natural environment. In meeting the present and future systemic challenges associated with bulk-cargo vessels, global initiatives will be necessary in which the Western maritime bloc should be prepared to play a role in league with Far Eastern countries, to which the merchant shipbuilding paradigm has shifted and is likely to remain for future years.

In many circumstances, transferable shipbuilding technologies are already in development or use within military and aerospace programs, but their implementation in the commercial shipbuilding industry is defeated by the absence of vigorous commercial vessel design and construction distribution throughout the world. The paucity of original maritime (non-military) investigatory research and technology transfer simply exacerbates the scientific void of "not knowing what we don't know." Historically, new and improved design and production technologies continued to advance when wooden sailing craft were replaced by steel and mechanically-powered commercial vessels. Similarly aircraft, aerospace, and automotive capabilities advanced through research, development, and technology transfer at an accelerated pace based on national need and leadership. In consequence of the post-1970s de-industrialization of American business events, this momentum requires government sponsorship for commercial shipbuilding technology renewal and not a continuation of partially-anachronistic empiricism. Without a technologically adequate and vibrant commercial shipbuilding base, any island nation will become (moreso) a "maritime paraplegic" plying the high seas with accident-prone workhorse vessels (especially bulk-cargo carriers) that will continue to be enlarged beyond the state of the art to cope with the insatiable appetite of world industrial demands.

PART TEN: EPILOGUE AND EPITAPH

The *S.S. Edmund Fitzgerald* bulk-cargo vessel for Great Lakes service and the *M.V. Derbyshire* Ore/Bulk/Oil (O.B.O.) oceangoing vessel names still resonate whenever they are spoken of in the United States and throughout Great Britain. While many know very little about the design, operation, and history of these vessels, the eulogized song entitled "The Wreck of the *Edmund Fitzgerald*" by Canadian folk singer Gordon Lightfoot has kept that vessel's name very much alive over the past thirty years.

The continuing public interest in the cornucopia of information available through universities, libraries, historical societies, and museums remains phenomenal. To partially illustrate the vitality of the *Fitzgerald* mystique, the Great Lakes Shipwreck Museum at Whitefish Bay, Michigan welcomed about eighty-seven thousand visitors in 2002.

The tragic premature loss of *M.V. Derbyshire* is nationally remembered in Great Britain by the dedicated search for justice through their Parliament and High Court of Justice, which was enabled by supporters of the *Derbyshire* Family Association (DFA). They were instrumental in clearing the victim master and crew of any blame for the catastrophic loss but received *no* monetary compensation for their pain and suffering.

As a retired member of the naval architecture profession, with a number of other "strings to my bow," I consider myself extremely privileged to have had an opportunity to directly participate in the design and construction of Hull No. 301, which became the *S.S. Edmund Fitzgerald* after her christening on June 7, 1958, at the

Great Lakes Engineering Works, River Rouge, Michigan, and to have gained understanding, as a past "insider," of commercial ship design and construction practices at the ex-Furness Shipbuilding Company responsible for the *M.V. Derbyshire* and other bulk-cargo carriers of the ill-fated Bridge Class.

The Mystique

The *Fitzgerald* "mystique," both before and after her loss, is somewhat ethereal to some and questionable by others who only perceive lakers as large, unattractive barges propelled by massive engines. Shipbuilder and mariner participants, however, see mystique in *all* vessels, regardless of their aesthetics or purpose, when every vessel takes on its own persona and achievements after emerging from a multitude of innocuous steel plates, structural sections, and a cacophony of chaotic noise. They take on a majestic character upon delivery when displaying unique paint colors, funnel insignia, and pennant.

In the eyes of her owners, the "Big Fitz" became an efficient transportation machine when, in 1964, she became the first Great Lakes vessel to carry more than one million tons of ore through the Soo locks at Sault Ste. Marie, Michigan. In the case of this well-maintained vessel, her stature was enhanced by being the largest and fastest "first-of-kind" that held ore-carrying records on the Great Lakes for about eleven years during her strenuous, short-lived, seventeen-year life.

Crews appreciated their air-conditioned accommodations and other amenities, and numerous shoreside admirers bestowed high esteem when they considered themselves fortunate to photograph her passing by. The stateroom and lounge spaces for V.I.P. passengers were superbly furnished and located on the forecastle deck, which was quiet and far-removed from the aft propulsion machinery space. Each master effused his own character throughout association with the vessel, especially Captain Peter P. Pulcer (circa 1966), who was as well known around the Lakes as his "Pride of the American Flag" command.

Without doubt, the *S.S. Edmund Fitzgerald* was worthy of a "unique-mystique" charisma.

The *Derbyshire*, regrettably, did not enjoy similar mystique for a number of reasons, including the fact that, as an oceangoing (versus inland waterway) workhorse, she was practically invisible to the public after initial media hyperbole and delivery from the shipbuilder. No "cottage industry" organizations or individuals sought gain by capitalizing on the tragic loss, which had far-reaching consequences for survivor families and the maritime industry at large. Public awareness and concern only re-emerged after the tragedy and the questions regarding structural adequacy of others in her Bridge Class and the safety of bulk-cargo vessels in general.

The Mystery
The "mystery" mantle attached to losses of *Fitzgerald* and *Derbyshire* has continued to prevail as the sunken vessels respectively rest in water depths of 530 feet and 13,812 feet (2.6 miles) without acceptable explanation. In both cases inquiries have thankfully absolved masters, officers, and crew members from any blame, and cause majeure (unexplainable acts of God) have again come to the fore, with corollary considerations of design and construction adequacy in relation to environmental forces encountered in full-load transit.

It was an expectation that both vessels would cost-effectively advance the state of the art in the transportation of bulk cargoes, and in doing so, their structural design processes were obliged to exceed the limits of extant ship classification society requirements that were excessively reliant on past experience. In the commercial maritime industry, technological advancements have always been gradual, cautious, and strongly based on semi-empiricism and extrapolation from precedent vessels of *similar* type, but usually without a comprehensive support base of scientific research, development, testing, and evaluation.

There is compelling evidence that "the oceangoing bulk loss problem" has grown too big to be overlooked. When one reviews the tragic casualty record, it is evident that numerous poorly-maintained vessels are apparently kept in service beyond the limits of their safe working lives.

In the period of 1980–1996, forty-three standard bulk-cargo vessels of over twenty thousand ton deadweight were lost under circumstances where structural failure could have played a part.

The ages of some failed vessels varied (1980–1996 era) from only eight years to thirty-nine, with an average of eighteen years, of which 78 percent were fifteen years or over. When designed and built, these forerunner bulk-cargo vessels would have been in compliance with a number of ship classification society and international regulations prevailing at that point in time. Ship classification societies knew, *or should have known*, that they were extrapolating from shallow scientific data bases to the earlier *Derbyshire* (O.B.O.) Bridge Class design and construction venture...when *no* directly applicable Rules were available from Lloyd's.

Most ship classification societies have traditionally been enshrouded in their own veil of mystery, and justifiably so for conventional-type vessels created by a technologically slow-moving merchant marine industry that is intermittently marked by certain "Eureka" periods, such as the advent of containerships, roll-on/roll-off vessels, *et al.* Regrettably the traditionally empirical approach for bulk-cargo vessels has fallen short of expected standards, mainly because they have failed to realize that traditional ship classification practices now require complementary years of research, development, and novel engineering—which are demanding and expensive. Based on their lack of broad and incisive initiatives, it would appear that their diagnostics have not adequately defined the severity of the oceangoing bulk-cargo carrier seaworthiness situation, and new international approaches should be sought and made viable.

In recent years the International Association of Classification Societies (IACS) introduced its Enhanced Survey Program (ESP) to reduce bulker losses. It is believed to have been somewhat successful as an initiative to raise the level of awareness regarding the operational safety of older bulk-cargo vessels in the resale brokerage market. They may have arrested or slowed the rate of "total loss" underwriter claims being paid to "can't lose" owners, who receive certification from lax ship classification societies of perhaps questionable business integrity.

As emerging industrial nations continue to enlarge their appetites for bulk-cargo vessels and the ranges of raw material they carry, they could be seeding a worse global casualty problem requiring global resolution, with a scope heretofore not seen. The same countries, having low-cost labor, are already ramping up their labor-intensive heavy industries including shipbuilding, and it is highly likely that the casualty history of oceangoing bulk-cargo vessels will repeat itself as vessels grow even larger and older to maximize their cost-effectiveness *without* the necessary scientific foundations and conscience to ensure safety. With globalization, their technological expertise should be called upon to play a leadership role in expanded international consortia. Concurrently it would appear prudent to develop a global ship data base applicable to every bulk-cargo vessel for use in the assignment of high-risk/low-risk (Figure of Merit) identifiers having utility to seafarer interests, insurers, and potential owners. At minimum, the data base would record vessel technical characteristics and the life-cycle history of service, casualties, repairs, etc., with possibly management by the International Maritime Organization (IMO).

In view of the historical casualty statistics, any bulk-cargo vessel reaching the age of fifteen years should become subject to service discontinuance unless the owner appeals to a suitably licensed inspection body having independence from regulatory governmental agencies and ship classification society affiliation.

The *Derbyshire* and her almost-sister vessels were unique Ore/Bulk/Oil (O.B.O.) cargo vessels of gargantuan proportions, with each carrying its own controversial history. With introspection and hindsight, it is highly probable that this relatively new Bridge Class of vessels could have reflected many hull structural problems of the presaging bulk-cargo fleet *in embryo*.

The "mystery" factors surrounding each loss do require more objective screening to determine what is unexplainable, unknown, or kept secret complemented by a blending of experience and research results.

In the case of *Fitzgerald*'s loss, much is explainable, and her loss could be primarily creditable to the vessel being at the "wrong place at the wrong time," under severe November storm conditions within convergent shoreline boundaries of Lake Superior. This explanation should dispel the aura of "mystery." The vessel's unpredictable encounter with episodic "Constructive Interference Waves" generated by a combination of abnormal trans-lake waves and magnifying clapotic waves reflected from underwater cliff-like convergent land masses and a reducing water depth regime, are believed to have released natural forces far in excess of (any) hatch cover bearing load capabilities or designer's vision. This resulted in their implosive buckling collapse, and uncontrollable cargo hold flooding. Indeed, this loss may be rightfully attributed to cause majeure (an unexplainable Act of God) circumstances, which conveniently subsumed other technical concerns, such as questionable Great Lakes environmental premising for reduced longitudinal strength standards, hatch cover strength criteria, hull springing and bending effects on fatigue and cracking, etc., associated with the *Fitzgerald*, as a 1958 forerunner of other Seaway-sized bulk-cargo carriers designs.

Many of the laker concerns expressed here were either reduced or eliminated by subsequent actions of the American Bureau of Shipping (ABS) in the late 1960s, when a need was recognized to reevaluate the existing strength standards for vessels operating on the Great Lakes and Gulf of St. Lawrence, mainly because of the growth in laker designs up to one thousand feet in length, and in the early 1970, as the ABS embarked on an extensive program to study wave-induced hull springing responses, and wave-load excitations.

The 1978 Rules For Building and Classing Bulk Carriers on the Great Lakes reflected a revised longitudinal strength standard and considerations of structural fatigue based on parametric, probabilistic analyses. While these ABS initiatives are to be applauded, a vital "missing link" intrinsic to *every* research element would have been the unique, and relatively unknown, nature of Great Lakes natural force fields generated within the constraining physical boundaries of surrounding land masses and lake floor topographic formations. To confidently accept scientific research based on first-principle analyses, the user needs to know that quantitatively-reliable (recorded) atmosphere and lake water interface data input are necessary, and that the natural force fields of the "atmosphere-*Great Lakes*" and "atmosphere-*Oceanic*" environments are mutually exclusive identities because of their uniqueness. In the absence of comprehensive data bases for Great Lakes interactive environments, parametric-probabilistic analytic approaches are commendable but should be used with reservation.

In the case of the *Derbyshire* loss, at the outset, the seeds of disaster appear to have been planted when Lloyd's approved the preliminary design executed by Swan Hunter Shipbuilders with direction to adapt 1971 Lloyd's Ship Classification Society Rule requirements for *tankers and dry-cargo vessels* in the *absence* of rules specific to such a large Ore/Bulk/Oil (O.B.O.) vessel's design and construction venture. The construction shipyard (ex-Furness Shipbuilding Company) drafting staffs subsequently developed production drawings, also *without* the use of O.B.O.-specific Rule requirements. It was not evident that advance or in-process research, development, or technical support were extensively provided by graduate engineers. Heuristic (rule-of-thumb) practices with semi-empiricism (past experience without reference to scientific principles) were used. In other words, standard commercial shipyard standards and design procedures were followed for a *pioneering* vessel.

The construction shipyard procedures for designer selection of Grade A plate steel having no guarantee of toughness and production management's receipt-inspection of structural materials; in-shop/on-berth alignment of prefabricated units; welding quality control; etc., were considered to be highly questionable and possibly contributory to hull structural failure(s).

The major misalignment and/or subsequent repairs of intercostal longitudinal structure immediately forward of the poop superstructure in way of Bulkhead 65 was considered (by some) as a major contributor to primary failures on *Derbyshire* and others of the Bridge Class. Albeit many reinforcing repairs were additionally carried out in other locations on the Bridge Class hulls.

For a considerable period of time, there was British government reluctance to proceed with formal investigation of the *Derbyshire* loss, until other Bridge Class casualties (*M.V. Kowloon Bridge, et al*) came to public attention. Throughout, there were many unknown, unexplainable, and potential secretive ("cover-up") elements that were brought into play with generation of obfuscation and enhancement of the mystery, to the chagrin of aggrieved members of the *Derbyshire* Family Association (DFA), who were seeking justice and not conjecture. As time progressed their perplexity transmuted to apoplexy. At that time it was reported that high-level civil servants in the U.K. Department of Transportation were persuading ministers to "...break from normal practice and *decline* to call for a public enquiry into the loss of *Derbyshire*." Since it is the rule rather than the exception to hold a public investigation whenever there is a heavy loss of life, such a proposition did *not* prevail.

In 1985, their initial unpublished Report (File MS7/9/0465) of preliminary investigations gave recognition to the reported alignment flaw at Bulkhead 65, and that the disaster could have been a cause of "structural hull failure" before being rescinded by later evidence that was reluctantly admitted during subsequent proceedings.

In 1986, when the report attributed the *Derbyshire* loss to cause majeure conditions, there was great angst on the part of survivor families.

The outcome of any accident inquiry is to objectively seek truth so that curative/preventative measures may be taken in potentially parallel future cases. There is a clear distinction between "inquisitorial" and "accusatorial" inquiry, in that the former is concerned with events that actually occurred or, given the known circumstances, most likely occurred; the latter having primary concern for the apportionment of culpability and liability. Whenever numerous parties are involved and have diverse self-interests, any inability to recognize where fault has arisen is a serious deterrent to good investigatory performance. Refusal to glean the fullest knowledge from mishaps can thus only be described as folly.

In the case of *Derbyshire*, I do *not* agree that the cause of her loss should remain a matter of speculation under the guise of force majeure circumstances.

In the cases of *Fitzgerald* and *Derbyshire* losses, preoccupation with causes of vessel loss has, to date, taken precedence over concerns for crew safety and means of survival when storm conditions and boarding seas preempted access to or deployment of (anachronistic) conventional lifeboats or life rafts. While considerable investment in safety and emergency escape has been made for motorists, aircrews and concepts befitting returning space travelers, there appears to be an international reluctance to objectively research and install modern mariner survival systems to replace equipment belonging to another century.

In testimony by a Great Lakes pilot, he said that "...if the damn ship is going to go down, I would get in my bunk and pull the blankets over my head and say, 'Let her go!' because there was *no* way of launching the boats."

Surely the time has come for jettisonable hard-shell survival module(s) with entry from within a deckhouse and release by explosive fasteners or other remotely-controlled device—and survival suits for all on board.

When the author decided to share his maritime thoughts and experience with readers, it was to be with focus on the *S.S. Edmund Fitzgerald*, with which I had an association while in the (circa 1958) employ of the now-defunct Great Lakes Engineering Works of River

Rouge, Michigan. This shipbuilding "cradle" had many historical accomplishments to its credit that provided a unique counterbalance to the scarcity of higher technology "bells and whistles" normally found in modern shipyards engaged in the design and construction of complex U.S. Navy vessels. The 1975 loss of "Big Fitz" and her crew is still mourned today and continues to be an enigma wrapped in "mystique" and "mystery" for some. While official investigatory reports, and a plethora of ad-hoc opinions, have been generated by interested, well-meaning parties, none of them appear to have ever made claim to close association with *Fitzgerald*'s design or construction involvement within the Great Lakes tradition-bound shipbuilding industry. Some authors and interested parties acknowledge and respect, the destructive environmental effects of Great Lakes storms, which have taken their toll of vessel and mariners, but with a paucity of supporting scientific rationale appropriate to these large, land-locked water masses.

While my original intent was to only share career insight (re: *Fitzgerald*), a course correction was subsequently made to include an abbreviated historical overview of inland marine commerce evolution for a fuller appreciation of our "Eighth Sea" in the nation's hinterland. It is fascinating that the *Fitzgerald* became the largest and an original Seaway-sized entry, which eventually evolved from the visionary aspirations and developments of pioneering explorers and settlers who used canoes, barges, and sailing craft in pursuit of Great Lakes trading.

The scope and depth of presentation were subsequently expanded to include the British *M.V. Derbyshire* Ore/Bulk/Oil (O.B.O.) vessel, which was tragically lost in 1980 and, at the outset, having Genesis and Exodus similarities to *Fitzgerald*. In the eyes of many, the High Court of Justice (Admiralty Court) findings and conclusions did *not* provide satisfactory explanation or resolution, and the closed case remains a continuing controversy (mystery?) within the gallant *Derbyshire* Family Association (DFA), and the maritime community at large. The various investigations and hearings were conducted under circumstances where (apparently) *no* liability may be assigned to the cognizent private shipbuilder businesses.

External to this matrix, a high ore-carrier casualty rate has simultaneously continued on an international scale, raising incisive safety concerns about the adequacy of ship classification society design and inspection standards, commercial shipbuilding production quality; the thoroughness of life-cycle maintenance; shiploading practices; and the presence and practices of sub-standard operating vessel owners using low-quality registers.

Although in a retired status, the author's interest in maritime issues remains unabated and active in circumstances such as those for *Fitzgerald* and *Derbyshire,* and for the safety of mariners on other bulk-cargo vessels that silently ply their trade throughout the world. Especially those at risk in newer, larger, and more complex designs that may exceed the limits of prevailing classification society rules and have metaphorical fissures in their research, development, testing, and first-principle engineering (RDT&E) foundations. The ramifications of these cases have systemic effect and touch on world-wide merchant marine industry interests as a whole, and the cases are believed to have the potential for establishing fertile ground to facilitate informed, professional, objective debate and research action through constructive mutual contribution.

The maritime industry should not be allowed to atrophy further or become a victim of its own long history. Any reluctance or refusal to glean the fullest knowledge from oceangoing or Great Lakes mishaps, without bias, should be critically viewed as professional folly and disregard for the lives of *all* mariners who continue to serve us well.

RECORD OF MISSING CREWMEN

S.S. EDMUND FITZGERALD

Ernest M. McSorley, master
John H. McCarthy, first mate
James A. Pratt, second mate
Michael E. Armagost, third mate
George J. Holl, chief engineer
Edward F. Bindon, first assistant
Thomas E. Edwards, second assistant
Russell G. Haskell, second assistant
Oliver J. Champeau, third assistant
Frederick J. Beetcher, porter
Thomas Bentsen, oiler
Thomas D. Borgeson, AB maintenance
Nolan F. Church, porter
Ransom E. Cundy, watchman
Bruce L. Hudson, deckhand

Allen G. Kalmon, second cook
Gordon F. MacLellan, wiper
Joseph W. Mazes, spec. maintenance
Eugene W. O'Brien, wheelsman
Karl A. Pekol, watchman
John J. Poviach, wheelsman
Robert C. Rafferty, steward
Paul M. Riipa, deckhand
John D. Simmons, wheelsman
William J. Spengler, wheelsman
Mark A. Thomas, deckhand
Ralph G. Walton, oiler
David E. Weiss, cadet (deck)
Blaine H. Wilhelm, oiler

M.V. DERBYSHIRE

K. ALLIS
F. A. BAYLISS
P. J. BEST
P. J. BINDON
T. V. BLEASE
R. BOND
T. BROWN
W. BUCKLEY
A. B. BUJANG
T. BURKE
N. COATES
L. T. M. COLTMAN
F. CHEDOTAL
J. J. CRONE
M. FREEMAN
A. GORDON
A. T. GORDON
J. H. GRAHAM
J. J. GREENLAND
B. J. HARDMAN
A. J. HODGES
W. L. HUNT

A-M. HUTCHINSON
G. HUTCHINSON
D. H. JONES
M. JONES
N. G. A. KANE
P. D. KING
P. LAMBERT
B. LANGTON
N. MARSH
A. B. H. MUSA
R. MUSA
J. NOBLETT
C. W. RAPLEY
D. M. RIDYARD
B. B. SEKAH
A. K. STOTT
P. J. TAYLOR
R. W. TAYLOR
G. V. UNDERHILL - MASTER
R. A. WALLER
G. W. WILLIAMS
E. F. WILLIAMSON

Epitaph
In solemn tribute to the mariners who serve
the industrial nations of the world
and the family survivors of
those who do not return.
We pray that their search for truth shall be rewarded.

Photo – *Detroit News*
Ship captains, family members and friends of the crew of the *Fitzgerald* attend a memorial service at Mariners Church in Detroit in 1988. A ship's bell was rung 29 times, once for each crewmember.

"The investigation of truth is in one way hard and in another way easy. An indication of this is found in the fact that no one is able to attain the truth entirely, while on the other hand no one fails entirely, but everyone says something true about the nature of things and by union of all a considerable amount is amassed."

Aristotle
Metaphysics, 2nd Book

References and Sources

Abbreviations.
A.B.S.	American Bureau of Shipping.
C.F.R.	Code of Federal Regulations.
D.F.A.	Derbyshire Family Association.
H.B.O.I.	Harbor Branch Oceanographic Institution.
I.T.F.	International Transport-Workers' Federation (UK).
L.R.	Lloyd's Register.
L.C.A.	Lake Carriers Association.
MARAD.	Maritime Administration.
N.O.A.A.	National Oceanic and Atmospheric Administration.
N.W.S.	National Weather Service
N.T.S.B.	National Transportation Safety Board.
R.I.N.A.	Royal Institution of Naval Architects.
S.L.S.D.C.	St. Lawrence Seaway System Development Corp.
S.N.A.M.E.	Society of Naval Architects and Marine Engineers.
T.S.B.	Transportation Safety Board of Canada.
U.S.D.O.T.	United States Department of Transportation.
U.K.D.O.T.	United Kingdom Department of Transport.
U.S.A.C.O.E.	United States Army Corps of Engineers.
U.S.C.G.	United States Coast Guard.

Reference Sources.
A Ship Too Far (*M.V. Derbyshire*). Ramwell and Madge, 1992.
Basic Naval Architecture. K.C. Barnaby, 1954.
Blue Water Research (M.V. Derbyshire). D. Mearns (UK), 2004.
Bowling Green University, Great Lakes Historical Collections.
Davie Shipbuilding Co. and Successors, S. Kack, 2000.
Derbyshire Family Association, D.C. Ramwell, P. Lambert.
Design of Merchant Ships. Schokker, Neuerburg, Vossnack: 1953.
Detroit Free Press/Detroit News Historical Archives.
Fifty Years of Furness. J.M. Evans, 2002.
Ford, The Men and The Machine: R. Lacy, 1986.
Great Lakes Maritime Institute, Dossin Museum: J. Polacsek, 2003.
Great Lakes Shipwreck Museum: T. Farnquist, 2004.
House of Commons Hansard (Derbyshire) Debates. July 1996.
Hydrographic Service, Ottawa, Canada.
I.T.F. Bulletin No. 6. 1991.
Introduction to Steel Shipbuilding. Baker, 1953.
MARAD Survey of U.S. Shipbuilding and Repair Facilities. E. Gearhart: 2003.
Marine Investigation Reports. TSB Canada.
Marine Casualty Report 16732/64216, USDOT/USCG, 1977.
Marine Accident Report MAR 78-3, NTSB, 1978.
Marine Engineering. SNAME, 1976.
Mechanics of Materials. Popov, 1957.
Ministry of Geology and Mines Report, Thunder Bay, Canada.
Nautical Magazine. (A British publication for merchant mariners) Ramwell: April 1991.
Naval Architect's and Shipbuilder's Pocketbook. Mackrow: 1954.
Oceaneering International. L. Karl: 2004.
Pride of the Inland Sea. B. Beck and C.P. Labadie: 2004.
RINA Paper, "A Theory on the Loss of *M.V. Derbyshire*" Bishop, Price, Temeral. 1990.
RINA Paper, "Design and Operation of Bulk Carriers," 2001.
RINA Paper, "An Analytical Assessment of the *M.V. Derbyshire* Sinking," Faulkner: 2001.
River Rouge Historical Museum, Michigan: D. Swekel, 2002.
Sault Evening News, Sault Ste. Marie, Michigan, Nov. 11, 1975.
Sea Technology. Compass Publications, Volume 35 No. 12, Dec. 1994.

Sea Breezes. (A British publication for merchant mariners) Ramwell Dec. 1989, Nov. 1992, Nov. 1994, Mar. 1998. Walsh Aug. 1987.
Ship Design and Construction. SNAME: 1969.
Ships for Victory. F.C. Lane, 2001.
Ship Construction and Calculations. Nicol: 1937.
SNAME Paper, St. Lawrence River Canal Vessels. Gilmore: 1957.
SNAME Paper, *S.S. Edmund Fitzgerald* Engine Room Design. Varian, Spooner, 1958.
SNAME Paper, "Naval Architectural Education Today." R.A. Yagle: 1966.
SNAME Paper, "Recent Research on Dynamic Behavior of Large Great Lakes Bulk Carriers." Stiansen: 1984.
SNAME Paper, "An Independent Assessment of the Sinking of *M.V. Derbyshire.*" Faulkner: 1998.
S.S. Edmund Fitzgerald Mystique and Its Evolution. Murphy: 2001.
Strength of Materials. Timoshenko: 1956.
Tall Ships and Tankers. E.R. Marcil: 1967.
Theoretical Naval Architecture. Attwood and Pengally: 1899–1946.
Toledo Blade, Ohio. Nov. 13, 1975.
The Night the Fitz Went Down. H.E. Bishop & Capt. Dudley J. Parquette: 2000.
UKDOT Court Report 8075 of Derbyshire Formal Investigation 1987.
UK High Court of Justice Report of the Reopened Formal Investigation into the Loss of M.V. Derbyshire Nov. 2000.
USCG Archives (G-IPA-4).
Wreck of The Edmund Fitzgerald. F. Stonehouse: 1977.

The foregoing is a representative, but not exhaustive, listing of reference sources used in the book preparation. They did augment personal memory recall which, by the grace of God, was not impaired by "senior citizen moments" of relapse. To any technical reader critical of the author's listing of dated reference sources, they may be assured that this was done with deliberate intent and as appropriate to the merchant ship design and construction of the 1950s era.

Glossary for Technical Bridging

Preamble
Force majeure, mystery, conjectural, and human error explanations have, to date, not been completely superseded by objective technical analyses. Therefore, the following contributions are cautiously made with an understanding that the outcomes should be accepted as estimates only, since absolute certitude is unattainable and basic (versus complex) premising is made for the benefit of readability.

1. Longitudinal Bending Stress
A vessel may be regarded as a large beam or girder, subject to bending in a fore and aft direction. Buoyancy support and the vertical distribution of vessel and cargo weight will vary considerably along the length of a vessel, even when floating in still water.

In some locations (e.g., engine room) the weight can exceed the upward support of buoyancy and vice-versa. The *total* vessel buoyancy must always equal the total weight to maintain equilibrium.

At each point along the hull girder there will be a tendency to flex up or down (hogging or sagging), caused by the manner in which a vessel is loaded and the height, length, and crest locations of wave formations supporting the hull. The girder must be made sufficiently strong to withstand this flexing and fatiguing tendency.

Hogging
The vessel is assumed to have the CREST of a wave amidships (Deck in tension) (Keel in compression)

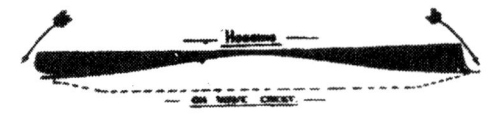

Sagging
The vessel is assumed to have the TROUGH of a wave amidships.
(Deck in compression)
(Keel in tension)

2. Listing

Listing is a *permanent* condition when a vessel is transversely inclined from a vertical position. This can occur subsequent to sustaining a casualty which causes a loss in buoyancy, or added asymmetric weight, and/or a shift in cargo weight on one side.

Listing is recognized as a contributor to increased hull girder stress levels.

3. Heeling

Heeling is a *temporary* condition when a vessel is transversely inclined from a vertical position by transient forces, such as wind or wave.

The emerged and immersed waterplane wedges extend to the bow and stern, and the volume of each wedge must be equal, since the vessel weight remains unchanged.

A compensatory righting moment will normally restore verticality.

4. Multi-Axial Hull Stressing

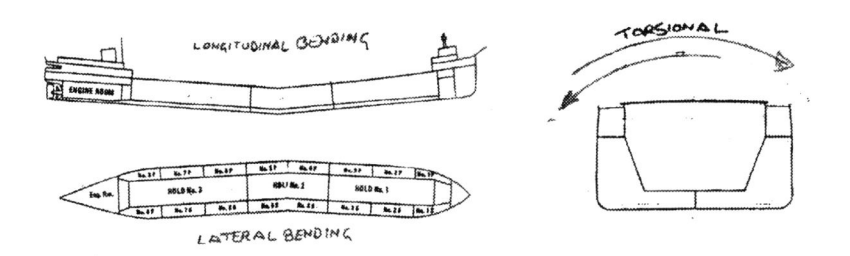

5. Buoyancy
With any immersed or partly immersed body, there is an upward thrust working against gravity and equal in amount to the weight of displaced fluid. The upward thrust is applied through, but not at, a point known as the center of buoyancy (i.e., the center of gravity of the displaced fluid).

6. Reserve Buoyancy
The difference between the displacement when a body is floating freely and when it is totally immersed (or at some desired maximum waterline) is known as reserve buoyancy. Excessive loss of reserve buoyancy can result in sinking.

7. Lost Buoyancy
A casualty condition when a vessel's compartment(s) is in *open* communication with the water in which a vessel is floating, and no longer can be considered as a contributor to that vessel's reserve buoyancy. (i.e., Applicable to Fitzgerald case, when below-waterline forward shell plating was probably ruptured by a large buoyant object. Pump-out was ineffective under continuous flooding from Lake Superior).

8. Added Weight
A casualty condition is treated as "added weight" whenever water enters a vessel's compartment that is *not* in continuous open communication with water in which a vessel is floating. (i.e., Applicable to *Fitzgerald* case, when an eight-inch diameter topside vent pipe was damaged on spar deck, causing tunnel flooding.)

"Added weight" can contribute to increased hull girder loading, and a listing attitude with contingency upon magnitude and location.

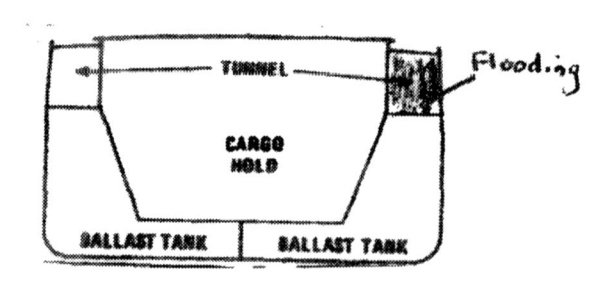

9. Water Density
For general computations: Salt water   35 cub. ft./ton
                                          64 lb./cub. ft.
                             Fresh water 36 cub. ft./ton.
                                          62.4 lb./cub. ft.

10. Water Pressure
Static pressure per foot of head height:
                             Salt water   0.444 lb./sq. inch.
                             Fresh water   0.433 lb./sq. inch.
                             (Atmospheric pressure excluded.)

11. Estimated Water Inflow VELOCITY During Flooding Casualty:
v = $C_d \sqrt{2g.H}$ ft./sec.
C_d = Discharge Coefficient.
g = 32.2 ft/sec/sec.
H = Waterhead (ft.) above orifice.

Estimated Water Inflow VOLUME During Flooding Casualty:
V = v x A cub. ft./sec.
V = v x A x 60 cub. ft./min.
A = Orifice area (sq. ft.)

Estimated Water Inflow WEIGHT During Flooding Casualty:
V = v x A x 60 / 35 tons per minute (salt water).
V = v x A x 60 / 36 tons per minute (fresh water).
Gallons per minute (U.S.)   =   V x 60 x 7.481
Gallons per minute (Brit)   =   V x 60 x 6.229

12. Dynamic Ship Motions with Six Degrees of Freedom
Ship motions may occur independently or with cross-coupling. When in a seaway, either rolling or pitching will predominate.

a) Rolling.
For small angles of roll, a vessel has a periodic transverse rotational oscillation when responding to external force(s) around a "quiescent point." This point closely approximates a vessel's center of gravity. A "stiff" vessel, such as *Fitzgerald*, has a short ("snap") roll period and

a large metacentric height (GM), while a "tender" ship has a longer period and a smaller metacentric height. Heavy rolling is a recognized contributor to transverse stress increases.

b) Pitching.
A pitching vessel results from the influence of heavy-sea heaving as she seeks a state of equilibrium with her mid-body first on a wave crest and afterwards in a wave trough (see heaving). Dangerous pitching may usually be reduced by changes in course and speed.

The bow and stern alternately emerge and immerse as they move upward and downward in a vertical plane.

When the wave direction is abaft the beam (as *Fitzgerald*) the period of wave encounter is increased, unless the component of the vessel's speed exceeds the wave speed (*Fitzgerald* on track 141° T had higher-speed abnormal rogue waves from about 135° T acting on the starboard beam quarter.)

In heavy seas, pitching contributes to a significant increase in the longitudinal bending moment and induces vertical accelerations of about 0.3g. which can increase multi-axial hull stresses.

c) Heaving.
A heaving vessel moves vertically up and down, usually without any alteration in trim, while seeking a state of equilibrium with her middle body first in a wave crest and afterwards in a wave trough.

When these wave crests and troughs are successively encountered within a short time, a vessel will not keep her balance, and there will be moments when the displacement does exceed a vessel's weight and vice versa. This causes a vessel to respond with vertical motion known as heaving.

In heavy seas, heaving contributes to an increase in the longitudinal bending moment, and some movement in the longitudinal center of buoyancy thereby causing pitching and some redistribution of accelerative forces.

d. Yawing.
Vessels are not, as a general rule, directionally stable, and bow headings require repetitive control by rudder movement.

When a vessel is pitching and rolling, the axis of roll is itself oscillating, and this sets up a gyroscopic couple which causes yawing. A more serious cause of yawing is the passage of a train of waves under the stern quarter of a vessel, which produces yaw oscillation.

e. Surging.
Fore and aft drifting that can become an oscillation is known as surging and may be caused by an uneven propulsion system power output (machinery and/or propeller).

f. Swaying.
Sideways drifting. Since a vessel does not gain in potential energy, there is no energy stored to generate a reverse drift.

13. True Bearings.
A true bearing is the direction of an object from an observer measured clockwise from true north (e.g., 145° T).

14. Navigation and Collision Avoidance.
Radar.
*R*adio *D*etection *A*nd *R*anging. Shipboard radiolocation equipment that detects and locates distance objects using pulses of microwave radiation.

Sonar.
*S*ound *N*avigation *A*nd *R*anging. Shipboard equipment that transmits acoustic pulse waves through water and measures time lapse for pulse to return from underwater object or seafloor.
Synonym: Echo sounder, fathometer.

15. Cause Majeure.
Other terminology, such as Force Majeure and Acts of God, are often used interchangeably to describe similar conditions such as:
- An event or effect that can be neither anticipated nor controlled.
- A superior or overpowering force.
- An overwhelming unpredictable event exclusively by forces of nature.
- All natural phenomena that are exceptionable, inevitable, and irresistible, the effects of which could not be anticipated, prevented, or avoided by the exercise of due care or foresight.

16. Ship Classification Societies and Rules.

Classification societies are organizations that establish and apply technical standards in relation to the design, construction, and survey of marine related facilities including ships and offshore structures. These standards are issued by the classification society as published rules. A vessel that has been designed and built to the appropriate rules of a society may apply for a Certificate of Classification from that society. The society issues this certificate upon completion of relevant classification surveys.

Such a certificate does not imply, and should not be construed as, an express warranty of safety, fitness for purpose, or seaworthiness of the ship. It is an attestation only that the vessel is in compliance with the standards that have been developed and published by the society issuing the classification certificate.

More than fifty organizations worldwide define their activities as providing marine classification. Ten of those organizations form the International Association of Classification Societies (IACS). It is estimated that these ten societies, together with the two additional societies that have been accorded associate status by IACS, collectively class about 94 percent of all commercial tonnage involved in international trade worldwide.

	Members	Origin
ABS	American Bureau of Shipping	1862
BV	Bureau Veritas	1828
CCS	China Classification Society	1956
DNV	Det Norske Veritas	1864
GL	Germanischer Lloyd	1867
KR	Korean Register of Shipping	1960
LR	Lloyd's Register	1834
NK	Nippon Kaiji Kyokai (ClassNK)	1899
RINA	Registro Italiano Navale	1861
RS	Russian Maritime Register of Shipping	1913
	Associates	Origin
CRS	(Croatian Register of Shipping)	1949
IRS	Indian Register of Shipping	1975

As an independent, self-regulating body, a classification society has no commercial interests related to ship design, ship building, ship ownership, ship operation, ship management, ship maintenance or repairs, insurance, or chartering.

Classification rules are developed to contribute to the structural strength and integrity of essential parts of the ship's hull and its appendages, and the reliability and the function of the propulsion and steering systems, power generation, and those other features and auxiliary systems which have been built into the ship in order to maintain essential services on board.

Class rules do not cover every piece of structure or item of equipment on board a vessel, nor do they cover operational elements. Activities which generally fall outside the scope of classification include such items as: design and manufacturing processes; choice of type and power of machinery and certain equipment (e.g., mooring bitts, capstans and winches); number and qualification of crew or operating personnel; form and cargo carrying capacity of the ship and maneuvering performance; hull vibrations; spare parts; life-saving appliances; and maintenance equipment. These matters may, however, be given consideration for classification according to the type of ship or class notation(s) assigned.

It should be emphasized that it is the shipowner who has total control over a vessel, including the manner in which it is operated and maintained. Classification is voluntary and its effectiveness depends upon the shipowner, and other interests, operating in good faith by disclosing to the class society any damage or deterioration that may affect the vessel's classification status. If there is the least question, the owner should notify the appropriate classification society and schedule a survey to determine if the vessel is in compliance with the relevant class standard.

It must also be emphasized that a class surveyor may only go on board a vessel once in a twelve-month period, for the annual survey. At that time it is neither possible, nor expected, that the surveyor scrutinize the entire structure of the vessel or its machinery. The survey involves a sampling, for which guidelines exist based upon empirical experience which may indicate those parts of the vessel or its machinery that may be subject to corrosion, or are exposed to the highest incidence of stress, or may be likely to exhibit signs of fatigue or damage.

Appendix

S.S. Edmund Fitzgerald:
Possible Effects of U.F.O. Encounter

I. In correlation with the USCG Report, it is possible that:
   (i) An Unidentified Floating Object (U.F.O.) could have caused underwater separation of the bow's stem bar, forepeak and No. 1 Ballast Tank shell plate welding on one side of the vessel.
   - This would have induced a "lost buoyancy" condition since uncontrollable ingress of water to forward compartments would have occurred.
   - *Effects*: Bow trim and a listing condition would be induced.
     : Ballast pumps would be emptying Lake Superior, and not the flooded tankage.

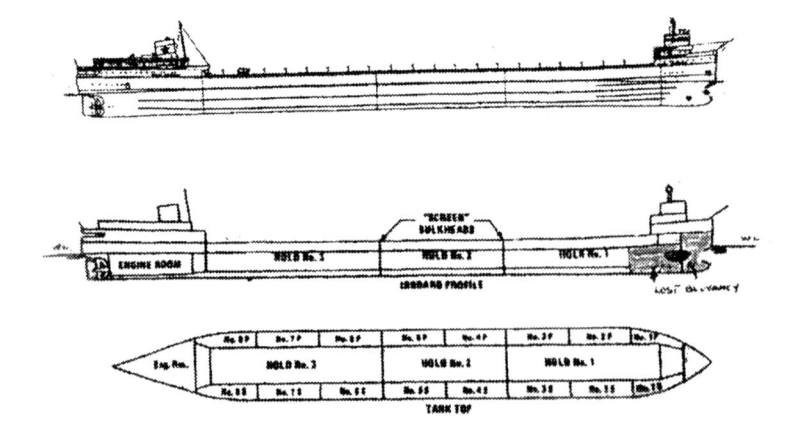

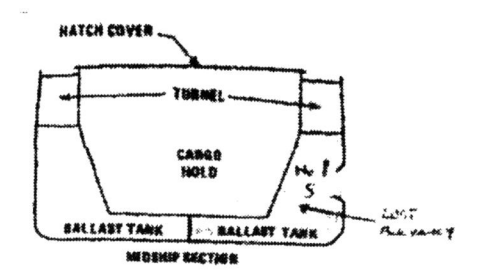

and
- (ii) Captain McSorley's "Couple of vents down" statement could have meant:
  - One eight-inch diameter broken vent pipe connected to the (ruptured) No. 1 Ballast Tank
    and
  - One eight-inch diameter broken vent pipe to a side tunnel, thereby allowing accumulation of water within a compartment having no water evacuation capabilities...because the aft gravity drain (to No. 8 Ballast Tank) was shut off.

  Effects: Uncontrollable water ingress would have resulted in asymmetrical topside "added weight" loading and an induced deteriorating list condition.

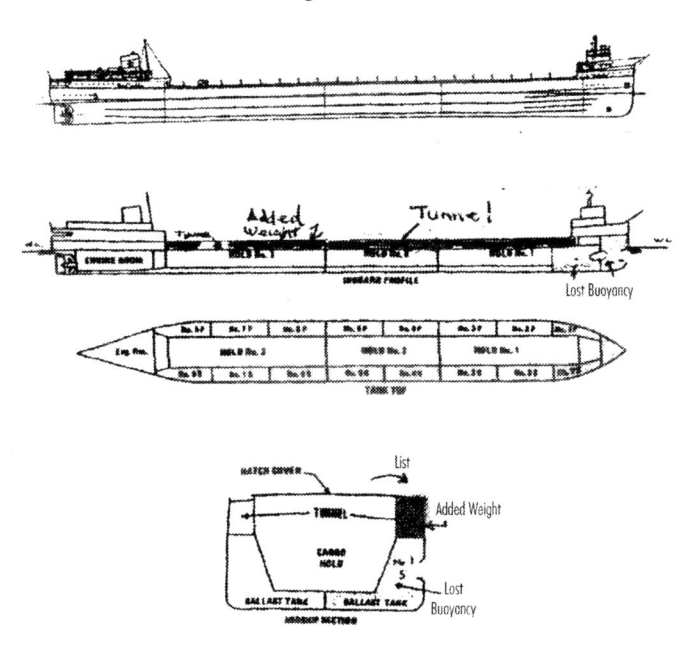

II. *S.S. Edmund Fitzgerald*:

Order of Magnitude Estimation of Water Ingress Through a Broken Spar Deck Air Pipe To Side Tunnel Compartment.

Calculations were based on steady state gravity flow conditions in a circular pipe of eight inches diameter subjected to various waterhead heights.

Under gravity flow, the rate of water ingress through a broken-off air pipe orifice is estimated as:

Volume (V) = $C_d \, A \, \sqrt{2gH}$ cubic feet per second.

or

(V) x 448.8 = Gallons per minute (U.S.).

Where

A is the orifice area in square feet.
H is the steady-state waterhead height in feet.
g is 32.2 feet/sec/sec.
C_d is Discharge Coefficient.

(An assumed theoretical Discharge Coefficient C_d = 0.60 was used in the absence of experimental data for parallel flow through vertical tubes, in the field of Moving Wave-Orifice Theory.

(Ref: RINA Paper: An Analytical Assessment of the Sinking of the *M.V. Derbyshire* – D. Faulkner 2001).

For reader perspective, the following provides estimations of water ingress through *one* eight-inch diameter orifice, to *one* side tunnel compartment when exposed to various steady-state waterhead heights:

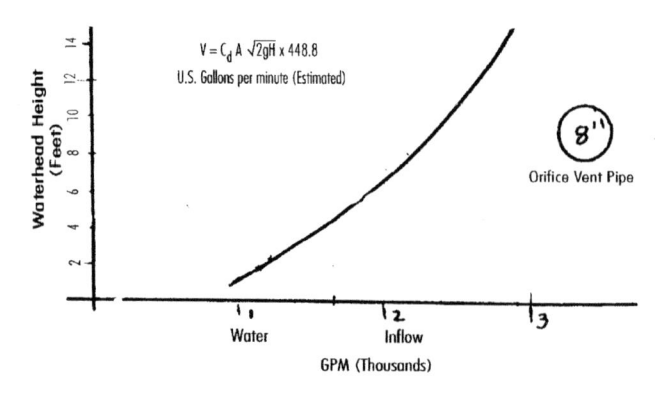

III. *S.S. Edmund Fitzgerald*: Order of Magnitude Estimation of Water Ingress Through <u>One (1) Breached Spar Deck Cargo Hatch Opening</u>

Calculations were based on steady-state gravity flow conditions through one breached (48 feet x 11 feet) spar deck cargo hatch opening subjected to various waterhead heights.

Under gravity flow, the rate of water ingress through a rectangular deck opening is estimated as:

Volume $(V) = C_d\ A\ \sqrt{2gH}$ cubic feet per second.
or
$(V) \div 36 = L$. tons per second (F.W.)

Where
A is the cargo hatch opening in square feet.
H is the steady-state waterhead height in feet.
g is 32.2 feet/sec/sec.
C_d is Discharge Coefficient.

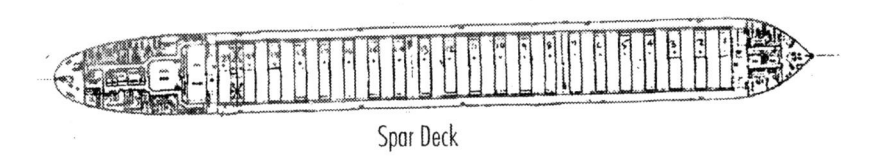

Spar Deck

The *Fitzgerald* had twenty-one cargo hatch covers, with each designed for a minimum four-foot waterhead height per 46 CFR 45.145. The spar deck openings measured eleven feet longitudinally and forty-eight feet transversely, and each had a twenty-four-inch high steel peripheral coaming. Every hatch cover was secured by sixty-eight pivoting Kestener clamps that engaged recessed buttons on each steel hatch cover upper surface.

In retrospect, it was noted that:

- The USCG Marine Casualty Report (1977) concluded that the hatch cover closure system failed to prevent the penetration of water into the vessel "*in any sea condition*", as required by USCG regulations.
- The NTSB, on March 23, 1978, unanimously voted to reject thee USCG's official report supporting ineffective closure of hatch covers due to operator negligence. (per N. Schlutheiss – Worldwide Web http://www.oakland.edu/boatnerd/efitz/com). November 10, 2000.
- 46 C.F.R. 45.145 promulgated revised cargo hatch cover structural design criteria (October 1, 2002), per Appendix.

For reader perspective, the following provides order of magnitude estimations of water ingress through each breached 48-foot x 11-foot cargo hatch opening, when exposed to various steady state waterhead heights:

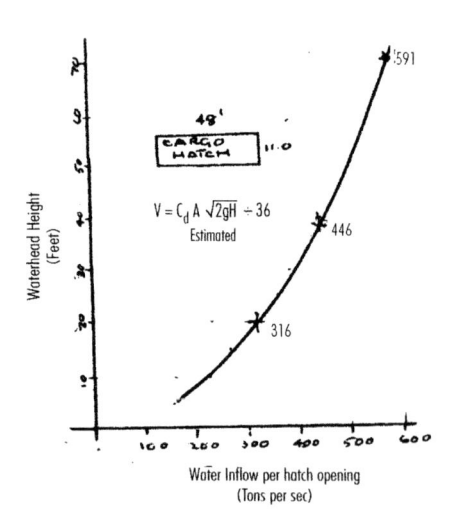

$$V = C_d A \sqrt{2gH} \div 36$$
Estimated

Waterhead Height (Feet) vs. Water Inflow per hatch opening (Tons per sec)

48' CARGO HATCH 11.0

Data points: 316, 446, 591

IV. Order of Magnitude Time Lapse Estimation for <u>Flooding Void Cargo Hold Volume (Above Taconite)</u>

Cargo hold gross volume 860,950 cub. ft.
Cargo hold total length 519 feet.
Cargo weight 26, 116 L.Tons
Cargo volume 417,856 Cub. Ft.

Cargo Hold	No. 1	No. 2	No. 3
Length in feet.	177	144	198
Gross Hold Volume (Cub. Ft.)	309,942	241,066	309,942
	(36%)	(28%)	(36%)
Ore Cargo Weight (Long Tons)	9,402	7,312	9,402
Ore Volume (@ 16 Cub. Ft/Ton)	150,432	116,991	150,432
Void Hold Volume (Cub. Ft.) Above Ore Cargo	159,510	124,075	159,510
*Flooding Capacity (Long Tons) (If void hold volume filled with water @ 36 Cub. Ft./Ton)	4,431	3,447	4,431

Estimated Time to Fill <u>No. 3 Cargo Hold Void Space</u> (After Breaching of After Hatch Covers Nos. 21 or 21, 20 or 21, 20, 19).

Waterhead Height and Inflow Rate	Hatch Covers Breached (No. 3 Cargo Hold Only)		
	21	21 and 20	21, 20 and 19
	Fill Time (secs)	Fill Time (secs)	Fill Time (secs)
20 ft. waterhead @ 316 tons/sec	14.0	7.0	4.7
40 ft. waterhead @ 446 tons/sec	9.9	5.0	3.3
70 ft. waterhead @ 591 tons/sec	7.5	3.8	2.5

* No allowance was made for cargo permeability since the time lapse for flooding and taconite penetration was minimal.

S.S. Edmund Fitzgerald
V. ORIGINAL
    Cargo Hatch Cover Structural Design Criteria.
Cite: 46 CFR 45.145.
Hatch cover design required minimum 4-foot waterhead.
Note: Theoretical highest point of hatch cover upper surface above winter load waterline under static and still water conditions

approximately fifteen feet, but *not* commensurate with actual in-service conditions.

Title 46 – Shipping
REVISED – Cargo Hatchway Cover Structural Design Criteria. (Rev. October 1, 2002) Cite: 46 CFR 45.145 Hatchway Covers.

(a) Hatchways in position 1 and 2 must have weathertight hatch covers with gaskets and clamping devices.
(b) The maximum ultimate strength of the hatchway cover material must be at least 4.25 times the maximum stress in the structure calculated with the following assumed loads:
   (1) For ships 350-feet or more in length, at least 250 pounds per foot in Position 1, and 200 pounds per foot in Position 2.
   (2) For ships less than 350-feet in length, at least AL in the following formula:
      (i) Position 1:
         $$AL = \underline{200} + C$$
      where $C = 50$
         $(L - 79)/271$
      (jj) Position 2:
         $$AL = \underline{150} + C$$
(c) Hatchway covers must be so designed as to limit the deflection to not more than 0.0028 times the span under the loads described in paragraph (b) of this section and the thickness of mild steel plating forming the tops of covers must be at least 1 percent of the spacing of stiffeners or 0.24 inches whichever is greater.

Author Comments:
Designer compliance with the foregoing revised CFR criteria is achievable although, as a "cookbook" engineering approach; they may *not* guarantee structural adequacy under actual operating conditions.

As a critical element in the preservation of vessel reserve buoyancy, the author considers cargo hatch design and construction should/could be more sophisticated.

Multi-disciplined support engineering should be implemented, with a first principle design approach, which (at least) recognizes quantifiable dynamic water loadings and resistance to elastic instability (buckling) followed by proof-of-concept full-scale replications subjected to research, test, and evaluation (RDT&E).